WITHDRAWN

Addiction Why Can't They Just Stop?

Rodale books may be purchased for business or promotional use
or for special sales. For information, please write to:
Special Markets Department, Rodale Inc.,
733 Third Avenue, New York, NY 10017

Printed in the United States of America

Rodale Inc. makes every effort to use acid-free ∞, recycled paper ♲.

Library of Congress Cataloging-in-Publication Data is on file with the publisher
ISBN-13: 978-1-59486-715-6
ISBN-10: 1-59486-715-1

Distributed to the book trade by Holtzbrinck Publishers

2 4 6 8 10 9 7 5 3 1 hardcover

We inspire and enable people to improve their lives and the world around them
For more of our products visit **rodalestore.com** or call 800-848-4735

Addiction Why Can't They Just Stop?

NEW KNOWLEDGE. NEW TREATMENTS.
NEW HOPE.

Edited by John Hoffman and Susan Froemke

Foreword by Sheila Nevins

Afterword by Susan Cheever

David Sheff
Larkin Warren
Katherine Ketcham
Katherine Eban

A NOTE FROM THE EDITORS

We would like to acknowledge the special contributions to this book made by author David Sheff, whose own family has lived through addiction, a story that he memorably reported in the *New York Times Magazine*. After seeing his piece, "My Addicted Son," we contacted Sheff, and our conversations with him then and over the past two years helped us better understand the impact addiction has on the family. He wrote Chapters 5 and 6 of this book as well as the opening pages of Chapter 1, adding the rich perspective of a parent and journalist who knows what it is like to face addiction—and persevere. His generosity and honesty benefit us all.

In 1987, The Partnership for a Drug-Free America launched an antinarcotics campaign.

It featured a simple message:

This is your brain,

this is drugs,

this is your brain on drugs.

Partnership For A Drug-Free America

Advances in brain-imaging science and other research have led us to a new understanding. This is your brain:

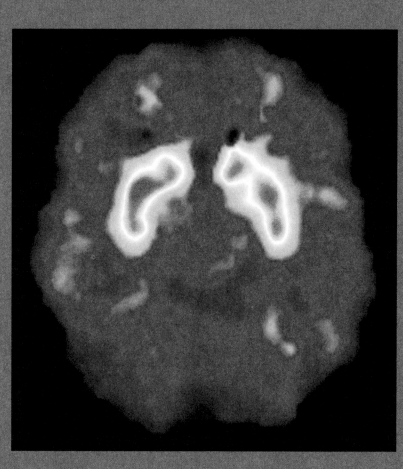

This is your brain addicted to:

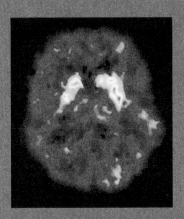

METHAMPHETAMINE

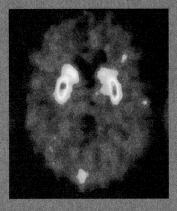

ALCOHOL

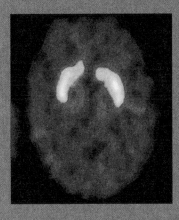

HEROIN

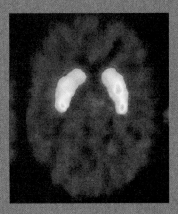

COCAINE

Using drugs and alcohol repeatedly over time alters brain chemistry and function.

Addiction is
a brain disease.
Treatment can
work.

Foreword

You discover someone in your family or a loved one is addicted to drugs or alcohol and your life is changed forever. Where do you go? What do you do? You realize how little you know.

In a state of a panic, you look for remedies to deal with this illness and you wonder to whom you can turn for the best kind of treatment—and at the same time, you feel the need to protect your privacy. With a mixture of frustration and sadness, you find that answers are hard to come by. And when they are found, they are often conflicting, hard to understand, expensive, and, frequently, not covered by insurance.

What is this disease of addiction? How is the chemistry of an addict's brain altered? Why do co-occurring disorders, such as depression, bipolar states, ADD, and OCD, among others, create in some a need for an addictive substance? What genetic factors make a person more susceptible to the ravages of drugs?

In many ways, an addicted individual becomes a bystander as his affliction takes over his rational thinking, and the burden of finding treatment belongs to those who care for him. The good news is that the addict, with proper treatment and the correct medications, can discover the commitment and the tools necessary to help in his own recovery. The hope is that he will find an alternative lifestyle that replaces the destructive patterns of addiction. The reality, however, is that addicts are often noncompliant and relapse.

This is what HBO's ADDICTION project is about—straightening out the dilemma of what the caretaker can give and what the addict is capable of accepting and changing.

It is the hope of the team of producers at HBO that you can discover in our collection of fourteen films, and in this companion book, an understanding that the person you care for has a brain disease—a chronic illness that you and the dependent person will continually struggle with.

HBO's ADDICTION project demonstrates conclusively that this disease is treatable. Recovery is possible for people suffering from addiction. But recovery is a monumental struggle, and facing the realities of addiction will require a lifelong commitment from those who care.

—Sheila Nevins
President, HBO Documentary Films

Introduction

John Hoffman and Susan Froemke

Three years ago, when Sheila Nevins asked us to research and produce a television special about drug and alcohol addiction, neither of us had an in-depth knowledge of the subject. We had each witnessed the struggles of family and friends, and had each seen the devastation that addiction can bring to relationships. But we really didn't understand addiction. We didn't truly comprehend what could cause someone to be incapable of stopping themselves from taking a drink or using a drug even when they knew it was ruining their life and, frequently, the lives of others.

Little did we know that coming to understand this dilemma would end up to be such a profound challenge. Even though we were given the time to consume as much information as we could on the topic—meeting with the best minds in this field, and gaining insight from the many people who shared their battles with addiction with us—we found it terribly difficult to attain a comprehensive, working understanding of the topic.

Addiction, as it turns out, is a problem that is messy—riddled with misconceptions, profoundly lacking in nationally recognized treatment standards, and highly stigmatized. Conversely, we also came to realize that although the science of addiction is relatively new, tremendous shifts in attitudes are occurring. The biggest change is the growing acceptance by the medical community and the general population that addiction is a chronic relapsing brain disease. A vivid contributor to this change in attitude is the fact that science now gives us the ability to see inside the brains of addicted people. We can see that the addicted brain is different; that it is altered. With brain research has come great advances in the medical treatment of addiction and the promise of even more effective treatments on the horizon.

We used the *Principles of Addiction Medicine* from the American Society of Addiction Medicine (ASAM) to help educate us as we were laying the foundation on which we built HBO's ADDICTION project and this book. With the help of our coproducer, Micah Cormier, we engaged in hundreds of hours of conversation with research scientists, physicians, psychiatrists, government leaders, treatment providers, treatment advocates, people in recovery, people actively using, families of active users, families of those in recovery, twelve-step advocates, and experts studying how addiction affects the workplace. Our goal was to become smarter about the subject and to find for our documentary those leading addiction experts who could communicate their knowledge in a compelling and accessible manner.

Our journey toward understanding the science of addiction started with a bit of serendipity. In May of 2004, the annual meeting of the American Psychiatric Association (APA) was being held in New York City and included a comprehensive seminar on addiction. Gathered together for five days, under one roof, were some of the leading thinkers in the field. We signed up. One message that was strongly reinforced at this conference was that drug addiction is a disease of the brain and that it is a chronic illness that needs continual care. One lecture, given by Kathleen Brady, MD, PhD, president of the American Academy of Addiction Psychiatry, made tremendous sense to us (the laypeople). It explored the impact of stress on the developing brain and the connection between stress and addiction. The ease with which Brady expressed these connections led to her being an important voice in our films.

Another speaker who went on to appear in our centerpiece film is Chuck O'Brien, MD, PhD, one of the nation's leading experts on the medical treatment of addiction. In his presentation, he remarked that the advances in medications for alcoholism were so great that there is now reason for every alcoholic to use these medications to help control their cravings. This was revolutionary to us. But the turning point in our education occurred at the standing-room-only lecture of Nora Volkow, MD, on "The Addicted Brain." We learned how drugs erode the voluntary acts of an individual. Volkow's vivid explanation of how the brain's ancient reward pathways are hijacked due to the spikes of the brain chemical dopamine through repeated drug use was eye-opening. That afternoon, we made an appointment to meet with her in Maryland at the National Institute on Drug Abuse (NIDA).

The vast majority of the funding in the United States for research on drug and alcohol addiction and treatment comes from NIDA and the National Institute on Alcohol Abuse and Alcoholism (NIAAA), two institutes of the National Institutes of Health. Their treatment recommendations are the most important guidelines that providers have. It became immediately apparent to us that if we wanted the viewers of the HBO films and the readers of this book to trust our messages, we needed the full cooperation of these agencies.

A month later, we were ushered into a conference room at NIDA crowded with staff members eager to brainstorm ideas. Many topics discussed in that room eventually became themes or storylines in our shows. Leading the list was the need to communicate the importance of comorbidity. Approximately 40 percent of addicts suffer from co-occurring mental disorders. NIDA stressed that any underlying mental disorder, as well as the addiction, must be treated simultaneously or the chances of a sustained recovery were slim. We learned about buprenorphine, a new FDA-approved medication for opiate addiction that is an alternative to methadone. The fact that it can be prescribed by a physician in his office (a less stigmatizing setting) is a valuable feature. As addiction is viewed more as a disease, the hope is that the medical community will play a larger role in treating it.

The next day was spent at NIAAA, which was another exciting experience. Again, we entered a room filled with scientists, academics, and researchers ready to educate us. New ideas were flying. They encouraged us to try to change the public perception of alcoholism; to communicate that alcoholism is not a middle-age disease but begins in youth, and that prevalence drops after the age of twenty-five. They also brought to our attention two new FDA-approved anticraving medications for alcoholism that the public is largely unaware of: naltrexone and acamprosate. We discussed at length how Alcoholics Anonymous is a great support system for the recovering addict, but alone is not treatment. We learned that addiction is a developmental disease, that people need to get help early, to continue treatment until they find what works for them, and to have hope.

We left Maryland impressed with the intellectual horsepower at work there and the compassion these scientists and staff had for people suffering from addiction.

From NIDA we had learned about the emergence of special courts, called drug courts, to handle cases involving substance-abusing offenders. To find out more, we traveled to South Boston to attend the conference of the New England Association of Drug Court Professionals. Drug courts were born twenty years ago out of the frustration of judges who were tired of sentencing nonviolent drug offenders to mandatory jail sentences, only to have the same people reappear before the court for the same charges once they were out of jail. So drug courts were designed to help these offenders get into long-term treatment by leveraging the authority of the criminal justice system. The fact that drug courts have been so successful demonstrates that coerced treatment is as effective as voluntary treatment. This exploded one of the myths we had adhered to (and one we realized we had to be a part of undoing): that an addict has to hit rock bottom for treatment to work. The organizer of this conference was Join Together, a potent think tank on addiction-related policy led by David Rosenbloom, PhD, a leader in the crusade to end discrimination against those with an addiction. He joined the esteemed list of experts who appear in our films.

But, outside of a drug court, how does a family access effective long-term treatment for a loved one struggling with addiction? None of the professionals we met could really give us a consistent answer, and our search for understanding why there were no standards for providers led us to Tom McLellan, PhD, co-founder and CEO of the Treatment Research Institute (TRI) in Philadelphia. With McLellan, we found a nonconformist who challenges the status quo in Washington, the medical establishment, the treatment community, and the insurance industry to handle addiction the same way they handle any other chronic disease.

McLellan was very clear that treatment can work, but accessing good treatment can be hard. Most addiction treatment facilities lack supervisors trained in addiction medicine. In the United States, there is no standard of care for addiction treatment providers, so buyer beware. A family must educate themselves and learn the elements of care. McLellan stressed that the two important questions to ask a provider are:

1. Are you accredited?

2. Is the medical leadership certified by the American Society of Addiction Medicine (ASAM)?

He emphasized that families must have a realistic understanding of what to expect from treatment, since there is no cure for this disease. The idea is to manage the disease, the way diabetes is managed. But there may be relapses, as there are with any chronic illness.

McLellan introduced us to one of his colleagues, Anna Rose Childress, PhD, whose research into the brain mechanisms responsible for addiction and relapse have led to a better understanding of why it is so hard for addicts to resist the pull of drugs, despite extremely negative consequences. We knew the one question every family member wanted answered was, "Why can't they just stop?" Through Childress, we learned that the answer lies in the brain's stop-and-go circuitry. Suddenly the brain disease model was beginning to make sense. It was an extraordinary moment for us—we had found the person who could explain this complex brain science in layperson's terms. We began to understand why relapse was so rampant. We began to understand the struggle each addict has to endure.

While we were spending time in some of the preeminent addiction research labs in the country and observing clinical trials for promising new medical treatments for alcoholism, the country was dealing with the rapidly spreading methamphetamine epidemic, and cocaine use was as strong as ever. Naïvely, we expected that since we had been pleasantly surprised to learn about advances in the medical treatment of various addictions, we would also learn about new medical treatments for stimulant addictions. Such was not the case. For the time being, the best weapon we have is a behavioral one, but it can be effective. We were put off at first by the acronyms thrown around in behavioral therapy—CBT, MET—but, at University of California at Los Angeles, we were introduced to Rick Rawson, PhD, who gave meaning to cognitive behavioral therapy (CBT) and motivational enhancement therapy (MET). His substantive work in this area led to NIDA's decision to deem his Matrix Model effective evidence-based treatment for cocaine and meth addiction.

When we learned that 75 percent of people struggling with addiction are employed, we were surprised, since this defied our stereotype of the typical addict. It became imperative to us that HBO's ADDICTION project include a workplace story. Finding a company that not only recognized the problem of addiction in the workplace, but was handling this problem in a progressive manner and was willing to go public with it proved to be impossible. Finally, Sam Bacharach, PhD, director of the Smithers Institute for Alcohol-Related Workplace Studies at Cornell University's School of Industrial and Labor Relations, steered us to a great labor story: the employee assistance program (EAP) of the Steamfitters Union, Local 638, in New York. The EAP was built by Don Perks, a steamfitter who attributes being alive to this program, and Perks's story offered inspiration to us in so many ways. It was Perks and Local 638 who took control of addiction treatment services away from the union's managed-care provider, leaving the steamfitters, who know their members, to make all the approvals for treatment services. With the steamfitters we also found a great story and a model for aftercare, now recognized as a crucial component for sustaining recovery.

As our research continued, we began meeting families in desperate struggles with severely addicted loved ones. Their complaints were eerily similar: they couldn't access inpatient treatment because their insurance company denied those benefits. We learned that after a decade of managed care, 92 percent of addiction treatment is outpatient. We met mothers who had lost children to drug overdoses while trying to get referrals from their insurance companies to inpatient or outpatient treatment.

The obstacles that managed care creates for families seeking addiction treatment were shocking. But one state stood out in its efforts to change this situation: Pennsylvania. Under the leadership of Deb Beck, president of Drug and Alcohol Service Providers of Pennsylvania, families of addicts took their fight to their state legislators, demanding the adequate insurance coverage they were due. Unknown to most Americans, there are forty-three states that require group health insurance plans, including managed care, to provide coverage for addiction treatment. But despite these laws that protect the consumer, managed-care providers continually deny adequate levels of care. This was a story that needed to be told.

We thank all the individuals we met while researching and producing HBO's ADDICTION project. Many continue to struggle with their recovery and others are doing very well.

Sheila Nevins's instinct that the time was right to explore the scientific advances in addiction treatment was prescient. Countless lives are now being saved. There are new medications that show great promise. We're confident that as more great minds enter the field of addiction medicine, and as the disease model is wholeheartedly embraced by the treatment community and the public, the stigma will fall away and addiction will become a far more manageable illness.

JULIE

Why Can't They Just Stop?

*It was like a hard-hitting reality—"I am an alcoholic."
I am one of those people I see on TV. I am one of those
people I used to criticize, thinking, How can they
be so weak?* JULIE, RECOVERING ALCOHOLIC

It was December, a peaceful evening, the sidewalks covered in fallen leaves. Along with a few colleagues, Timothy* ducked out of his office. The 42-year-old engineer wore a new blazer and gray wool slacks underneath a gray overcoat, which he pulled tighter when he felt the cold night.

Timothy, tall with hazel eyes and dark hair parted on the side, ran a small, elite R&D division at a software company. He was a popular boss. He loved his job, though not the required seasonal office parties like the one he was walking to that evening.

En route, Timothy held back from his colleagues for a moment. Retrieving his cell phone from underneath his coat, he dialed home. Lara*, his wife, answered on the first ring. Their 14-month-old was singing in the background and banging on a toy drum.

After asking about the kids and Lara's day, Timothy promised, "I'll be home in a couple of hours. I'll escape as quickly as humanly possible." When Lara told him to have fun, he half groaned. "You know what these things are like," he said. "I'll pay my respects and be home soon. I love you."

"I love you."

The restaurant was decorated for the holidays with twinkling white lights, a flocked Christmas tree, and red-leafed poinsettias on white-clothed tables. A jazz combo, set up in a corner of the room under mistletoe, played a vaguely recognizable version of "O Holy Night."

Timothy's colleagues dispersed, making their way toward other early arrivals, and meanwhile a waiter approached him and asked what he would like to drink. Without giving it a second thought, he asked for a sparkling water. In recovery for three years, he had made sparkling water a habit. At AA meetings, he joked that it had become his drug of choice—having replaced the drugs that previously had vied for that title: cocaine, methamphetamine, and prescription pills such as Valium and Vicodin. It was those drugs, when mixed and combined with a new Toyota Prius, that landed him in a hospital emergency room. The car was totaled but he was fine. Miraculously. The greatest miracle, however, was that he had driven his car into a tree and not an oncoming car. Afterward, he dwelled on this detail. A head-on collision probably would have been fatal, but that wasn't the worst scenario. Much worse, Timothy knew, would have been to have survived the accident but harmed someone. Or killed someone. He could not have lived with that. It was a sobering realization. Figuratively and literally.

Timothy claimed that even if not for the DUI and threatened criminal charges, he would have checked into rehab. It was his second time. In the initial rehab three years earlier, he learned that there's a myth that addicts and alcoholics have to hit bottom—whatever that is—before they become sober, but the reality is that everyone is different—there is no predicting what will impel someone to seek treatment. That first time, he had been in wretched shape. His wife had threatened to leave him if he didn't get help. But the accident was the clarion call of the variety that many addicts speak about in twelve-step meetings. "I got it," he would say when he told his story. "Only by the grace of God was I still here. That was that. I checked myself into treatment." For the second time. He promised his wife—he vowed—there would not be a third time.

Since then, he and Lara had another child, a beautiful daughter with large brown eyes and a serene smile. His career, which had floundered while he used, was back on track. He was committed to recovery, a regular attendee at Alcoholics Anonymous meetings. He had a full life, a happy life.

At the Christmas party, soon after his call home and after he ordered the sparkling water, something caught Timothy's eye. Later, he describes it. "It sat there on an isolated table," he says. "The rest of the room—the people, the sounds, the light—it all faded away. I sort of laughed it off. Like God was testing me. *You can't fool me,* I thought." A glass of Scotch, abandoned, set by a poinsettia on a white table, illuminated as if by a spotlight. He walked over, picked it up, and sniffed it. "A billon thoughts went through my mind," he explains afterward. "A billion thoughts and no thoughts." He spoke wistfully. "The glistening amber liquid. The intoxicating smell. Wood smoke. Euphoria."

Maybe, in that moment, he could have made a different decision—or maybe that moment was too late. "My mind simultaneously raced and froze," he says. "I thought, *After three years a sip won't hurt. I am so bored. What a waste of good liquor. I deserve it. I hate parties. It's a night of celebration. Christmastime. I am impervious. I am one of the lucky ones. My gorgeous children. My family. Three years sober and a sip. A sip.* Half thoughts like those and no thought at all."

He says it was almost like watching someone else— someone in a movie. Like he left his body. He felt a sense of horror, he says. Horror and also, incongruously, reckless delight. He sipped the Scotch. He breathed it. The taste was "heaven." He sipped again. "Glorious." He drained the glass. The reaction inside his head was instantaneous and intense. "I was filled with electric warmth," he recalls. "A smoldering fire was rekindled. I felt enlivened. The taste was . . . and I felt so . . ." He could not find the exact words. "I was horrified and felt perfect, both, but perfect won."

He said the required goodbyes and left the party. Again wrapped in his overcoat, walking to his car, he thought, *See? They say that I can't have one drink. I can and I did. A glass of Scotch. One glass. I am in recovery. Three years. My judgment isn't impaired. It's sharper than ever.*

Driving, he thought, *One drink. I missed the taste. The faint buzz. No problem. I've licked my addiction. Maybe "they"—"they" in the rehab programs, "they" in AA meetings—can't have just one, but I am not like them. I never have been. I talked the talk and walked the walk. I played along. But I'm not like them.* He laughed. Aloud.

He drove home, had every intention of driving home. His car came to the same intersection he drove through every morning and every evening before and after work. The car turned. By itself. Left instead of right. He smiled. Nervous now. The car had a mind of its own. Right would have led home. Left led to . . .

Peter*.

For a little holiday cheer, he told himself. *I deserve it after three years. Everything is in my life is great. Celebration. I am not like them. One line.*

Some addicts think it's okay to drink or smoke— "Just a little pot," "One beer"—as long as they don't use whatever was their drug of choice. However, according to Richard Rawson, PhD, associate director of UCLA's Integrated Substance Abuse Programs, an addict is far more likely to relapse on hard drugs if they drink or smoke marijuana.

Driving this familiar route, Timothy felt what he later describes as "a secret thrill. It filled my body." Driving itself, the car wound down a quiet suburban street—he chuckled as he always did when he turned on the road because it was called High Street—and pulled over in front of a cheery house. Peter. His friend. His buddy. The house dressed brightly for the holidays with a wreath on the front door.

Inside, after a bear hug from Peter, he noticed a clock. It was 7:30. Early. Plenty of time. At nine o'clock, he ignored his chiming cell phone. It rang again at 9:12. Then again. At 9:30, after the incessant ringing, he shuddered and turned off the phone. At dawn, he thought, *I am making up for lost time. I'm flying. How I have missed this in my life. Who have I been kidding?* Later he explains that there was something else inside him, a barely remembered sense somewhere in some part of his consciousness: Lara. The children. Home. Christmas. His job. Friends—a life.

Addiction is
a disease that
impacts 1 in 4
families.

Someone else's life. That life was an abstraction so distant as to be unreal. What was completely and utterly real was the moment: life coursed through his veins. "I felt powerful and alert. Whole."

Earlier there had been a first line—the first line in three years—followed by another. At eleven or so, he asked Peter if he had rigs (syringes). Peter smiled. "What took you so long?" he asked, embracing his friend. "I've missed you, bro."

Addicts or their family members must contend with what may be one of the most difficult concepts of all to comprehend: at various points on the road to recovery, addicts may relapse.

Timothy shot up, thinking, *And I have missed this! How could I have lived without it? I am in control. I'm fine. A celebration. One night after three years. I'll go home soon and sleep it off.* He says later, "High again, I felt immune, invulnerable, at peace."

He was awake. At four in the morning. Shooting. It was as if no time had passed between him and Peter, his dearest, truest friend. They drank Scotch and smoked weed. They talked. How he had missed talk like this—genuine and open and alive. "I'm glad I'm over this shit," Timothy said at one point. "Now I can take it or leave it."

The following day, he thought for a fleeting moment that maybe he should call Lara, but he pushed the thought aside. He shot up more and another day and another night were gone.

Lara's husband had not returned home for seventy-two hours. Three days. Lara did what wives and parents and children and lovers and friends of addicts do. She imagined every scenario, no matter how implausible. Timothy had been murdered. He had been kidnapped. She imagined a terrorist attack and accidents. Horrible accidents that involved dozens of cars. Ludicrously, sleepless in the middle of the night, she imagined a 747 hitting the freeway. She concocted preposterous scenarios, while all the while knowing that the truth was simpler. He had relapsed. It was the obvious but most discouraging explanation. She had already done what people who love addicts do. She had called his friends and colleagues and then, bracing herself, called the hospital emergency rooms and the police. Nothing.

Not knowing but knowing. She felt what family members feel: the horror, the dread, the terror. After the imagined 747 crash, she replayed much more likely fantasies—horrific fantasies. He has overdosed. He has gone out to kill himself. High, he crashed. Again. He is dead. She thought, *What did I do wrong?* Besides the self-blame, she also felt guilt for something else that flooded her—another thing that most people who love addicts feel and simultaneously feel guilty for feeling: she was enraged. By habit and for the children, her rage was contained. But tormented, she thought, *How could he do this to us? The bastard. Again.* She felt rage toward him and blamed herself. Both. *How could I have trusted him? I am a terrible mother. How can I put my children through this? The bastard. Poor Timothy. Poor Timothy? Poor us. The bastard. Where is he?*

Dawn on Monday the sky was smoky gray. Normally, Timothy would be on his way to work, stopping for coffee and a newspaper. That morning, however, he shakily drove across town and parked in front of another building that was familiar to him. A pallid, jittery ghost with sunken eyes, he walked up a flight of stairs and pushed through the glass door of the same rehab facility he had graduated from three years ago. By coincidence, the first person he saw was a counselor with whom he had been close. She glanced up and noticed him. She looked again, closer, and knew. She shook her head and without a word came up and hugged him. He wept.

Through tears, he whispered the obvious: "I relapsed."

"But you're here now," she said.

RELAPSE: PART OF THE ROAD TO RECOVERY

Addicts or their family members must contend with what may be one of the most difficult concepts of all to comprehend: at various points on the road to recovery, addicts may relapse. In some cases, it may be a failure of their treatment. "Some addicts fail to respond," says Nora Volkow, MD, director of the National Institute on Drug Abuse (NIDA). "There are many reasons. It wasn't a good program. The treatment was good, but it did not fit the person." In most cases, however, a relapse does not mean the efforts in recovery thus far haven't been effective.

Like other chronic illnesses, addiction—with the proper treatment—can be managed, so that an addict can live a life without drugs.

"Some heavy users will go through treatment once," says UCLA's Rawson. "They will stay sober after that. But for many, it will take multiple tries." Michael Dennis, PhD, a senior research pyschologist in the Lighthouse Institute of Chestnut Health Systems in Bloomington, Illinois, says that 70 percent of the patients relapse after their first time in treatment. "It's not like fixing a broken bone," he says.

Gantt Galloway, PharmD, a scientist in the Addiction Pharmacology Research Laboratory at the California Pacific Medical Center Research Institute in San Francisco, explains, "If we look at recovery as a lifelong process that may include one or many relapses, a far more realistic view of success emerges. We need to think of a treatment trajectory: it may take five, seven, nine times before they get it. Chronic depression has similar success rates. Seizure patients? The noncompliance rate is just as high. High blood pressure? All they have to do is take their medicine. It's not as difficult as staying sober, but the rate of noncompliance is just as high."

"Relapse is not a failure of treatment," says Anna Rose Childress, PhD, research associate professor at the University of Pennsylvania School of Medicine. "Relapse is part of the disorder." Kathleen Brady, MD, PhD, director of the Clinical Neuroscience Division at the Medical University of South Carolina and president of the American Academy of Addiction Psychiatry, explains, "[Addicts] have changed their brain in ways that make them vulnerable to relapse."

While relapse is common following treatment, the good news is that, in the long term, slightly more than half of the drug addicts who receive treatment ultimately achieve a state of stable remission. For alcoholics, the recovery rate is encouraging, according to Mark Willenbring, MD, of the National Institute on Alcohol Abuse and Alcoholism (NIAAA). Though a third may relapse, they still are much improved. Over the course of many years, about two-thirds of them eventually recover. For young people, the numbers are even more optimistic. Twenty years after the onset of alcohol dependence, only 7 percent were still dependent, with 20 percent improved. The rest were in full recovery. "Compare that to diabetes, asthma, arthritis, heart disease, or hypertension!" says Willenbring. "When was the last time you knew someone with diabetes who no longer required treatment and was fully recovered?"

Though these statistics are encouraging, no one—not the addict, not their family—wants to hear that addicts in recovery often relapse. After Timothy's relapse, when Lara came to visit him at his rehab program, she angrily asked, "Why, Timothy? Why? What was it?" He shook his head and said, "I don't know. It was like I didn't have a choice."

"You had a choice," she responded with a flash of anger. She was crying again. She had cried throughout the morning session. She cried throughout the afternoon session.

Timothy said, "I may not have felt as if it was a choice, but, yes, on some level I must have chosen it. No one forced me."

THE LONG REACH OF ADDICTION IN AMERICA

Addiction is a complex disease. It has profound effects on the health and well-being of the individual addict, as well as those around them, and society at large. Like other chronic illnesses, addiction—with the proper treatment— can be managed, so that an addict can live a life without drugs. The road to recovery, however, is often fraught with devastating consequences, some of which are short-lived and others, lifelong. Health, reputation, livelihood, and

Addiction is a National Concern

During 2004, there were 198 total drug-related deaths in **OREGON** reported by the State Medical Examiner Division. Ninety-four of these deaths were heroin related, 78 were methamphetamine related, 66 were cocaine related and 40 deaths involved a combination of drugs.

An estimated 5.5 million adults in **CALIFORNIA** are binge drinkers.

Approximately 10% of **NORTH DAKOTA** 12th graders surveyed in 2003 reported using methamphetamine at least once during their lifetimes.

Per capita, **HAWAII** has the highest population of meth users in the nation.

According to the **IOWA** Department of Corrections, meth-related offenses made up 62% of new prison admissions in state fiscal year 2004.

Approximately 10.5% of **KANSAS** students surveyed in 2006 reported being drunk or high at school within the past year.

The number of methamphetamine labs seized in **OKLAHOMA** by the Oklahoma Bureau of Narcotics has increased from 10 during 1994 to 1,277 during 2004.

The number of deaths in **TEXAS** in which cocaine was mentioned increased from 223 in 1992 to 699 in 2004.

During 2004, there were 38,606 drug-related hospitalizations in **MISSOURI**.

A survey of **INDIANA** youth in 2005 revealed that 7.3% of 6th graders reported using inhalants at least once in their lives.

In **KENTUCKY**, the Daniel Boone National Forest continues to suffer from the collateral effects of marijuana cultivation. These effects include property damage to natural resources, archeological sites, and wildlife, including endangered species.

More than 22% (22.3%) of **MISSISSIPPI** high school students surveyed in 2003 reported that they have been offered, sold, or given an illegal drug on school property within the past year.

Methamphetamine use was the lowest among young adults in **NEW YORK** (0.3%).

TENNESSEE accounts for 75% of the meth lab seizures in the southeastern United States.

During 2000, the **NORTH CAROLINA** Department of Health and Human Services reported 359 prescription drug thefts.

On March 16, 2006, drug possession offenses accounted for the most common offense among **GEORGIA**'s active probationers. Approximately 36% of all probationers had drug offenses as their primary offense.

Approximately 7% of **FLORIDA** high school students surveyed in 2005 reported selling drugs within the past year.

Heroin has equaled crack cocaine as the greatest drug threat in **CONNECTICUT**.

Heroin is abused throughout **MARYLAND** but is most problematic in and around the city of Baltimore. Baltimore is home to higher numbers of heroin addicts and heroin-related crime than almost any other city in the nation.

An increasing number of pharmacy burglaries and armed robberies have been attributed to the increase in OxyContin abuse in **MASSACHUSETTS**. During 2002, 148 of the 166 pharmacy thefts reported in New England took place in Massachusetts.

One in five adults said they had an immediate relative (spouse, parent, brother, sister, son or daughter) who at some point had been addicted to alcohol or drugs. That translates into roughly 40 million American adults with a spouse, parent, sibling or child battling addiction.

31% of women interviewed who had an addicted relative mentioned their spouse, compared with only 12% of men.

Three out of four respondents with addicted close relatives said they thought their family member could make a full recovery. However, two-thirds of them thought recovery was possible only with professional help.

SOURCE: USA TODAY/HBO FAMILY DRUG ADDICTION/ GALLUP POLL TAKEN APRIL–MAY 2006

interpersonal relationships are just a few areas that can be severely affected by drug and alcohol abuse—and that, in many cases, can be repaired in recovery.

Today's epidemic of addiction to drugs or alcohol is a subject that is talked about candidly only with extreme difficulty. Why? The stigma and shame associated with drug and alcohol dependence have helped to build an invisible wall that can isolate addicts and their loved ones in times of deep crisis. Common misconceptions as to both the causes of addiction and the ways in which it can be successfully (or not) treated add to the fog of mystery and confusion. As Timothy and Lara and so many others have learned, the cost for society's prejudices and misunderstandings is simply too high. Not just because of individual lives ruined or lost (as if they weren't cause enough for concern), but because the disease of addiction is everywhere; it is spreading—and it never affects just one person.

Among addiction treatment professionals, conventional wisdom holds that an addict has a direct negative impact on anywhere between four and fifteen people. Count up the people you know, the ones you regularly talk to or see. Husbands and wives. Parents and children. Your spouse's siblings and your own. Your boss, your colleagues. Your children's friends, classmates, teammates. The church, the book club, the Scout troop. It's easier than you think for each of us to tote up fifty, perhaps even one hundred people who are regularly in our lives. Multiply that number by 22.2 million addicts and you have a rough idea of the devastating impact of addiction on this country.

For all of us, it is important to see that addiction doesn't exist "over there," on the other side of the figurative tracks. Addiction has many faces: black and white and all the colors in between. It is rural and urban, rich and poor. The disease does not confine itself to socioeconomic groups or specific neighborhoods, whether the South Bronx or Beverly Hills. It fills emergency rooms, clogs our court system, and overcrowds our jails. It ends marriages, shatters families, kills our children, and drains our tax dollars. Of its many faces, one thing is almost guaranteed: it is a face you know.

In Cranberry Township, a community outside Pittsburgh—the type of sedate, leafy suburb that is likely to be voted "best place to live" by its residents—a program called Bridges to Hope regularly draws together a group of women who share stories of children suffering from continued drug relapses, brushes with the law, and dead-end life situations. In the meeting at her home, Joan Ward tells the group, "The message I want people to receive is, we are in the middle of suburbia and we could go down any cul-de-sac in this whole area and we would find addiction, we would find everything that goes with it," she says. "First we have to be courageous enough to say, 'It's in my living room,' and that's hard to do."

Addiction has many faces: black and white and all the shades in between. It is rural and urban, rich and poor. Of its many faces, one thing is almost guaranteed: it is a face you know.

The USA Today/HBO Family Drug Addiction Poll conducted by Gallup in 2006 of 902 adults with an immediate family member who suffers from addiction begins to show the impact of this problem. About half the respondents with an addicted spouse said the experience has taken a major negative toll on their emotional health. Almost half said they suffer from shame over having an addicted family member. Although women were more likely than men to say that their family member's addiction had "hurt their mental and physical health, as well as their marriage," the words that everyone used were powerfully negative: "devastating," "abusive," "horrible."

Each addict leaves a unique footprint on their family and community. Depending on who the addicts are, what they're using, how they get it, and the behavior the addiction encourages—erratic mood swings, manic spending, inexplicable fears, sullen apathy, spousal abuse, petty theft, the list goes on—the impact of the addiction can range

Some people who start as casual drinkers or drug users will stay that way. But others will become substance abusers or dependent, feeling that they need a drug to feel alive. The difference between abuse and dependence is not always clear to the general public, but medical professionals use a set of criteria to distinguish between these two categories of problem use.

The essential feature of abuse is a pattern of substance use that causes someone to experience harmful consequences. Clinicians diagnose substance abuse if, in a twelve-month period, a person is in one or more of the following situations related to drug use:

→ Failure to meet obligations, such as missing work or school
→ Engaging in reckless activities, such as driving while intoxicated
→ Encountering legal troubles, such as getting arrested
→ Continuing to use despite personal problems, such as a fight with a partner

Dependence is more severe. Medical professionals will look for three or more criteria from a set that includes two physiological factors and five behavioral patterns, again, over a twelve-month period. Tolerance and withdrawal alone are not enough to indicate dependence. And not all behavioral signs occur with every substance.

The physiological factors are:
→ Tolerance, in which a person needs more of a drug to achieve intoxication
→ Withdrawal, in which they experience mental or physical symptoms after stopping drug use

The behavioral patterns are:
→ Being unable to stop once using starts
→ Exceeding self-imposed limits
→ Curtailing time spent on other activities
→ Spending excessive time using or getting drugs
→ Taking a drug despite deteriorating health

from quietly devastating to openly dangerous. Whether it's the child addict whose habit upends her family's ability to get through the day or the hooked adult who commits crimes to support his fix, every addict spreads tentacles of consequences through their home and neighborhood. Yet the problem remains cloaked in shame, denial, and stigma, discussed in hushed tones, as if the people who suffer from the disease are somehow responsible for it. After all, addicts invited this particular problem on themselves, didn't they?

Well, yes. And no. Addiction was first defined as a disease by the American Medical Association in 1956, and it has taken a full half-century of research and treatment for even medical and psychological professionals to shed old beliefs. So perhaps it should come as no surprise that society at large has difficulty seeing an old disease in a new way.

ADDICTION IS A DISEASE

Addicts are weak, the myth goes. Weak of mind, weak of character. Or they're willfully self-destructive. Or they're unbearably selfish. They must be. Otherwise they'd stop hurting themselves and hurting others as well, right? "That's the real mistake that people make," says senior research psychologist Dennis. "They think it's about a morality play, a moral shortcoming. That somehow you've failed as a person."

According to a recent survey by the National Council on Alcoholism and Drug Dependence, half the public believes that addiction is a personal weakness. In the 2006 USA Today/HBO Family Drug Addiction Poll, while 76 percent of those polled identified addiction as a "disease," they identified "lack of willpower" as the main problem facing addicts.

In fact, the new understanding of drug and alcohol addiction that top scientists like Volkow and Willenbring agree on suggests the opposite. A more accurate way to put it would be that any so-called lack of willpower in an addict has been caused by changes in the brain. Dependence on drugs or alcohol caused these very changes. The inability to make clear decisions is a by-product of the same disease from which the addict is trying to escape. What could be more insidious? More clearly than ever, today's addiction specialists understand this conundrum: repeated use of drugs and alcohol alters the way the brain works. These alterations can now be observed and described in precise detail. The sea change in our understanding of addiction has begun to yield new treatments, including new types of medications that help restore the brain's normal functions. The first step, therefore, is to call addiction what it is, instead of the well-worn metaphors that polite, embarrassed, or justifiably frightened people have used for generations. It is not a "problem." It is not "a phase she's going through." It is not "shaking out the jams before he settles down." It is a chronic, relapsing brain disease.

POPULAR MISCONCEPTIONS

It is hard to dismiss the mythical role that pop culture depictions of "altered states" have played in each generation's responses to drug and alcohol use. Just look at D. W. Griffith's *A Drunkard's Reformation* in 1909, or 1915's *Charlie's Drunken Daze,* when Charlie Chaplin's wild night on the town ends in a hotel room mix-up with a pretty girl. In 1936, *Reefer Madness* was supposed to serve as a warning about marijuana, but instead has come to be viewed as an inadvertently camp comedy; in 1981, Dudley Moore was a hilarious yet ultimately pathetic drunk in *Arthur*. In 1988, *Clean and Sober* depicted a cocaine addict hiding out from the law in a rehab center, where he's confronted by the one person anyone would devoutly wish to have not just as an addiction sponsor but a life coach: Morgan Freeman. And 2004's *Sideways* begins as a sophisticated buddy movie about a California wine country tour, but devolves into a story of an alcoholic whose life is in shambles.

In spite of the chaos portrayed in films and plays about addiction, there is still at the root of them something melancholy, almost romantic—an often confusing message containing both attraction and revulsion. Even the most tragic addict is somehow viewed as heroic or noble in his suffering (see Nicolas Cage in *Leaving Las Vegas*). The "tragic artist as addict" motif runs through music and literature as well; writers such as Hemingway, Fitzgerald, and Faulkner all worried that sobriety would kill their creativity, and that alcohol was somehow necessary to the Muse. Do we see

Kurt Cobain, Brian Jones, or Jim Morrison as tortured artists whose creativity required drugs, or do we see them clearly as addicts with compromised lives who somehow managed to make some music—but possibly not as much as they might have? When kids hear hip-hop lyrics that tout a life of champagne and blunts, are they attracted to what they're hearing or are they able to understand the context, and reject it?

There are hopeful signs that attitudes are changing in the music industry (at least toward the plight of the musicians themselves) with the inception of support groups such as MusiCares, the Musicians' Assistance Program, and Road Recovery. Musicians such as James Taylor and Bonnie Raitt have often spoken out about their own battles with addiction. Some veteran rap musicians have also spoken of their desire to see hip-hop lyrics move away from the one-note deification of "thug life" behavior. Nevertheless, our culture's continuing fascination with celebrities often dilutes the grim seriousness of their struggle.

In October of 2006, Susan Murray, an assistant professor of culture and communications at New York University's Steinhardt School of Education, reported that alcohol use in reality TV programs was "a pretty common ploy to make the plot line move along and make it interesting." Murray, the coeditor of a compilation of scholarly essays titled *Reality TV: Remaking Television Culture*, said the excessive drinking, arranged and sanctioned by the programs' producers, was a clear attempt to manipulate the situations and the people who were in them. An 18-year-old might have no trouble realizing these are real people with some real problems—but would a 14-year-old?

Perhaps even more damaging than pop culture's gauzy view of drug and alcohol use is its skewed version of treatment and rehabilitation for the same substances. A casual flip through *People* magazine suggests that 2006 was a year for the famous and the infamous to hit rock bottom and then rise from the ashes. A drunk Mel Gibson gets pulled over by the cops, spews an anti-Semitic tirade, and then makes public apologies and proclaims his addiction and his intention to get help.

The story line seems ubiquitous: some famous movie

Myths of Addiction

1. Addicts are bad, crazy, or stupid.
Evolving research is demonstrating that addicts are not bad people who need to get good, crazy people who need to get sane, or stupid people who need education. Addicts have a brain disease that goes beyond their use of drugs.

2. Addiction is a willpower problem.
This is an old belief, probably based upon wanting to blame addicts for using drugs to excess. This myth is reinforced by the observation that most treatments for alcoholism and addiction are behavioral (talk) therapies, which are perceived to build self-control. But addiction occurs in an area of the brain called the mesolimbic dopamine system that is not under conscious control.

3. Addicts should be punished, not treated, for using drugs.
Science is demonstrating that addicts have a brain disease that causes them to have impaired control over their use of drugs. Addicts need treatment for their neurochemically driven brain pathology.

4. People addicted to one drug are addicted to all drugs.
While this sometimes occurs, most people who are dependent on a drug may be dependent on one or two drugs, but not all. This is probably due to how each drug "matches up" with the person's brain chemistry.

5. Addicts cannot be treated with medications.
Actually, addicts are medically detoxified in hospitals, when appropriate, all the time. But can they be treated with medications after detox? New pharmacotherapies (medicines) are being developed to help patients who have already become abstinent to further curb their craving for addicting drugs. These medications reduce the chances of relapse and enhance the effectiveness of existing behavioral (talk) therapies.

6. Addiction is treated behaviorally, so it must be a behavioral problem.
New brain scan studies are showing that behavioral treatments (i.e., psychotherapy) and medications work similarly in changing brain function. So addiction is a brain disease that can be treated by changing brain function, through several types of treatments.

7. Alcoholics can stop drinking simply by attending AA meetings, so they can't have a brain disease.
The key word here is "simply." For most people, AA is a tough, lifelong working of the Twelve Steps. On the basis of research, we know that this support system of people with a common experience is one of the active ingredients of recovery in AA. AA doesn't work for everyone, even for many people who truly want to stop drinking.

SOURCE: ADAPTED FROM THE UNIVERSITY OF TEXAS ADDICTION SCIENCE RESEARCH AND EDUCATION CENTER, WRITTEN BY CARLTON K. ERICKSON, PhD

star or politician has a potentially career-ending lapse in behavior and the explanation, that drugs or alcohol are to blame, is immediately followed by seclusion in rehab, a cycle implying that recovery and resurrection are sure to follow.

Numerous myths stand between addicts and effective help. And unfortunately, 2006 proved to be a good year for perpetuating them, as the drama of who was or wasn't fighting an addiction played out repeatedly on the public stage.

"It's not as simple as just saying no, or just stopping. Once someone's arrived at the chronic condition of alcohol or drug dependence, it's not that easy for them to quit."

When Congressman Bob Ney of Ohio pleaded guilty last year to making false statements and conspiring to commit fraud, admitting that he accepted thousands of dollars in free travel, meals, and sporting events from disgraced lobbyist Jack Abramoff, he said, "I have come to realize that dependency on alcohol has been a problem for me."

What could Congressman Mark Foley of Florida possibly say to excuse his behavior, after news broke that he had been sending sexually explicit text messages to teenage male pages on Capitol Hill? He had fought for laws against sexual predators as head of a House caucus on missing and exploited children, but now appeared to be one. His lawyer publicly announced that Foley had checked into a treatment center. "The combination of alcohol and mental illness can result in inappropriate conduct," the lawyer said, citing experts.

Rush Limbaugh, the radio shock jock, admitted to being hooked on OxyContin and hydrocodone after being investigated by Florida authorities for illegally buying narcotic painkillers. He told his radio audience that he was checking into a treatment center for a month to "once and for all break the hold this highly addictive medication has on me."

REAL-LIFE ADDICTION

That one could hit rock bottom, look in the mirror, decide to overhaul one's life, check into a thirty-day rehab program, and emerge healed is certainly a seductive notion. But it's based on pernicious myths about addiction and does little to help those struggling with the lifetime grip of addiction and the hard work of quitting.

Brady, president of the American Academy of Addiction Psychiatry, says, "The whole idea that an individual needs to reach rock bottom before they can get any help" is "absolutely wrong." In fact, recovery is easier when there is more to live for—before someone has lost a spouse or a job, or has a criminal record.

Real-life addiction rarely has a tidy or triumphant story line, as the USA Today/HBO poll makes clear. It elicited tragic and all-too-real stories of families torn apart, people dead of liver disease or drunk-driving accidents, and the unfathomable grief of parents who had lost children (and children who had lost parents). After the poll ran, numerous readers responded with accounts of their own twelve-step successes and failures, multiple treatments at rehab centers, and family homes sold at auction because of the high cost of repeated attempts at treatment and recovery.

Senior research psychologist Dennis, a leading expert in the treatment of adolescent addicts, has heard hundreds of similar stories through the years. "It's not as simple as just saying no, or just stopping," he argues. "Once someone's arrived at the chronic condition of alcohol or drug dependence, it's not that easy for them to quit."

Before talking in more detail about the ins and outs of treatment and recovery—what works, what doesn't, and why—it is important to remember that each addict deserves a treatment tailored to their personal circumstances and addiction, specifically the substance(s) in question and any co-occurring mood or anxiety disorders. The origins of addiction are as varied as the addicts themselves. Each case needs to be understood as a human faced with a particular set of variables—parents, economic status, psychological environment—all of which are relevant but no single one of which can rightly be called decisive. Some addicts come from families where alcoholism or drug addiction appear unfairly predestined; others seem to have every advantage in the world, genetic and otherwise, and still addiction lays them low. Attempts to pass judgment seem misguided after one considers the extreme range of circumstances that have resulted in addiction for different types of people.

For Jimmy, a successful criminal defense lawyer in Massachusetts, addiction was always someone else's problem. Addicts and drug dealers were Jimmy's clients, whom he represented with so much skill. They were the people who came into the courtroom drunk, day after day. But in 1999, after a car accident literally turned his world upside down, he began a journey into addiction that would change his perspective—and his life—forever.

After a head-on collison, Jimmy landed on the roof of his car with his briefcase whizzing past his face and awoke, minus his spleen, to a long, painful recovery. Three years later, his wife, whom he had relied on entirely, died of a brain aneurysm. Those agonizing events led him to take refuge in the painkiller OxyContin, which his doctor had prescribed after the accident. Before long, he was into almost anything he could scrounge up, from cocaine to heroin to crystal meth.

The only way to quit, he concluded, would be if he was "plucked off the face of the earth and thrown into a jail cell"—which finally happened. Before, he had seen the scourge of addiction through his perspective as a lawyer. This time, the addict—the person standing before the judge, lying to his family—was him.

For some, addiction can turn up in the middle of their lives seemingly without any warning or for any valid reason at all. "Even though I lived through it, I still don't understand it," says Emma*, "and I don't know if I ever will." The mother of four and former wife of a successful businessman speaks in the quiet tones of someone who's squared off against catastrophe and is still standing.

"People will ask, 'What did you do this weekend?' I'm

always saying, 'My son and I did this and my son and I did that.' They'll ask, 'Doesn't he ever spend time with his dad?" And I say, 'Well, he can't. His dad's in prison.' It always gets a gasp. Long story—basically drugs, alcohol, and white-collar crime."

Emma and her family lived in a nice, middle-class neighborhood, in a big house, with a nice life—church every Sunday, the kids in Catholic school, everyone doing well and every reason to believe it would only get better. "The kids were our lives," she says. "And my husband was so dedicated to them, and so was I—people kind of thought of us as the *Leave It to Beaver* family."

The origins of addiction are as varied as the addicts themselves. Each case needs to be understood as a human faced with a particular set of variables.

Then Emma's husband began to struggle with depression. Wisely, he sought therapy. The counselor sent him to a physician, who gave him prescriptions for dextroamphetamine (Dexedrine) and amphetamine-dextroamphetamine (Adderall). "I didn't find out until later," Emma says, "but the doctor had actually prescribed four times the recommended amount of Adderall per day. And four times the amount of Dexedrine. And four times the amount of whatever he was supposed to take at night to sleep."

Very quickly, the husband and dad they all knew vanished. "He just got strange all of a sudden. He'd disappear into the attic for hours, maybe seven hours, and come out and tell us how well he had insulated it," says Emma. "I took all my kids down to my daughter's cheerleading competition, and when we came home, we were excited because we'd taken first in the state. And he said, 'That's great. You know what I did this weekend? I took apart the washer and dryer and fixed them.' I said, 'I didn't know they were broken.' He said, 'Well, I just wanted to make sure.'"

When Emma's father-in-law died, her husband decided he needed to quit his prescription drugs cold turkey— a decision that could have killed him, the medical experts later told her. Instead, it drove him crazy. "He threw furniture in the pool," she says, "and then he started drinking. Just replaced one for the other. He'd look me straight in

In total, the 2005 National Survey on Drug Use and Health estimated that 22.2 million Americans, age 12 and older, suffer from dependence on, or abuse of, drugs and alcohol.

the eye and say, 'I'm not drinking.' I'd known this man since I was 13, I knew what kind of person he was, I knew how he'd raised my kids. And all of a sudden, there was this man I didn't know. And I didn't know that the mortgage wasn't being paid. I didn't know that the bills weren't being paid—he'd intercept the mail and all the phone calls."

If her husband had received better treatment for his depression in the first place, would the rest have ever occurred? Impossible to judge. The fact that he became a drug addict only verifies that a predisposition was there: the wrong drugs for the wrong brain at the wrong moment.

The worsening financial crisis led to court proceedings, which Emma's husband missed; in fact, he simply disappeared. A warrant was issued for his arrest. The next she heard, he was being held in prison on federal charges stemming from a bad financial mess at his workplace. When she returned home from his hearing, there was a notice on her door that the bank had foreclosed on their home. The cars were repossessed and the bank accounts were all overdrawn. It was a scenario she'd expect on *The Jerry Springer Show*, not in her own life. It was the result, she says, of a "scary disease" called addiction. "There are days when I'm so mad that I can't even think straight. There are days when I cry for the dream I had for our family. I cry for that dream because that dream is gone."

A NATIONAL HEALTH ISSUE . . .
White middle-aged Americans like Jimmy and Emma's husband are the nation's fastest growing population of drug abusers, according to a 2007 article from the *New York Times*. Author Mike Males, PhD, a senior researcher at the Center on Juvenile and Criminal Justice also noted that deaths from illegal-drug overdoses among people in their forties and fifties have risen by 800 percent since 1980, and 300 percent in the past decade.

In total, the Substance Abuse and Mental Health Services Administration found that between 2002 and 2005, the rate of illegal drug use among adults ages 50 to 59 rose from 2.7 percent to 4.4 percent. According to recent data, abuse and dependence have increased for senior citizens as well, in what one expert calls a "silent epidemic" because it is so rarely diagnosed or treated correctly. (Substance abuse is most common between the ages of 18 and 25.) In total, the 2005 National Survey on Drug Use and Health estimated that 22.2 million Americans, age 12 and older, suffer from dependence on, or abuse of, drugs and alcohol. Of these, approximately 3.3 million people were dependent on or abused both alcohol and illegal drugs; 3.6 million were dependent on or abused illegal drugs (excluding alcohol) only; 15.4 million were dependent on or abuse alcohol alone.

One nationwide survey in 2001 reported that six million children in America live with at least one parent who abuses alcohol or drugs, and substance abuse by parents is a major contributing factor in the number of children currently in foster care—half a million to date. It is estimated that approximately one-third of the 500,000 people currently homeless in America have addiction disorders.

Drug overdose deaths have increased 540 percent since 1980. One-quarter of all emergency room admissions are alcohol related (although many ER doctors will tell you that the actual figure is likely much higher). Traditionally,

Drug and Alcohol Facts

→ According to NIDA, drug-related deaths have more than doubled since the early 1980s. There are more deaths, illness, and disabilities from substance abuse than from any other preventable health condition.

→ According to the Centers for Disease Control, excessive alcohol use causes 75,000 American deaths each year. These are split about evenly between chronic causes such as liver disease and acute causes such as accidental injuries and automobile crashes.

→ According to a 2003 study by the National Highway Traffic Safety Administration, drugs, other than alcohol, are involved in about 18 percent of motor-vehicle driver deaths. These other drugs are generally used in combination with alcohol.

→ According to a study published in 2004 in the *Journal of American Medical Association*, appoximately 17,000 deaths in 2000 were caused by illicit drug use.

SOURCES: NIDA, CENTERS FOR DISEASE CONTROL, ACTUAL CAUSES OF DEATH IN THE UNITED STATES, 2000.

Addiction in America: The Substances of Abuse

Number, in thousands, of Americans age 12 and older dependent on or abusing substances

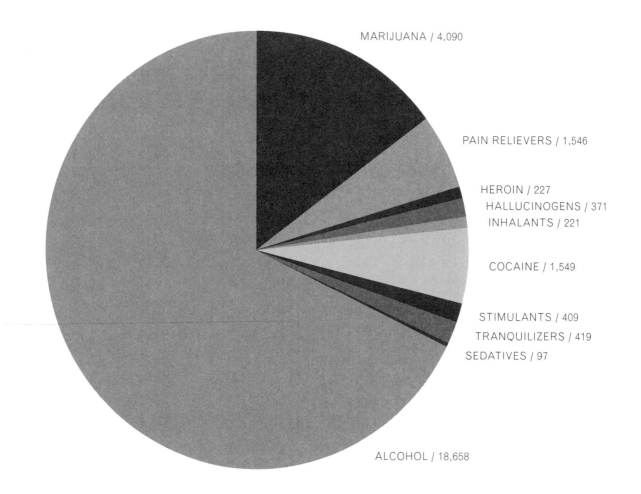

MARIJUANA / 4,090

PAIN RELIEVERS / 1,546

HEROIN / 227
HALLUCINOGENS / 371
INHALANTS / 221

COCAINE / 1,549

STIMULANTS / 409
TRANQUILIZERS / 419
SEDATIVES / 97

ALCOHOL / 18,658

SOURCE: *SAMHSA, 2005 National Survey on Drug Use and Health*

doctors have not been trained to diagnose addiction, so its presence as a factor in injuries or diseases is often overlooked. One-third of all suicides, and more than half of all homicides and domestic violence incidents, are alcohol related as well. Excessive alcohol use—the third most common cause of preventable death, behind smoking and obesity—kills 75,000 Americans a year.

. . . WITH GROWING COSTS

According to Samuel Bacharach, PhD, director of the Smithers Institute for Alcohol-Related Workplace Studies at Cornell University, the most recent federal data from 2002 estimate that alcohol and drug use cost U.S. employers over $128.6 billion in lost productivity and an additional $15.8 billion in substance-use related employee healthcare costs. Addiction alone accounts for 500 *million* lost workdays each year, not to mention job-site accidents and increased insurance premiums. "Addiction and alcohol problems are probably the most underdetected, undertreated health problems in the American workplace," says Eric Goplerud, PhD, director of Ensuring Solutions to Alcohol Problems, which reviews state insurance policies for the Department of Health Policy at George Washington University in Washington, DC. "It affects eight workers out of a hundred, and yet most of them never get the treatment that they need or could benefit from."

But with all of this sameness, and the drumbeat of intractability surrounding this problem, there is something new: the medical and scientific paradigm shift whose significance has just begun to be fully exploited.

THE NEW PARADIGM: THERE *IS* HOPE

The Massachusetts lawyer, Jimmy, was addicted long before he realized it. In his mind, he took drugs in order to function, in order to wake up every day and go to work, not to get high. But he now realizes that he was kidding himself about the seriousness of his addiction and says that he probably should have been institutionalized after his wife's death. "I had no right being out of this house," he says, when he considers that he drove while high. "Thank God I didn't kill anybody."

Jimmy agrees that naming the problem is an important first step toward recovery. For him, it began when he was arrested while buying drugs. "From that moment I was plucked off the street . . . I knew, *Okay, this is how it is that there's an end.* From that second, it's like everything changed."

It is not that recovery was easy for him. It was agony, both physical and mental. But his arrest collapsed the myths he'd constructed: that using drugs was helping him to function as a professional and earn a living to support

Brains harmed by addiction can be repaired. It may take more than one try; it most certainly won't be an easy road, but it can be done.

his kids. In treatment, he had to confront a far more painful reality: that he had not stopped despite the needs of his children. "I said to my therapist, 'I'm ashamed because I looked into the eyes of my children—and that wasn't enough to make me stop.' When I said that to her, she threw a book at me and said, 'It's *physical*. It's a physical addiction.' And I've come to forgive myself."

If you're an addict or you love one, quitting often seems like an impossible dream, something you talk about and never do. "I became a great liar," says Jimmy. "I looked people dead straight in the eye and told them I wasn't on drugs time and time again." All the while, he was completely hooked. "I'd have to do drugs to go to sleep," he recalls. If I woke up in the middle of the night, I'd have to do them to get back to sleep. I'd wake up in the morning and have to do them to get up."

For seven years, Jimmy could not function without drugs. And in the process, he lost everything: his house, cars, law license, and his public standing. But today, Jimmy has finally quit.

"People take the drug despite tremendous social and personal cost," says NIDA's Volkow. "Even though they know they are going to end up in jail. Even though they know their spouse is going to abandon them. Even though they know their children are going to be taken away. It's not that these people don't care about these things—they care very much—it's that something very fundamental has changed in their brain."

That *something* is the question Volkow has been exploring for the past two decades. Breakthroughs in imaging technology have allowed her and other researchers to literally peer inside the human brain and observe what it looks like while addicted to any number of different substances, and what it looks like in recovery. What Volkow and others have discovered (or perhaps more accurately, reaffirmed and given new meaning to) bears repeating: addiction is a progressive, chronic, relapsing disorder of the brain. Addiction *can* be successfully treated. It is not a moral failing but something much closer in its nature to diseases like asthma or diabetes.

"The science of understanding addiction has just been exploding in recent years through the use of any number of different technologies, including genetics, animal studies, studies in humans, and brain imaging," says NIAAA's Willenbring. "We are really starting to piece together some of the brain mechanisms involved in the development of and resolution of drug dependence and alcohol dependence." Such advances mean a new ability to objectively measure the success of different treatments and to develop new treatments that can be clinically proven to work. This watershed moment promises to help sweep away decades of moralistic cant and punitive condemnation surrounding the fate of addicts in this country. No longer should addicts be expected to just tough it out when the true, slippery nature of their disease can be so much more finely calibrated.

This new understanding has already helped addicts like Jimmy. Addicts seemingly lost forever to their families or themselves have come back from oblivion. What scientists like Volkow and Willenbring have helped the public to understand is that brains harmed by addiction *can* be repaired. It may take more than one try; it most certainly won't be an easy road, but it can be done. Perhaps the most startling recognition is that new medications—pills that have been clinically tested and are available by prescription from a doctor—can help restore the brain's normal functioning and control or eliminate the craving for certain drugs and alcohol.

Tom is among the addicts who have been spared years of suffering, if not death, thanks to one of these new medications. By his own description, Tom was always a "functional drunk." He was never in trouble with the law, rarely missed work selling building materials, and got along with his neighbors. But he drank hard every day. Once he retired he found himself drinking "twenty-four hours a day, seven days a week." In about eight years of retirement, he only played two rounds of golf. His life was "in the toilet."

And then he learned that a good friend had cancer and was yearning to stay alive. "Here I am, with the gift of life, and I'm pissing it away at the bottom of a whiskey bottle," Tom realized.

He enrolled in a treatment program that was testing a promising new medication called topiramate, typically used to reduce seizures by quieting abnormal brain activity. From the day he enrolled in the program, he never drank again. He attributes this both to the medicine and to his will to stop. "There's no light-switch therapy," he says. "You've got to mentally want to, and then medication can help you."

He continues, "In days gone by, I know what I'd do. I'd be sitting here drinking in the middle of the day." Now, instead of spending the entire day drinking, he chooses what to do with his days.

His only regret? "It's too bad I didn't come to this realization a long time ago. I can't change that. But I can determine what's going to happen tomorrow. And I'm not going to drink."

Addiction is
a chronic,
relapsing—
and treatable—
brain disease.

Sally MISSOURI

A mother of three, Sally has recently stopped using meth.

They say that meth is the hardest to kick. The recovery rate for meth addicts is very low. I wish they had more money for treatment, instead of throwing us in jail and locking us up for the rest of our lives. We're good people. We've just made bad choices. And we need help. We need to be able to reach out for that help, and not have people shun us and look down on us.

What a lot of people don't understand is that addiction is a disease. It's a disease in your brain. And the cravings that you get just make the disease worse, to where it consumes your life, like it did mine.

I have to work on a daily basis to keep what I have, to keep clean and to stay away from meth. That includes having people and places you have to stay away from too. It's like they say, if you hang around the barbershop long enough, you're gonna get a haircut. And it's true. Whenever I got clean before, I stayed around the same people and hung out at the same places. I wasn't doing the work. I was just dry. I would go through life

as I always had, just not using. But it was only a matter of time and I was right back in it.

You have to want to stay clean for yourself and no other reason. Because if you don't do it for yourself, you're not gonna make it. You'll end up back in your addiction. I never believed it when they said you'll pick up right where you left off and you'll get worse. And that's exactly true. When I would start back up again, it was even more than where I left off. It'll go until it kills you. And that's what it was doing to me. It was killing me slowly. It killed my spirit. It killed everything that I cared about, my morals, my standards.

What goes on inside my head—an addict's or alcoholic's head—is self-torture. It's really hard just to think normal thoughts. Instead of facing our problems, we run to the bar, run to the pipe, get drunk, or get high and erase all those problems.

I know right from wrong. I know that getting high is bad. I know it's breaking the law. The

thoughts that go through my head are hard to explain. It's like a ping-pong game. It's back and forth and back and forth. You know what's right, but it feels good. It makes me forget. I can do it just this once. Nobody's gonna know. And it's just a daily struggle.

The obstacle is everyday life. I run into situations where I get stressed out, or I'll get angry and I'll wanna use. It takes away the pain. It

It takes a lot to get your self-respect back. I know that it's gonna take a long time for my family to trust me again, respect me again. Every time I go over to my mom's, she's looking me in the eye, trying to see if I'm high or not. It's gonna take a lot of work on my part, and a lot of understanding on theirs, for them to accept me again.

I've done ten years of damage. And it's gonna take ten years plus to make everything okay

You have to want to stay clean for yourself and no other reason. Because if you don't do it for yourself, you're not gonna make it.

helps me forget what I'm going through. But after awhile, it didn't even cover up the pain. The pain was still there. The problems were there. They just got bigger. I just ignored 'em and put 'em off. And now I have to deal with everything that I've put off for the past ten years.

again. But as long as I'm doing what I'm supposed to do, and as long as I'm doing everything right and praying and asking for help, reaching out, it'll work. It's not easy. I'm gonna need help for the rest of my life.

GREGORY

Addiction Is a Brain Disease

It's very embarrassing at this stage of the game to actually have to admit having an addiction because, in my heart of hearts, I don't believe it. But my actions speak louder than words. I know that this is a problem for me. GREGORY, RECOVERING ALCOHOLIC

"Patients say, 'Why can't I just stop? I've lost so much, I've paid such a high price,'" says Anna Rose Childress of the University of Pennsylvania. "Parents say, 'They've completely wrecked their lives. Our lives, too. Why can't they just stop?' What we're beginning to understand now, at the level of the brain, is that there are lots of cards that are stacked in
the wrong direction here."

When the primary focus of someone's life is getting and using a substance that alters their way of thinking, everything else eventually falls by the wayside. Personal relationships are strained, education is interrupted or ended, and bills go unpaid. Add to this list any number of untreated physical and mental illnesses, and a potentially crippling social isolation.

And that's just the damage we can see. Unseen is the actual biochemical alteration of the parts of the brain that are necessary for us to make decisions and control our behavior. That's why, even when an addict has a strong desire to change their life, what happens next is not as simple as walking into the first AA meeting they find. "They can't stop because their brain has been changed," says David Rosenbloom, PhD, director of Join Together, a program of the Boston University School of Public Health. "Most people typically have three or four false starts before they're able to successfully maintain a year of sobriety," reports Michael Dennis of Chestnut Health Systems. "That can often take eight or nine years."

Even when an addict has a strong desire to change his life, what happens next is not as simple as walking into the first AA meeting he finds.

Recovery is possible, but it can depend to a great degree on how old the person is who comes to treatment, how long they have been using, to what degree their addiction may be complicated by co-occurring mood and anxiety disorders, and what substances, or combinations of substances, they have been using. "The brain has a tremendous capacity for recovery, because it's what we call 'plastic,'" says NIDA's Volkow. "But as we grow older, we lose some of the plasticity of the brain necessary for recovery."

Recovery is a process far more complicated and complex than just ending the use of chemical substances; it involves the rewiring of brain circuits altered by drugs or alcohol. However, there are significant barriers to that process, one of them being the longstanding stigma against addiction and the person who suffers from it.

"Addicts are discriminated against in ways that people suffering from no other disease are," says Rosenbloom. "It starts with a healthcare system that doesn't cover the disease very well. And [because] many addicts have been in the criminal justice system, they can't get jobs. We throw

Drugs and alcohol change the brain—they change its structure and how it works.

The Addicted Brain: Beyond Willpower

Nora D. Volkow, MD

Director, National Institute on Drug Abuse

The human brain is a complex and fine-tuned communications network containing billions of specialized cells (neurons) that give origin to our thoughts, emotions, perceptions, and drives. Often, a drug is taken the first time by choice—to feel pleasure or to relieve depression or stress. But this notion of choice is short-lived. Why? Because repeated drug use disrupts well-balanced systems in the brain in ways that persist, eventually replacing a person's normal needs and desires with a one-track mission to seek and use drugs. At this point, normal desires and motives will have a hard time competing with desire for the drug.

How does the brain become addicted? It typically happens like this:

→ Drugs of abuse activate the same brain circuits as do behaviors linked to survival, such as eating, bonding, and sex. The drug causes a surge in levels of a brain chemical called dopamine, which results in feelings of pleasure. The brain remembers this pleasure and wants it repeated.

→ Just as food is linked to survival in day-to-day living, drugs begin to take on the same significance for the addict. The need to obtain and take drugs becomes more important than any other need, including behaviors (like eating) that are truly necessary for survival. The addict no longer seeks the drug for pleasure, but for the need to relieve distress.

→ Eventually, the drive to seek and use the drug is all that matters, despite devastating consequences. Control and choice and everything that once held value in a person's life, such as family, job, community, are lost to the disease of addiction.

What brain changes cause such a dramatic shift?
Research on addiction is helping us find out just how drugs change the way the brain works. These changes include the following:

→ Reduced dopamine activity. We depend on our brain's ability to release dopamine in order to experience pleasure and to motivate our responses to the natural rewards of everyday life, such as the sight or smell of food. Drugs of abuse produce very large and rapid dopamine surges, and the brain responds by reducing normal dopamine activity. Eventually, the disrupted dopamine system renders the addict incapable of feeling any pleasure—even from the drugs they seek to feed their addiction.

→ Altered brain regions that control decision-making and judgment. Drugs of abuse affect the regions of the brain that help us control our desires and emotions. The resulting lack of control leads addicted people to compulsively pursue drugs, even when the drugs have lost their power to reward.

The disease of addiction can develop in people despite their best intentions or the strength of their character. Drug addiction is especially insidious because it affects the very brain areas that people need to "think straight," apply good judgment, and make good decisions for their lives. No one wants to be an addict, after all.

them out of public housing. They can't get welfare, they can't get food stamps for their kids."

As with almost all forms of discrimination, this one carries a big price tag, both to the individual and to society. And just as we've learned with other forms of discrimination, the only way to reverse this one is with knowledge. We must understand not just what addiction does to the lives of the addict, their loved ones, and the population overall, but what it is—a brain disease.

"One of the exciting things about this moment, in terms of our understanding addiction, is that for the first time in all of human history we can peek inside the brain and see what may be broken," explains Childress. "And if we can see what's broken, we have an idea how to go about fixing it."

PEERING INSIDE THE BRAIN

Inside the brain, the actual neurological response to alcohol and drug consumption (and the effects of addiction) can clearly be seen. And we do mean *seen,* in vivid, multicolored, multidimensional images relayed by high-tech scanning machines. In the past several years, scientists have learned more about how the human brain works than in all the previous centuries, primarily because of the development of a series of machines that allow them to look inside a living brain while the brain's owner is awake and responsive to stimuli.

Different types of messenger chemicals inside the brain, called neurotransmitters, carry information from one brain cell, or neuron, to another. Imaging technologies can reflect the activity in these transmitter systems, measuring how well (or how poorly) they do their jobs when alcohol or drugs have affected the brain. Some of the key neurotransmitters whose communication functions are disrupted by abused substances are dopamine, serotonin, GABA, and glutamate. And while all drugs of abuse directly or indirectly affect dopamine, there are also specific drug effects on other neurotransmitter systems. For example, LSD and Ecstasy alter serotonin function; heroin and morphine affect opiate receptors; and alcohol interacts with almost every neurotransmitter, but especially GABA and glutamate.

"GO!": THE DOPAMINE PLEASURE PATHWAY

Research has shown that all drugs of abuse directly or indirectly activate the brain's pleasure pathway, the intricate network that controls and regulates our ability to feel pleasure. When we experience something good— lovemaking, a good meal, a beautiful sunset—our brain experiences a surge in the level of the neurotransmitter dopamine. We feel warm, calm, and happy. After awhile, dopamine returns to a baseline level, and we go about our lives, looking forward to the next pleasurable experience.

We look forward to the next time because the experi-

Structures of the Brain

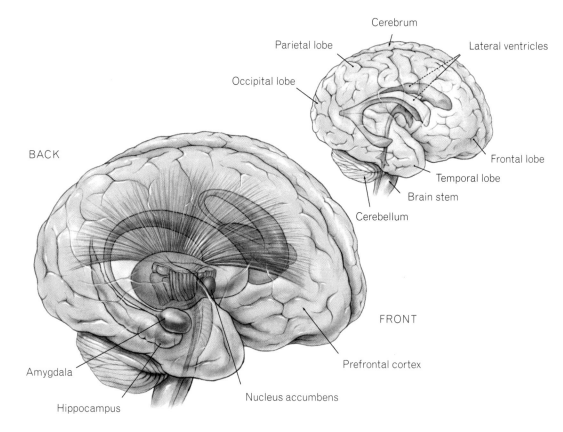

Cerebrum

Parietal lobe

Lateral ventricles

Occipital lobe

BACK

Frontal lobe

Temporal lobe

Brain stem

Cerebellum

FRONT

Prefrontal cortex

Amygdala

Nucleus accumbens

Hippocampus

ence is logged into the brain's limbic system, which, in addition to being the center for pleasure and emotion, houses key memory and motivation circuits. This is what the brain's dopamine pathway does; it records both the actual experience of pleasure and ensures that the behaviors that led to it are remembered and repeated. In between pleasurable events, there is a quiet period when the neurotransmitters return to their baseline levels. It is useful to remember that the whole system evolved from the biological imperative of survival. Food meant survival, sex meant survival, and going back for more of both meant survival of the species, in the most literal sense.

The first time we experience a drug or alcohol high, the amount of chemical we ingest often exceeds (by a factor of anywhere from two to ten) the levels of naturally occurring neurotransmitters in our body. Dopamine levels may spike higher than they do even with eating, and that initial spike typically lasts longer. That experience, no matter how brief, is stored in the hippocampus and amygdala, important centers of motivation that are sometimes called the "Go!" system. Getting drunk with your buddies, getting high at the beach—they both initially flood the brain with dopamine, along with a picture-memory of the event and the body's pleasurable response to it. And so we look forward to doing it again.

But it's a trick.

After each upward spike, dopamine levels again recede, eventually to below the baseline. The following spike doesn't go quite as high as the one before it. Over time, the rush becomes smaller, and the crash that follows becomes deeper. The brain has been fooled into "thinking" that achieving that high is equivalent to survival (even more so than with food and sex), and the "Go!" light is on all the time. Eventually, the brain is forced to turn on a self-defense mechanism, reducing the production of dopamine altogether—and weakening the pleasure circuit's function. At this point, the addicted person is compelled to use the substance not to get high, but to feel "normal"—since there's little or no dopamine response to be had. It is like repeatedly jamming your ATM card in the slot even though your bank account has been long since overdrawn.

"STOP!": THE BRAIN'S BRAKES

In addition to the "Go!" system, the brain also has a built-in "Stop!" system: the prefrontal cortex, sometimes referred to as the seat of sober second thought. With this system, we pull all the information together, weigh it, examine the risks and consequences, and strategize the next move. Is this a good idea? Is this illegal or immoral, or will it make me sick? Will I be able to drive safely, will I be too hung over to get to my job in the morning?

The Dopamine Pleasure Pathway

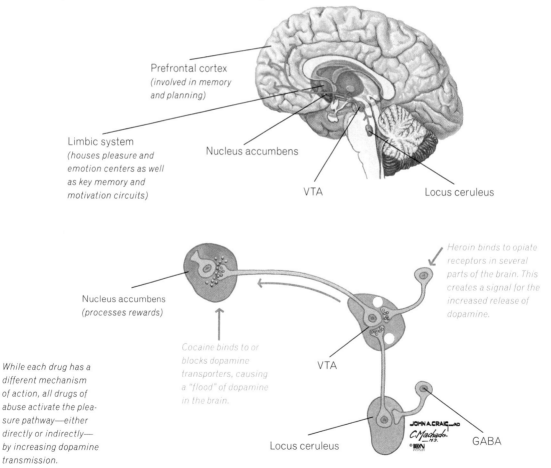

Prefrontal cortex
(involved in memory and planning)

Limbic system
(houses pleasure and emotion centers as well as key memory and motivation circuits)

Nucleus accumbens

VTA

Locus ceruleus

Nucleus accumbens
(processes rewards)

Heroin binds to opiate receptors in several parts of the brain. This creates a signal for the increased release of dopamine.

While each drug has a different mechanism of action, all drugs of abuse activate the pleasure pathway—either directly or indirectly—by increasing dopamine transmission.

Cocaine binds to or blocks dopamine transporters, causing a "flood" of dopamine in the brain.

VTA

Locus ceruleus

GABA

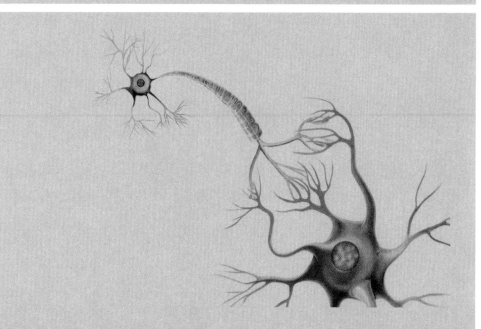

The brain contains billions of brain cells called neurons that exchange signals throughout the brain and body. The processing of these signals is what enables planning, logic, memory, motor skills, language, our senses, and our moods.

A neuron resembles a tree; it has roots, called dendrites, which connect to other neurons. It has a trunk, called an axon, which carries signals from the roots to the branches. A neuron's branches reach out to the dendrites of other neurons so they can communicate with one another. The junction between the branches of one neuron and the next is called the synapse. Neurons are constantly sending signals to other neurons, and as you learn new things, neurons grow and change.

The signals traveling down the axon are electrical in nature, but this current cannot cross the synapse. Instead, chemicals called neurotransmitters ferry signals across this gap. When a signal reaches the end of a neuron (the axon terminal), neurotransmitters are released. They wash over the dendrite of the neighboring neuron, which has special molecules on it called receptors. The neurotransmitters stick, or bind, to these receptors, and the receiving neuron responds to the signal and continues the process of transmitting information through the nervous system.

Often, these chemicals work in combination with one another. For example, dopamine, norepinephrine, and serotonin together affect mood and cognitive function. There are more than sixty different neurochemicals involved in neurotransmission. Here are some examples:

→ Acetylcholine: controls voluntary movement of the muscles

→ CRH (corticotropin-releasing hormone): regulates the stress system

→ Dopamine: controls voluntary movement and emotional arousal

→ GABA (gamma aminobutyric acid): modulates motions, memory, and motor behavior

→ Glutamate: modulates motivation, learning, and memory

→ Norepinephrine: controls wakefulness or arousal

→ Serotonin: regulates mood, memory, wakefulness, sleep, and temperature

"When things are working right, the 'Go!' circuitry and the 'Stop!' circuitry really are interconnected and are talking to each other to help you weigh the consequences of a decision and decide when to go or not to go," says Childress. "It's not that they're separable. They're interactive. They're interlinked at all times."

The addictive process moves in, undoes or weakens what the brain knew before, and then teaches it something else entirely.

With addicts, however, "it is as though [the systems] have become functionally disconnected. It is as though the 'Go!' system is sort of running off on its own, is a rogue system now and is not interacting in a regular, seamless, integrated way with the 'Stop!' system," Childress says.

Drugs of abuse directly activate the pleasure pathway, but recent research shows that addiction also involves the same pathways that manage memory and learning; that is, the addictive process moves in, undoes or weakens what the brain knew before, and then teaches it something else entirely. One amazing illustration of how this works is with Childress's patient William, a longtime cocaine addict in supervised recovery. When William undergoes a PET scan and is shown images of a beautiful sunset or laughing children during the scan, his brain produces little or no dopamine response. But when he's given brief flashes (each a barely perceptible fraction of a second) of a coke spoon or heroin needle, or images of the old neighborhood in which he used to score drugs, his hippocampus and amygdala light up like a Christmas tree—in spite of his sobriety and what his conscious mind knows about that "old" life, where it led, and what it cost him. The "Go!" system is in charge; the "Stop!" system is mute.

That is what we mean when we say that successful addiction recovery truly involves a rewiring of the brain.

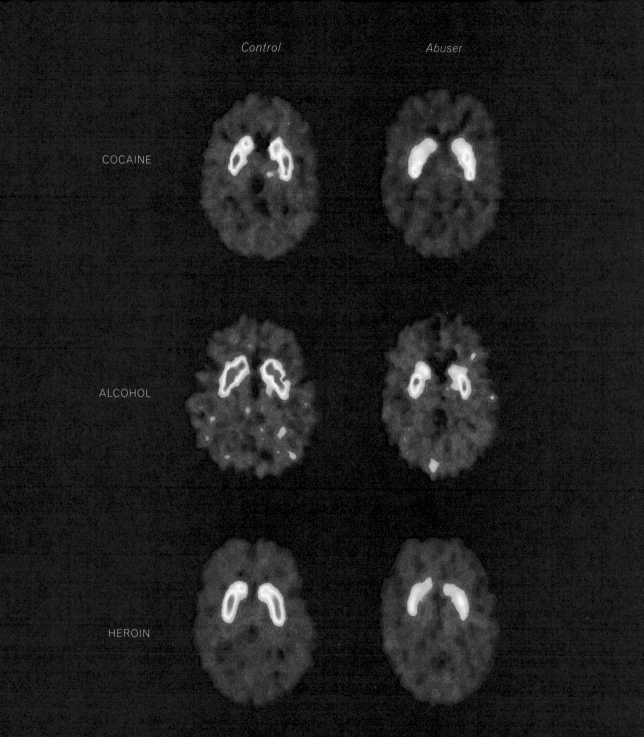

COCAINE

ALCOHOL

HEROIN

Control

Abuser

POSITRON EMISSION TOMOGRAPHY (PET) SCANS OF DOPAMINE RECEPTOR ACTIVITY
PET scans show similar significant decreases in dopamine receptor activity resulting from addiction to different substances. The reward area of the brain shows up as bright red/yellow in the nonusing subjects (controls), indicating numerous dopamine receptors. Conversely, the brains of addicted individuals show a less intense signal.

Expert Advice

What Is Craving?

Anna Rose Childress, PhD

Research associate professor, Department of Psychiatry, University of Pennsylvania School of Medicine

"Craving" is a word that is used—by addicted individuals and by professionals in the treatment field—to mean desire. Cravings are part of the human condition. Our brains are "hard-wired" to appreciate and to pursue natural rewards such as food and sex because of their critical survival value.

Drugs used by addicted people activate the same circuits that motivate eating and sexual behavior. Signals, called cues, can be sights, sounds, smells, or thoughts. Cues activate the brain's powerful "Go!" circuit, creating cravings. The cravings for alcohol and other drugs can be even stronger than those for food or sex.

Managing the cravings associated with food, sex, and drugs is the responsibility of the brain's inhibitory "Stop!" circuitry. Research suggests that some people have better "Stop!" systems, better "brakes," than others. Individuals with weaker "brakes" may have much greater difficulty managing cravings, putting them at increased risk for addiction and relapse. Exposure to some drugs may actually weaken the brain's braking system.

Cravings may have their beginnings outside conscious awareness. Recent brain imaging research shows that drug and sexual cues as brief as thirty-three milliseconds can activate the "Go!" circuit even if a person is not conscious of the cues.

In addition to cue-induced craving, desire can also be fueled by:
→ A small sample of the drug/food/rewarding activity (this is the "salty peanut" effect: "just a little" often leads to much more)
→ The wish to avoid negative effects (such as drug withdrawal, negative moods, etc.). Many people with addictions have a co-occurring mood disorder (anxiety or depression). These moods can themselves become triggers for food or drug craving, increasing the risk of relapse.

Hope through research

There is much ongoing research aimed at the development of more effective anticraving interventions, for food, drug, sex, gambling, and other addictions.

Anticraving medications and anticraving behavioral strategies may be helpful to inhibit or "Stop!" drug craving. Many of these medications have been well-studied; others are in the early stages of testing. New anti-craving interventions may be available in a location close to you. Research treatments are usually available at no cost (as they are supported by research grants), and they may offer a new treatment option that is not yet available in your community.

With a combination of evidence-based treatments and prescribed medication (when available), it is possible that the brain can recover and undergo the retraining needed to block out the signals that trigger addiction and relearning to respond positively to the experiences that brought happiness before the brain was hijacked by drugs.

CO-OCCURRING DISORDERS

When addressing addiction recovery, it is critical to recognize the possibility of a co-occuring mental illness. Being addicted raises the risk of having depression; being depressed increases the risk of self-medicating, which then leads to addiction. According to the 2004 National Survey on Drug Use and Health, there were 4.6 million adults with co-occurring serious psychological distress and a substance use disorder. Studies based on the National Epidemiologic Survey on Alcohol and Related Conditions (NESARC), which collected data from 2001 to 2002, have found that a quarter to almost half of the people in treatment have both alcohol use disorders and other mental illnesses. Specialists can and do argue about whether the mental illness caused the substance abuse disorder or the other way around, but ultimately, it is imperative that both disorders be properly diagnosed and treated at the same time.

If people stop using early enough—and if they were only battling one substance—they can often achieve sobriety on their own. But if someone is ten or twenty years into addiction, the odds are good that he or she is struggling with multiple co-occurring psychiatric problems.

"Which are those mental disorders that make you more vulnerable to taking drugs?" asks NIDA's Volkow. "Schizophrenia, depression, anxiety disorders, post-traumatic stress disorder, conduct disorder, learning disabilities, attention deficit hyperactivity disorder. The other side is also true; if you are an addicted person, the likelihood of your having a mental disorder is much greater. It can be anything from attention deficit to depression to psychosis to anxiety disorder. . . . To treat the addiction, without dealing with that depression, is most likely going to lead to relapse."

Of necessity, treatment might include prescriptive

Cocaine interferes with the reabsorption of dopamine, a neurotransmitter key to the brain's pleasure pathway. By blocking absorption of dopamine, cocaine causes a buildup of the neurotransmitter that floods neurons and causes euphoria.

Cocaine causes lasting changes in the brain

→ The overload of dopamine causes brain cells to reduce the number of dopamine receptors.

→ A reduced number of receptors alters the brain's capacity for pleasure. According to imaging studies, cocaine disables parts of the brain's reward system so that normally positive experiences don't register as such in cocaine users' brains.

The ability for the brain to recover depends on the extent and pattern of past cocaine use. Animal studies have shown that dopamine receptors that have diminished after one week of cocaine use can recover within a few weeks of abstinence. But after one year of use, recovery varied. Some primates recovered within three months, but others had still not recovered after one year of abstinence.

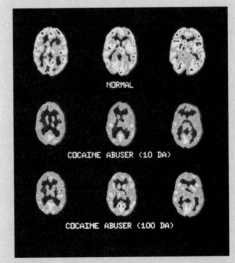

Once addicted to a drug like cocaine, the brain is affected for a long time. The level of brain function is shown here in yellow. The normal brain (top row) shows a lot of brain activity. Even after one hundred days without cocaine (bottom row), an addict's brain still has not recovered normal brain function.

Drugs and Alcohol at a Glance

Depressants	SHORT-TERM EFFECTS
Alcohol Booze, liquor, juice How drug is used: ingested	Impaired judgment, coordination, and vision. A delayed reaction time to outside stimuli.
Benzodiazepine (BZD) Xanax, Valium, Ativan, Klonopin, sleeping pills, tranks, bennies How drug is used: tablets	Produces a drowsy or calming effect. Can also cause poor concentration, muscle weakness, vertigo, and mental confusion. In rare cases, may lead to increased excitement, irritability, aggression, hostility, and impulsivity may occur.

Stimulants	SHORT-TERM EFFECTS
Cocaine / crack cocaine Coke, marching powder, nose candy, snow, blow, crack, candy, rock How drug is used: snorted, ingested, smoked, or injected	Disturbances in heart rhythm, increased heart and respiratory rates, elevated blood pressure, dilated pupils, decreased appetite, excessive activity, talkativeness, irritability, argumentative behavior, nervousness, agitation
Methamphetamine Meth, speed, ice, crystal, black beauty, poor man's coke How drug is used: ingested, smoked, snorted, or injected	Increased activity, euphoria, decreased appetite, fever, irritability, insomnia, confusion, tremors, paranoia, aggression, increased heart rate and blood pressure, irreversible damage to blood vessels in the brain, jaw clenching, teeth grinding
Amphetamine Adderall, Dexedrine, pep pills, speed, sweets, uppers How drug is used: ingested, snorted, or injected	Anxiety, euphoria, irregular heartbeat, irritability, paranoia, insomnia
Methylphenidate Ritalin, west coast, Vitamin R How drug is used: ingested, snorted, or injected	Stimulates the central nervous system, with effects similar to, but less potent than, amphetamines.

Inhalants	SHORT-TERM EFFECTS
Aerosol cans, plastic cement, nail polish remover, lighter fluid, insecticide, cleaning solvent Whippets, poppers, snappers, buzz bomb, laughing gas How drug is used: sniffed from an open container or "huffed" from a rag soaked in the substance and held to the face	Rapid high similar to alcohol intoxication. Slurred speech, headache, drowsiness, unconsciousness, numbness and tingling of hands and feet, loss of muscle control, decrease or loss of sense of smell, nosebleeds, nausea, and irregular heartbeat.

LONG-TERM EFFECTS	RELATED DANGERS	WITHDRAWAL	TREATMENT
Liver and heart disease, high blood pressure, pancreatitis, and cancer. Long-term abuse may cause brain damage.	Driving while intoxicated, alcohol poisoning, fetal alcohol syndrome	Insomnia, anxiety, seizures, hallucinations, delirium (DT's)	pg. 152
Long-term abuse can lead to dependence. Suddenly stopping chronic use may cause withdrawal side effects, including seizures.	Not applicable	Insomnia, anxiety, and depression. The brain's bid to rebound from prolonged use can cause seizures.	pg. 152

LONG-TERM EFFECTS	RELATED DANGERS	WITHDRAWAL	TREATMENT
Brain cells reduce their numbers of dopamine receptors. Snorting can lead to loss of sense of smell, nosebleeds, problems swallowing, and nasal cavity irritation. Ingested cocaine can cause bowel gangrene. Smoking crack cocaine can harm the lungs.	Premature births, low birth weights, and shorter length at birth. Injecting cocaine with shared needles can spread HIV, hepatitis B, and hepatitis C.	Cravings, fatigue, lack of pleasure, anxiety, irritability, sleepiness	pg. 152
Psychotic behavior, hallucinations, respiratory problems, irregular heartbeat, extreme anorexia, stroke, death	Injecting methamphetamine with shared needles can spread HIV, hepatitis B, and hepatitis C. "Meth Mouth": users tend to lose their teeth abnormally quickly.	Cravings, depression, anxiety, fatigue, paranoia, aggression	pg. 152
Increased blood pressure, mood or mental changes	Injecting amphetamine with shared needles can spread HIV, hepatitis B, and hepatitis C.	Depression, "the shakes," tiredness, unusual tiredness	pg. 152
High doses can lead to compulsive use, paranoia, dangerously high body temperatures, and irregular heartbeat.	Injecting methylphenidate with shared needles can spread HIV, hepatitis B, and hepatitis C.	Withdrawal symptoms are similar to that of amphetamines.	pg. 152

LONG-TERM EFFECTS	RELATED DANGERS	WITHDRAWAL	TREATMENT
Cognitive abnormalities ranging from mild impairment to severe dementia. Difficulty coordinating movement, limb spasms, loss of feeling, hearing, and vision. Chronic exposure can produce significant damage to the brain, heart, lungs, liver, and kidneys.	Possible birth defects	Mild withdrawal symptoms may occur.	pg. 153

Opiates

Heroin

Smack, junk, brown sugar, black tar, H, hard candy

How drug is used: snorted, smoked, or injected

A surge of euphoria followed by a drowsy state. Mental functioning becomes clouded due to the depression of the central nervous system.

Prescription painkillers

Oxycodone, OxyContin, Percocet, Percodan, Vicodin, hillbilly heroin, oxycotton, oxy, OC, killer

How drug is used: ingested, snorted, or injected

Produces effects similar to heroin. Drowsiness, constipation, nausea, and, depending on the amount of drug taken, respiratory depression.

Hallucinogens

SHORT-TERM EFFECTS

LSD

Acid, A

How drug is used: tablets, capsules, liquid, or on absorbent paper

Dilated pupils, higher body temperature, increased heart rate and blood pressure, sweating, loss of appetite, sleeplessness, dry mouth, and tremors. The user may feel several different emotions at once or swing rapidly from one emotion to another. Depending on the dose, the drug can produce delusions and hallucinations.

MDMA

Ecstasy, XTC, X, Adam, happy pill, love pill

How drug is used: tablets or capsules

Increased heart rate and blood pressure, higher body temperature, jaw/teeth clenching, muscle tension, hypertension, dehydration, chills and/or sweating, nausea, blurred vision, faintness, confusion, insomnia

Ketamine hydrochloride

Special K, Vitamin K, kit kat, super acid

How drug is used: tablets, liquid, or powder

Increased heart rate and blood pressure, impaired motor function, numbness, nauseau, and vomiting. At high doses, ketamine can cause delerium and respiratory depression and arrest.

Phencyclidine

PCP, angel dust, crazy coke, rocket fuel, wack

How drug is used: tablets, capsules, or colored powder. It can be snorted, smoked, or ingested.

Increased blood pressure and heart rate, nausea, blurred vision, dizziness, and decreased awareness of pain. Muscle contractions may cause uncoordinated movements. Some users report hallucinations, panic, and violent behavior.

Cannabis

SHORT-TERM EFFECTS

Marijuana

Bud, pot, weed, ganja, grass, herb, reefer, skunk

How drug is used: smoked, sometimes mixed with food

Memory and learning problems, distorted perception, increased heart rate, anxiety

LONG-TERM EFFECTS	RELATED DANGERS	WITHDRAWAL	TREATMENT
Scarred and/or collapsed veins, bacterial infections of the blood vessels and heart valves, abscesses, liver and kidney disease, lung complications	Injecting heroin with shared needles can spread HIV, hepatitis B, and hepatitis C.	Restlessness, muscle and bone pain, insomnia, diarrhea, vomiting, cold flashes, leg movements	pg. 153
Use of prescription painkillers can lead to physical dependence and addiction.	Injecting prescription painkillers with shared needles can spread HIV, hepatitis B, and hepatitis C.	Withdrawal symptoms are similar to that of heroin.	pg. 153

LONG-TERM EFFECTS	RELATED DANGERS	WITHDRAWAL	TREATMENT
LSD users may experience flashbacks, which can occur suddenly and may occur within a few days or more than a year after use. LSD users may also manifest relatively long-lasting psychoses, such as schizophrenia or severe depression.	Although LSD is generally considered nontoxic, it may temporarily impair the ability to make sensible judgments and understand common dangers, making the user susceptible to accidents and personal injury.	Not applicable	pg. 153
Depression, sleep disorders, anxiety, liver and brain damage. Ecstasy alters the function of serotonin and dopamine pathways in the brain.	Other, more dangerous chemicals are often added to Ecstasy tablets, or simply sold as Ecstasy.	Fatigue, severe anxiety, loss of appetite, difficulty concentrating, depression	pg. 153
Depression, memory loss	Reportedly used as a date-rape drug	Not applicable	pg. 153
Tolerance, possible psychological dependence	Users of PCP can become violent or suicidal and can become a danger to themselves and others.	Not applicable	pg. 153

LONG-TERM EFFECTS	RELATED DANGERS	WITHDRAWAL	TREATMENT
Increased risk of chronic cough, bronchitis, emphysema, and cancer of the head, neck, and lungs	A decrease in testosterone levels and lower sperm count for men.	Cravings, irritability, insomnia, anxiety	pg. 153

medicine for the mental disorder (such as antidepressants, mood stabilizers, or antianxiety medicines). For example, "antidepressants can be useful in the treatment of addiction," says Kathleen Brady, current president of the American Academy of Addiction Psychiatry, "when the individual has an anxiety disorder or depressive disorder underlying the addiction." However, this increases the need for close medical and psychological supervision during addiction treatment. (See Chapter 4 for more information on co-occurring disorders.)

In addition to being treated for co-occurring disorders, the addict's natural brain processes that have been overrun by drugs need to be helped to regain their natural functioning. And meanwhile, the maladaptive processes that characterize addiction—the compulsive craving and seeking, and the constant need to take the drug to simulate the pleasurable neurotransmitter responses—need to be reversed in the brain.

WHO'S AT RISK?

The reasons and causes for addiction can often seem as varied as the number of people it touches. Some of us walk down the street, see someone drunk or high, and think, *That could never happen to me or to anyone I love.* Only later, we are humbled by the reality that someone we know is indeed suffering with addiction. Both genders are susceptible, as are all ages, every economic level, and each ethnic group. As with any other disease, vulnerability to addiction differs from person to person. But as different as addicted persons may seem from each other, they actually do have many predictor factors in common. In general, the more risk factors an individual has, the greater the chances that taking drugs will lead to abuse and addiction.

BIOLOGICAL FACTORS: IT'S IN THE GENES

Just as we inherit eye color and musical or athletic ability (or lack thereof) from our parents and grandparents, we also inherit from them any genetic predispositions to certain diseases. Most researchers state unequivocally that heredity is a critical factor in developing a substance addiction.

Someone with an alcoholic parent—or worse, two—has a greater chance of developing addiction than someone whose parents are not alcoholics. And nature can often outfox nurture: some studies show that when children of alcoholics are adopted early and subsequently raised in nonalcoholic homes, their risk of addiction is still three to four times higher than it is for the general population (which runs a one-in-twelve risk).

In order to "switch on," certain genes must interact with or be triggered by environmental factors. If that doesn't happen, the addiction will not occur.

Unlike a disease such as cystic fibrosis, which is caused by a defect of a single gene, addiction is classified as genetically complex, which means that many genes play a role in shaping addiction risk. Although genetics researchers are trying to identify the genes that confer vulnerability to alcoholism, this task is difficult because the illness is thought to be related to many different genes, each of which contributes only a portion of the vulnerability. According to the NIAAA, "The methods used to search for genes in complex diseases have to account for the fact that the effects of any one gene may be subtle, and a different array of genes underlies risk in different people."

The Human Genome Project (HGP), a thirteen-year effort coordinated by the U.S. Department of Energy and the National Institutes of Health, was established to identify all of the approximately twenty to twenty-five thousand genes in human DNA and to determine the sequences of the three billion chemical base pairs that make it up. Somewhere in all that information, which scientists estimate will take many years to analyze, is quite possibly a key to managing chemical addiction.

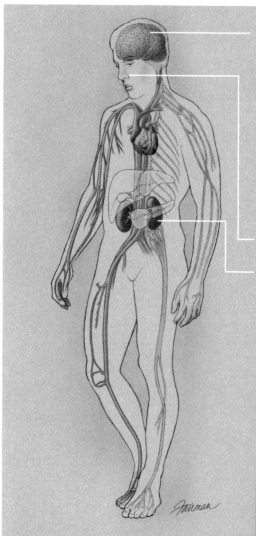

Brain The brains of chronic heavy drinkers shrink, specifically in the frontal cortex, which is responsible for higher-level cognitive functions such as planning and reasoning, and in the cerebellum, which governs gait, balance, and some kinds of learning. Long-term alcohol use also damages the hippocampus, which is the brain's center of learning, memory, and mood, and the factory that supplies the entire brain with new brain cells.

Some very heavy drinkers may develop Wernicke-Korsakoff syndrome, in which the alcoholic cannot remember new information for more than a few seconds. This condition is irreversible.

Nose Chronic heavy drinkers may lose their sense of smell.

Organs Long-term or heavy drinking can damage the liver, cause high blood pressure, and shrink the arteries.

Bones In teens, alcohol abuse may stunt bone growth, and in adults, it may cause osteoporosis.

Reproductive system Alcoholics may experience reduced sperm count and sperm abnormalities in men, and irregular menstrual cycles, infertility, and early menopause in women. Pregnant women who drink increase the risk of birth defects and fetal alcohol syndrome.

Disease Alcoholics have an elevated risk of several different cancers.

Many of these ill effects can be reversed with the cessation of drinking. Improvements begin about a month after abstention and may continue for a year or more.

RIGHT: MRI of a 41-year-old alcoholic woman. When brain tissue shrinks or is lost due to alcoholism, the lateral ventricles, in red, expand to fill the space (right). When brain tissue expands, the ventricles shrink (far right) and provide an index of recovery.

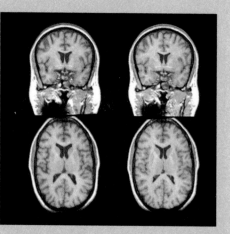

2 months sober   14 months sober

In the meantime, just having a genetic predisposition to a certain condition doesn't guarantee that the condition will happen. In order to "switch on," certain genes must interact with or be triggered by environmental factors. If that doesn't happen, the addiction will not occur. In fact, there are even identical twins, one of whom suffers from an addictive disorder and one who does not, in spite of their having the same parents and DNA. It is also not unusual to see someone with no known family history of substance abuse become an addict—because of environmental circumstances, or an unrealized genetic predisposition in previous generations, or both.

While genes are not destiny, a known multigenerational family history of drug and alcohol abuse is, or should be, a very large warning sign. It is commonplace these days that a family history of other serious disorders—such as heart disease, high blood pressure, diabetes, and various cancers—is sufficient argument for regular testing and monitoring, which ideally leads to early diagnosis, treatment, and improved outcomes. So it is reasonable to hope for the same kind of vigilance when there is a genuine risk of addiction. (As yet, however, there is no definitive biological test that indicates who might be at risk for addiction.) The question then becomes what that vigilance would entail.

For the time being, the only nonmedical, noncoerced option seems to be abstinence. That is a difficult argument to make before somebody takes a first pill or drink, but it carries significant weight, especially with Sis Wenger of the National Association for Children of Alcoholics. NACOA recently started including an abstinence message in its material targeted to kids. "You can't get this disease if you choose not to drink or take drugs," Wenger says.

ENVIRONMENTAL INFLUENCES:
THE WORLD WE LIVE IN
We cannot underestimate the impact, both positive and negative, of the family. From our first awareness as infants, we take it all in—the way adults act, interact, work, live, react to stress and crisis, recreate, and replenish their bodies and spirits. We take our cues from the people,

There is no single factor that determines whether someone will become addicted to alcohol or drugs, but researchers have identified many biological and environmental factors that may contribute to a person's vulnerability. Both nature and nurture influence a person's risk of becoming addicted to drugs or alcohol. Some people inherit a genetic predisposition to drug or alcohol dependence from their parents. Others inherit a personality or behavioral disorder that makes them more susceptible to addiction. Some mental health problems, such as anxiety and depression, are also associated with addiction but may not directly cause it.

The world a person lives in has an enormous influence on his or her drug and alcohol use. Children who grow up in an environment where drug or alcohol abuse is common or accepted are more likely to abuse these substances themselves. Children who have little parental supervision or support, or who experience harsh or inconsistent discipline, abuse, or rejection are also more likely to use drugs or alcohol. Those who start using in their teens are more likely to become addicted later.

Any of the following factors may increase your risk of becoming addicted to drugs or alcohol:

→ Having parents or siblings who are addicted to drugs or alcohol

→ Being diagnosed with a conduct disorder or exhibiting aggressive behavior that might indicate a lack of self-control

→ Having an untreated attention deficit or hyperactivity disorder

→ Being depressed or anxious

→ Having experienced trauma, such as exposure to violence or physical or sexual abuse

→ Experiencing a stressful life transition, such as leaving home for the first time, losing a job, getting divorced, or losing someone close to you

→ Having experienced conflict at home with parents, spouse, or children

→ Being exposed to drugs and alcohol and peer pressure to use them

→ Using drugs and alcohol before age 15

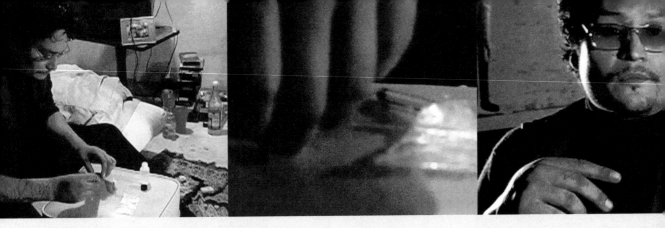

Damien

Damien has a history of heroin use in his family and is seeking treatment for his own addiction.

I have a close relative who has been a heroin addict pretty much since I was a kid. I never really wanted to fuck with it. I don't even know why I did it. I always told myself I wouldn't. And then I did. And before I knew it, it caught up to me. There came a point in time when I got real severe bouts of depression. And I really didn't care whether I was around or not. I actually didn't expect to be alive past 27. I discarded my whole belief system. I guess in some weird psychological way I was saying, "Well, fuck it."

I actually saw him not too long ago. That was the first time I'd seen him in fifteen years. I showed him my track marks and I told him, "Look, this is what happened." And I made a joke of it.

I don't necessarily want to blame him for it. I knew what I was doing. It's totally on me. I'm gonna be responsible for my own actions. I can't blame anybody else for what I've done because I was aware of what the consequences could be. I knew one-hundred percent what I was getting myself into. The first year that I did it, I really

wasn't addicted. I could take it or leave it. I also wasn't really getting sick then because I wasn't really using a lot. I did it maybe once a week or once every two weeks at first. And I smoked it at first. So, I never got sick from that.

I didn't start using the needle until a year after I was smoking it. But with heroin, once you start using a needle, you don't want to do anything else but heroin. I noticed that it started changing me when I stopped drinking as much. The drinking started slowing down and the drug intake got bigger.

When I started using the needle, at first it was like once a week. And then, maybe two weeks later, it was twice, three times a week. I didn't even notice when it changed from that to a habit. My habit started off at a $20 piece a day. I didn't really want to spend more money than that. When it wasn't doing anything to me anymore, I ended up having to spend more. I went up from twenty bucks, to forty, to sixty. It just kept going up, you know, trying to reach

that high again. You get it at first, but then you never, ever get that again. Eventually, you get to a point where you're just doing it so you're not sick.

My close friends started noticing it. And they said, "You're addicted." I wasn't paying attention. I didn't think that I was addicted because me. It fucks up my bones, my lower back. I can't move around. There's no way I could work. I get so cranky and irritated. There's a sense of desperation that comes over me. It's just this intense, intense desperation that comes with trying to get off the heroin.

And I'm sick of it, so I'm actually pretty happy

When I started using the needle, at first it was like once a week. And then, maybe two weeks later, it was twice, three times a week. I didn't even notice when it changed from that to a habit.

I was functioning. I'm definitely not a functioning addict right now. And that's why I'm going into treatment tomorrow.

I never got sick when I didn't do the other drugs. With this drug, I get physically ill. And the illness that comes with giving up heroin is so intense I just can't do it. I can't deal with just living a regular life being that sick. It really, really affects about entering treatment. I don't really have a doubt in my mind that I'm not gonna do it. I've convinced myself. I've been working on it for the last two, three weeks. You know, just like, "Okay, I'm gonna do it." And I'm gonna do it, you know. I know it's feasible. If I just stay on track and stop lying to myself or stop running, I can do it. I've been running for so fuckin' long now that it's just time. It's time for me to do it.

events, and messages that surround us, and we may reflect them back, in our own behavior.

As we mirror what we see, we also absorb it. One of the things we absorb is the trauma associated with difficult events, a list that might include divorce, illness, or the death of a family member, or a serious financial reversal that creates instability and means a move from one home to another. Each of these creates uncertainty and loss for both parent and child, but usually the most damaging effect of this kind of stress is on the developing brain of a child, at a time when that child is developing core beliefs about security and safety: Who will take care of me? Whom can I count on? Does everyone I love go away? It is at this point—when parents are most distracted by their own struggle to respond to the crisis—that addressing the needs and fears of the child is imperative. And that doesn't always happen.

While emotional, physical, and sexual abuse rank highest on the scale of traumatic events, even the death of a beloved pet or a series of bad school grades can cause deep psychological wounds that in a dysfunctional environment might not heal properly, which then creates a vulnerability to all kinds of mental disorders, including addiction. Some addicts will attest that they picked up a first drink or snuck a first pill out of a parent's medicine cabinet to "feel better." This does not mean, of course, that the children who face challenges in their lives are automatically destined for addiction.

"We know that there are some environments that afford a higher risk," says Volkow. "For kids, it would be a household with no parental surveillance. For adults, it may be high levels of stress, or a history of abuse, or high levels of accessibility to the substance… The past history of an individual can induce changes that make them vulnerable to taking drugs and then to the process of addiction."

In addition to coping with life changes that create domestic, psychological, and economic instability, we also deal with the impact of our peer groups—which basically comes down to the question of how everyone else behaves. Do we feel the need to behave similarly, just to fit in or be comfortable? Do our friends drink too much or use illegal or prescription drugs as "feel better" mechanisms? Is drinking to excess, or using illegal drugs, something that's accepted among the people we hang out with? This is particularly important in relation to adolescent substance use and abuse, since that's the age where the influence of peers begins to outweigh parental influence, no matter how good and involved a parent might be. And it's also the age when addiction usually begins.

The past history of an individual can induce changes that make them vulnerable to taking drugs and then to the process of addiction.

There are cultural rituals to contend with as well—the ones our families observe and the ones that exist in the larger society around us. Alcohol is not only legal, but it has always been part of rites of passage—think of pledges getting "wasted" during fraternity rush. Think of how often you've heard or said, "Let's get together for a drink." Or, "What a terrible day, I could really use a drink." It doesn't always follow that the person who utters these sentences, or responds positively to them, has a problem. It just means that in the case of the first statement, there is an understood shorthand for social discourse; in the second, there is an understood shorthand for managing stress. Whether it's the first job, the bad job, the next job, the retirement party, a wedding, a divorce, graduation, even a funeral—most rites of passage involve alcohol.

NEW DISCOVERIES IMPROVE
ADDICTION TREATMENT
The discoveries of Volkow and hundreds of scientific colleagues across the globe have significantly expanded what we know. The past two decades have seen breakthroughs in technology, pharmacology, behavioral therapeutic practice, and our understanding of social science that

Addiction to Multiple Substances

Nora D. Volkow, MD

Director, National Institute on Drug Abuse

It is not unusual for an addicted person to be addicted to alcohol, nicotine, and illicit drugs at the same time. Addiction to multiple substances raises the level of individual suffering and magnifies the associated costs to society. No matter what the addictive substance, they all have at least one thing in common—they disrupt the brain's reward pathway, the route to pleasure.

What is the best way to treat people who are addicted to more than one drug?

→ **Medications** In some cases, medications developed for one addiction have proven useful for another. For example, naltrexone, which can help former heroin abusers remain abstinent by blocking the "high" associated with heroin, has been found to be effective in treating alcoholism.

→ **Behavioral therapy or other psychotherapy** Behavioral therapies do not need to be specific to one drug and can be adapted to address use of multiple or different drugs. It is the disease of addiction that the therapy addresses.

→ **Combined medications and behavioral therapy** Research shows that this combination, when available, works best.

→ **Multipronged approach** Treatment for multiple addictions should be delivered at the same time. This is especially true because there are always triggers, such as trauma, depression, or exposure to one drug or another, that can put the recovering addict at risk for relapse. In addition, treatment must consider all aspects of a person—age, gender, life experiences—in order to best treat the addiction. Although the type of treatment may differ, it should always strive to address the entire person through a multi-pronged approach that tackles all co-occurring conditions at once.

have dramatically increased opportunities for recovery. Discoveries have led to the scientific testing of various treatment approaches to establish evidence-based care. The new science has paved the way for pharmacological advances. Doctors are prescribing medications, such as buprenorphine, sold as Suboxone. Healthcare professionals use buprenorphine as a medical replacement therapy for people addicted to opioids such as heroin or OxyContin. Currently, there are no FDA-approved medications for people addicted to stimulants, but researchers have promising new medications undergoing clinical trials.

The science doesn't just affect pharmacology. It has also changed the way that behavioral (talk) therapists have involved addicted people and their families in therapy and treatment. "So the hope of the future is medications and behavorial treatments that can combine to literally reset the brain," says Childress.

There are many challenges to sustained recovery, including learning how to manage the stress that the addicted individual didn't know how to manage before the drug abuse, and learning to navigate past the "triggers" of addiction that led to relapse. In spite of these challenges to managing the disease of addiction, many former addicts are successful at recovery.

Expert Advice

Understanding Relapse: The "Stop!" and "Go!" Systems

Anna Rose Childress, PhD

Research associate professor, Department of Psychiatry, University of Pennsylvania School of Medicine

Relapse is a hallmark feature of addictions, and one of the most painful.
Most people who struggle with addiction will have one or more relapses—the return to drug use after a drug-free period—during their ongoing attempts to recover. This can be extremely frustrating for patients and for families, as they have already experienced great pain.

What leads to relapse?
Multiple—and often interactive—factors can increase the likelihood of relapse. These are some of the commonly cited precursors to relapse:

→ Drug-related "reminder" cues (sights, sounds, smells, drug thoughts, or drug dreams) tightly linked to use of the preferred drug

→ Negative mood states / stress

→ Positive mood states / celebrations

→ Sampling the drug itself, even in very small amounts

All of these relapse precursors have a final common-path action on ancient brain motivational circuits. The motivation to seek a drug—once triggered—can feel overwhelming, and sometimes leads to very poor decision-making: the user will pursue the drug despite potentially disastrous future consequences (and many past negative consequences).

Are there brain vulnerabilities that may lead to relapse? Are some more vulnerable?

Brain-imaging research is helping us to understand the paradox of relapse—choosing to pursue a drug reward despite potential negative consequences. For example, very recent imaging research shows that visual drug cues as short as thirty-three milliseconds can activate the ancient reward ("Go!") circuitry, and that this does not require conscious processing—it can begin outside awareness.

By the time the motivation does reach awareness, and is recognized and labeled, the reward circuit has a strong head start. This head start means the brain's frontal regions—responsible for weighing the consequences of a decision, and for helping to "Stop!" or inhibit the impulses toward drug reward—may be less effective.

When it comes to the vulnerability to relapse, and to addiction itself, we are not all created equal. Imaging research also shows that some individuals have less effective "Stop!" circuitry. For these people, the job of managing the powerful impulses toward drug reward may be even more difficult. We differ both in our brain response to drug rewards and in our ability to manage the powerful impulses toward drug reward. The tools of brain imaging and genetics promise to help us understand our vulnerabilities—and our strengths—toward the goal of more effective relapse prevention.

Hope through research

Relapse is a frustrating feature of addiction disorders. It is a long-term vulnerability, but intensive ongoing research is targeting the problem. Many different clinical research trials are underway across the nation, and new anti-relapse interventions (behavioral or medication-based) may be available in a location close to you.

Find out more

You can contact the National Institute on Drug Abuse at the National Institutes of Health for information on clinical trials (using medications, behavioral strategies, or both) that are currently testing the newest treatments for addictions. These clinical trials offer treatment at no cost to those meeting eligibility criteria. NIDA can offer referrals to community resources if you do not match the specific criteria of ongoing trials. For more information, visit www.clinicaltrials.gov.

NORMAL

METHAMPHETAMINE ABUSER
(1 month abstinence)

METHAMPHETAMINE ABUSER
(24 months abstinence)

POSITRON EMISSION TOMOGRAPHY (PET) SCAN OF A PERSON WHO USED METHAMPHETAMINE
These images show the brain's potential to recover, at least partially, after a long abstinence from drugs—in this case methamphetamine. Red and yellow areas indicate dopamine receptors.

Addiction is NOT a moral failure.

ANGELICA

A Disease of Young People

The alcohol became an addiction, but once I confronted my emotional demons, that's when I was able to deal with it. ANGELICA, RECOVERING ALCOHOLIC

Addiction is frightening, chaotic, sometimes tragic, and always destructive. But when the addict in question is an adolescent—for all practical (and legal) purposes, a child—addiction is all of these negatives multiplied many times over.

The younger a person starts drinking or using drugs, the more likely they are to go past occasional illicit experimentation into frequent abuse and then addiction. For example, kids who use before the age of 15 are four or five times more likely to become addicted than they are if they wait until they're 21, the Substance Abuse and Mental Health Services Administration reported in 2004.

"Most of the people entering treatment now have been sick for twenty years or more," says NIAAA's Mark Willenbring. "As we become more aware of that, we're starting to really change our focus, to look at the disorder as it's developing in young people. How can we prevent it?

Early Use Leads to Higher Chances of Addiction

There is an association between first use of alcohol and later dependence and abuse.

PERCENT DEPENDENT OR ABUSING IN PAST YEAR

ABUSING ALCOHOL

DEPENDENT ON ALCOHOL

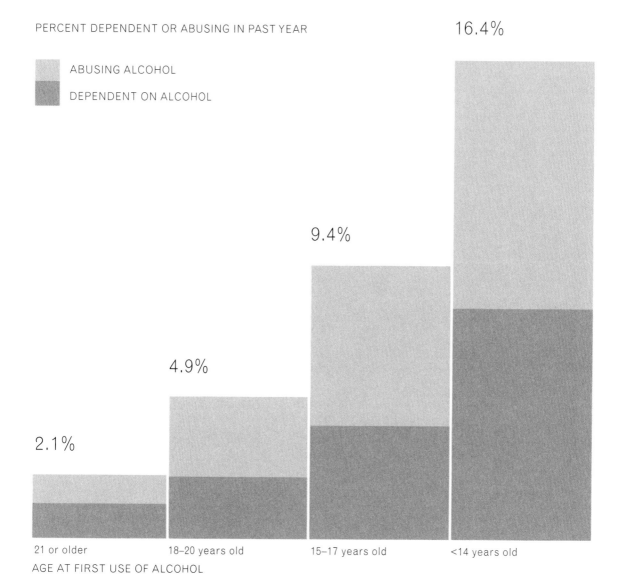

2.1%

4.9%

9.4%

16.4%

21 or older   18–20 years old   15–17 years old   <14 years old

AGE AT FIRST USE OF ALCOHOL

The study also found that among adults age 18 or older who first tried alcohol at age 14 or younger, 17.8 percent were classified with alcohol dependence or abuse compared with only 3.9 percent of adults who had first used alcohol at age 18 or older.

How can we prevent the progression of chronicity in those who develop alcohol problems during adolescence? And in those who do move on to a more severe form of the disorder, how can we arrest it earlier? How can we mitigate the consequences? How can we slow the rate of progression? This is where our research is moving."

WHERE IT STARTS: THE BRAIN

The key to adolescent addiction is the adolescent brain. At one time, scientists believed that the brain reached full "adult" development during puberty or near its end. However, current research indicates that, in fact, the maturation process isn't complete until 24 or 25 years of age.

The fact that the brain is an organ "under construction" during the teen years and beyond makes it easier for us to understand some characteristic adolescent behavior, such as the propensity for risk-taking and the attraction to potentially dangerous situations, including drug and alcohol experimentation. Developmental changes also offer a possible physiological explanation for why teens act so impulsively, often not recognizing that their actions have consequences.

The nucleus accumbens (the portion of the brain that processes rewards) matures before the brain's prefrontal cortex (the home of the "Stop!" mechanism discussed in Chapter 2), located directly behind the forehead. The prefrontal cortex is involved in what researchers call "executive function"—memory, planning, making decisions. In a mature, unaddicted brain, the prefrontal cortex acts as a guardian at the gate, prioritizing responsibilities and weighing the risks and consequences of choosing, or not choosing, certain behaviors. The adolescent's immature prefrontal cortex, coupled with a more mature nucleus accumbens, may explain why they might engage in high-excitement activities that provide immediate gratification (video games, skateboarding—and drug and alcohol experimentation) at the expense of long-term consequences.

No parent wants to compare their child to a lab rat, but it's useful to do exactly that when trying to understand what happens when a kid takes substances. For example, adolescent lab rats seem to be less sensitive to the effects

Expert Advice

Adolescent Brain Development

Thomas J. Crowley, MD *Director, Division of Substance Dependence, University of Colorado School of Medicine*

Elizabeth Whitmore, PhD *Associate professor of Psychiatry, University of Colorado School of Medicine*

1. The brain's "front end" (the part above the eyes) exists to slow us down or stop our impulsive behaviors. It considers the risks and benefits of our actions, and it helps us hit the brakes when we consider doing things that are too risky.

2. This front part of the brain is still developing connections to the rest of the brain until we are in our twenties, so adolescents' brains lack some of the wiring that carries "brake" or "stop" messages to the rest of the brain.

3. Drugs and alcohol are often available to adolescents. These drugs make them feel good but they can be very harmful. Lacking some of the wiring for the "stop" message, adolescents' brains may not fully weigh the risks of drug use.

4. The two drugs that cause the most deaths are also the most available: tobacco and alcohol. Late adolescence, before the brain is fully matured, is the peak time for developing dependence on these and other drugs.

5. Heavy drug use during times of critical brain development may cause permanent changes in the way the brain works and responds to rewards and consequences. Therefore, it is important to address a developing substance abuse problem as early as possible.

of alcohol than are adult rats; in fact, they can consume two or three times as much as adult rats do, without exhibiting the obvious signs of intoxication as quickly. But adolescent rats are more sensitive to the social disinhibition created by alcohol use, and they perform worse on memory tasks than do the "drunk" adult rats—which indicates that it's the hippocampus (the "seat of memory") that's being harmed. In fact, in 2004, the Treatment Research Institute

The fact that the brain is an organ "under construction" during the teen years and beyond makes it easier for us to understand some characteristic adolescent behavior, such as the propensity for risk-taking and the attraction to potentially dangerous situations, including drug and alcohol experimentation.

cited evidence that teens with a history of extensive alcohol abuse can show a reduced hippocampus volume of anywhere from 10 to 35 percent. It is unknown how much of that difference was there before the alcohol use, but it does show that there is an association between heavy alcohol use and a brain that is losing the ability to learn. Says one treatment specialist, "It's not unusual in recovery to see someone in their late thirties or early forties struggle with planning and problem-solving—being on time, balancing a checkbook—in exactly the way a teenager does. That's because the process of learning those skills stopped when he began using. Now he's struggling to catch up."

The younger a person is when they start drinking or using drugs, the more likely they are to develop an addiction. Kids who start drinking before age 15 are four times more likely to develop alcoholism than they are if they wait until age 21, no matter what their additional genetic or environmental factors may be. The serious risks to a teenager who is drinking or taking drugs are physical (liver and heart damage, impaired reproductive organ development, weakened immune system, impaired brain function, stunted bone growth), psychological (depression, sleep

Kids who start drinking before age 15 are four times more likely to develop alcoholism than they are if they wait until they're 21, no matter what their additional genetic or environmental factors may be.

disorders, conduct disorders, brain damage), and academic (impairment has an inevitable impact on educational achievement and economic earning power). Kids who use eventually find themselves in the wrong place at the wrong time: in a car with an impaired driver (or driving it themselves); in unfamiliar neighborhoods where their safety might be threatened; in risky situations where pregnancy and sexually transmitted diseases such as HIV are threats; in buying or using situations that involve the police and, ultimately, the justice system.

HOW IT STARTS

The causes of addiction are complex, with heredity, environment, traumatic stressors, and social factors all being important contributors (as described in Chapter 2). "We know from twin and family studies that about 50 percent of a person's vulnerability to addiction is genetic," says Nora Volkow, director of the NIDA. "But if you're never exposed to

Effects on Adolescent Health

During adolescence—the transitional phase of human development that starts around the age of 12 and ends around the age of 20—the body undergoes many rapid changes. Drugs and alcohol can adversely affect the body in many ways during this sensitive transition.

Limbic system

The limbic system is the brain's reward system. Most drugs and alcohol target this system to make the user feel high, but also alter it in the process.

→ Drugs such as cocaine, MDMA, and methamphetamine alter the structure of this system in such a way that it becomes difficult for the brain to feel pleasure without the drug.
→ These changes may lead to addiction.

Liver

While adolescents rarely develop liver cirrhosis and other conditions caused by chronic alcohol abuse, heavy adolescent drinkers and obese adolescents who are moderate drinkers often have elevated liver enzymes, which are signs of liver damage.

Endocrine system

The endocrine system stimulates reproductive and growth hormones that cause the reproductive organs and muscle and the skeletal system to mature.

→ Alcohol, especially binge drinking, decreases the levels of these hormones and can disrupt normal development of the ovaries, testes, and the brain regions that govern the endocrine system.
→ Steroids may also cause changes that affect sex hormones. Boys may develop breasts; girls might grow facial hair.

Immune system

The immune system fights infections.

→ Marijuana, cocaine, methamphetamine, and heroin can damage parts of the immune system, leaving the body more vulnerable to infections.
→ Alcohol also damages immune function.

Bone growth

In boys, alcohol use during adolescence has been linked to stunted bone growth.

illegal drugs, or if you grow up and live in an environment without trauma or too many stressors, you probably won't become addicted."

About 50 percent of a person's vulnerability to addiction is genetic.

But there are a number of risk factors that are specific to adolescent abuse and the development of addiction, primarily because of their intersection with the immature reasoning process inherent to the still-developing adolescent brain. These can include:

→ Insufficient parental supervision
→ Lack of communication between parents and children
→ Poorly defined and enforced rules and expectations regarding substance use
→ Family conflict
→ Parental alcoholism or drug use
→ The perception that parents, teachers, and other key adults in the community approve of drug-abusing behavior
→ Poor social and academic performance in school
→ Friendships with kids who have been in trouble
→ Co-occurring disorders, such as attention deficit disorder, hyperactivity, or other emotional or psychiatric disorders

"People who experience early trauma actually undergo changes in the stress systems in the brain—they do not respond to stress in the same way that an individual who doesn't have a history of early trauma does," says Kathleen Brady, president of the American Academy of Addiction Psychiatry. "And this disrupted stress response . . . makes them less able to cope with stressors, and more vulnerable to addiction."

"Adolescence is that period of trying to pull back from

Expert Advice

Reducing the Risks of Adolescent Substance Abuse

Paula D. Riggs, MD

Associate professor, Department of Psychiatry, University of Colorado

Advances in research have helped us identify and understand the risk factors that can contribute to the development of drug and alcohol problems in adolescents, as well as ways to reduce those risks. Parents must address other issues in their adolescents' lives, in addition to drug and alcohol use.

What are some of the risk factors?
Research has shown that children who have significant mood and behavior problems, such as prolonged temper tantrums, excessive aggression, impulsivity, or risk-taking behaviors, have a greater chance of developing substance abuse in adolescence, compared to those who do not exhibit these behaviors. In addition, children who have learning disabilities or other academic or behavioral problems during the elementary- and middle-school years may also be at higher risk of early drug or alcohol involvement during adolescence.

What can parents do to reduce the risks?
1. Seek early evaluation and treatment. The good news is that early evaluation and treatment can help reduce the risks if your child does develop some of these problems. There are a number of proven approaches for childhood behavior problems that focus on helping parents learn the tools of effective behavioral management, such as how to notice and reward good behavior. Another important part of treatment is teaching the skills that help children achieve greater control over their own behaviors, moods, and thoughts. Early diagnosis and treatment of learning disorders, ADHD, and mood and anxiety disorders may also reduce the risk of substance abuse in adolescence.

2. Be an involved parent. Research shows that parental support, monitoring, and involvement in a child's life are important factors in protecting against adolescent drug abuse. Involvement in a child's school life reduces behavioral and academic problems and also helps parents to know their children's friends and those friends' parents.

3. Encourage open and honest communication. Regular family discussions. characterized by respectful conversation about behavioral expectations and consequences, including attitudes and family rules about drug and alcohol use, can reduce the risk of adolescent drug abuse and other serious problem behaviors. The tricky part for parents is achieving a balance between being clear, consistent, and authoritative while at the same time making it safe for kids to tell the truth. For example, I often advise parents to make it clear to their teenager that they can call you any time if they feel they might be in an unsafe situation and you will come and pick them up, no questions asked—at least not on the way home.

4. Get the additional help you need for your own well-being. The majority of us have had a family member or a close friend suffer from the impact of substance abuse or addiction, or have abused substances ourselves. All of us are affected and connected by the enormous personal and social impact of substance abuse and addiction.

Donna PENNSYLVANIA

Donna's daughter, Aubrey, is addicted to heroin. She had her daughter arrested in hopes of forcing her into treatment.

I had heard about people having their children arrested to get help. And I thought, *What a desperate measure.* I used to hope I'd never get to that point. I thought, *I could never arrest my own child. I mean, how could you do that?* But it's like an addict getting desperate. I'm desperate now. I will do anything to help my child. My daughter has been an addict for seven years. I've seen her overdose twice. She almost didn't make it last time.

She was in the gifted program at school, captain of the cheerleading squad. She had a lot of friends. She had a beautiful voice. But she never liked herself.

When you talk to people who do not have addicts in their families, they just don't understand. You'll hear, "Well, where were the parents? Where were you when this was happening?" I was right here. I was with my daughter. I had her in everything. I kept her busy. Or they might ask, "Why don't you do something about it?" I've done everything I could possibly do about it.

When I put her in treatment I was led to believe—and maybe it was just me because I didn't know and they didn't explain it to me— that when you put your daughter into treatment she's gonna go through the treatment and learn what she has to do. When she came out of treatment I thought, *This is it. You know, this is good.* But it wasn't.

Her goal is to stay clean. My goal is to maybe, someday, not worry. I've got a 23-year-old daughter. Most people who have children that age can take off and start living all over again. To me it's like having a 10-year-old that I have to babysit.

What I really lost besides material things, which are not important, and trust, which will come back, is the ability to dream. I have to live one day at a time. A mother would dream about her child getting a good job, going to college, graduating, and then she'd dream of being a grandmother. I don't have those dreams anymore. I can't.

Nobody's promised tomorrow. But I miss dreaming. I miss looking ahead.

Aubrey PENNSYLVANIA

Aubrey has been in and out of rehab twelve times during the past seven years.

I was done running. I just couldn't do it anymore. You gotta find a place to sleep every night. You gotta find ways of getting money every day. It's too much. I didn't care what happened just as long as I got high. But then near the end the money ran out. I had nowhere to go. I was like, "Now I care. This isn't what I want."

I don't really know what bottom is. I guess it's different for everybody. Can I say I'm never gonna take another drug or have another drink for the rest of my life? No, I cannot say that. Can I say I'm not gonna take a drug or drink today? Yeah, I can. It works like that.

I know what I need to do. I need to not be bored. I need to get a job. I need to make new friends who don't use. I know enough about addiction and recovery. I've been going to rehab since I was 16—for, what, seven years. I could run a rehab.

Every time I tried and failed, the next time I went in I had less hope that I would do it. My goal now is to stay clean. That would never have been my goal. I used to want to become a dancer,

to become a mother. Now my goal is to not get high. Losing faith in myself was the worst loss of all.

The problem is that when you use for so long you feel like that's what you are. I don't know how many times I said to people, "I'm a junkie. I'm a heroin addict." That's what you really believe you are. Even when you go to an AA meeting, it's like, "Hi, I'm Bree, I'm an addict." You're constantly using that label for yourself.

But to actually get through it and to love yourself you have to think of yourself not just as an addict. Yeah, I will be an addict for the rest of my life. I know that I could never control using. But that's not only who I am. I'm not just an addict. I'm a daughter and I'm a friend and I'm an athlete and I'm a singer. I'm lots of things. But when I'm getting high, I'm none of those.

the parents and establish your own identity," says Michael Dennis, an expert on treating adolescent addiction with the Lighthouse Institute of Chestnut Health Systems in Bloomington, Illinois. "This is often done by establishing a relationship with a peer group. And what those peers are doing—using, or not using—has a great deal of influence on kids . . . If, at the very time you're learning to cope with stress, control your emotions and control your behaviors, you find yourself preoccupied with drugs, you're not learning those things. As a consequence, you get into trouble."

More than half of young people with a substance-abuse diagnosis also have a diagnosable mental illness.

CO-OCCURRING DISORDERS

It is important to understand the possibility that an adolescent sliding into addiction may also be suffering from a co-occurring or dual disorder—or, as the specialists call it, "comorbidity." (See Chapter 2 and Chapter 4.) In fact, having a mood disorder increases the likelihood of addiction, and vice versa, whereas missing or misdiagnosing either disorder increases the likelihood that an adolescent will be improperly treated. "Co-occurring disorders are the norm in adolescents entering substance-abuse treatment," says Dennis. "If you really want to break the pattern, you have to identify all of the co-occurring disorders and address them at the same time."

Just as there can be a genetic predisposition to chemical addiction, there can be a genetic component to anxiety and panic disorders, ADHD, hyperactivity, depression, bipolar disease, and schizophrenia. And the discomfort or confusion that results from any of these can lead a kid to look for a way to self-medicate. According to the National Alliance on Mental Illness, "more than half of young persons with a substance-abuse diagnosis also have a diagnosable mental illness."

"I think what happens with substance use and psychiatric disorders and symptoms is that people are just looking for relief of the pain," says Brady. But that "relief" can come at a terrible cost, when what's at stake is the developing adolescent brain.

DRUGS OF CHOICE

When the topic is drug use among kids, the focus is most often on tobacco, alcohol, and marijuana—the drugs that make up the largest percentage of adolescent substance use.

Alcohol is the first drug of choice among young people, due primarily to its accessibility and social acceptance. According to the U.S. Department of Health and Human Services (HHS), the Surgeon General has established a 50 percent reduction in heavy episodic drinking among college students by the year 2010 as one of the nation's health goals. But the problems, of course, begin long before college age. In the past forty years, the average age at which a person takes their first drink has slipped from 17 to 14, according to a 2002 Substance Abuse and Mental Health Services Administration (SAMHSA) survey.

The 2006 Monitoring the Future Survey indicates that almost three-fourths of twelfth graders, almost two-thirds of tenth graders, and about two in every five eighth graders have consumed alcohol at least once in their lifetime. The 2003 Youth Risk Behavior Survey found that 45 percent of the high school students polled reported that they drank alcohol, and 64 percent of those teens participated in binge drinking, which is defined as five or more drinks on the same occasion.

According to the HHS, approximately five thousand young people under the age of 21 die as a result of underage drinking every year—about 1,900 deaths from motor vehicle crashes, 1,600 as a result of homicides, 300 from suicide, as well as hundreds from other injuries such as falls, burns, and drownings. The NIAAA reports that about 1,700 college students die each year due to alcohol-related injuries. In 2002, the National Advisory Council on Alcohol Abuse and Alcoholism put the annual number of students who drive under the influence of alcohol at more than two million.

In June 2006, Duke University researchers, working from data collected in a 2003 survey of 10,424 freshmen at fourteen U.S. colleges, published a study that branded the

While alcohol is the leading cause of emergency room admissions for adults, for adolescents, it's marijuana.

drinking habits of college students as "extreme drinking"— meaning they consumed two to three times more alcohol than what is defined as binge drinking. An estimated 500,000 college students ages 18 to 24 suffer unintentional injuries while under the influence of alcohol. Colleges with high rates of heavy drinking also have high rates of sleep and study disruption, vandalism, and verbal, physical, and sexual violence; approximately 600,000 college students are assaulted each year by students who have been drinking. More telling, a 2005 study published in the *Archives of General Psychiatry* found that 18 percent of U.S. college students—nearly one out of five—suffered from clinically significant alcohol-related problems.

While alcohol is the leading cause of emergency room admissions for adults, for adolescents, it's marijuana. Complaints include delusions and hallucinations, automobile accidents, and more serious psychological and physical reactions when marijuana has been combined with other addictive substances.

The 2006 Monitoring the Future Survey found that 42.3 percent of twelfth graders, 31.8 percent of tenth graders, and 15.7 percent of eighth graders reported having used marijuana. One alarming factor is the strength of the

95% of all adults dependent on or abusing alcohol started drinking before age 21.

hybrid cannabis being grown today, often estimated to be up to three times stronger than it was thirty years ago. "It's a more potent drug than it was, so dependence comes on more quickly," says David Rosenbloom, director of Join Together.

Contrary to the relatively benign cultural perceptions of marijuana, the evidence of its harmfulness is strong. It is addictive, and a majority of young people entering treatment for substance abuse report marijuana as their primary drug of abuse. A 2002 SAMHSA report on the initiation of marijuana use concluded that the younger kids are when they first use marijuana, the more likely they are to use cocaine and heroin and become dependent as adults. Because it is smoked, marijuana can damage the lungs and may lead to a chronic cough and bronchitis. Students who smoke marijuana tend to get lower grades and are less likely to graduate from high school. There is an increased risk of mental illness, including depression, anxiety, schizophrenia, and other psychiatric problems, in those who smoke marijuana regularly. It also affects short-term memory, making it difficult to concentrate and learn, particularly complex information.

If there is any good news on the marijuana front, it is that the rate of use among young people ages 12 to 17 has actually declined in recent years—from 8.2 percent in 2002 to 6.8 percent in 2005, according to the National Survey on Drug Use and Health (NSDUH). In addition, the age of first use, which had dropped from 18 or older in the 1960s to under 15 in the late 1990s, has been steadily moving upward ever since, to 17.4 in 2005. Given that the odds of marijuana dependence in adulthood are six times higher for those who start using pot before age 15 than for those who begin after 18, the upward age trend is encouraging.

Another area of growing concern is the use of inhalants—household products that contain volatile solvents or aerosols that create a high if they're "huffed" from a solvent-soaked rag or breathed in directly from the container. On the list of harmful substances, the NIDA includes glues, nail polish remover, lighter fluid, spray paints (silver and gold in particular), paint thinners, gasoline, felt-tip markers, aerosol deodorant, hair spray, whipped cream canisters, butane lighters, and cleaning fluids.

"Even a single session of repeated inhalant abuse can disrupt heart rhythms and cause death from cardiac arrest, or lower oxygen levels enough to cause suffocation," reports Volkow. "Regular abuse can result in serious harm to vital organs, including the brain, heart, kidneys, and liver." A

The odds of marijuana dependence in adulthood are six times higher for those who start using pot before age 15 than for those who begin after 18.

2006 NIDA-supported survey reported that 16.1 percent of eighth graders, 13.3 percent of tenth graders, and 11.1 percent of twelfth graders have tried inhalants at least once in their lives. A PRIDE (Parents' Resource Institute for Drug Education) Questionnaire survey found in 2003–04 that 2.5 percent of U.S. fourth graders had tried inhalants in the previous year.

Abuse of prescription drugs presents an increasing danger to young people. The 2006 Monitoring the Future Survey also found that the use of prescription-type drugs remains high among middle- and high-school students. In the past year, 9.7 percent of twelfth graders reported using acetaminophen-hydrocodone (Vicodin) and 4.3 percent reported using oxycodone (OxyContin). Another 6.6 percent of twelfth graders reported using prescription tranquilizers, 6.6 percent reported using barbiturates such as pentobarbital (Nembutal), and 8.1 percent reported using amphetamines—all for nonprescribed, nonmedical use.

Some kids assume that because something is in Mom and Dad's medicine cabinet, it's safe to take. But these are powerful medications that, when used inappropriately, can have devastating consequences. This is particularly true for prescription pain relievers, such as OxyContin and Vicodin. When taken as directed, these can be valuable medications.

Things to Know About Getting Drugs Over the Internet

Robert F. Forman, PhD

Adjunct assistant professor, Center for Studies of Addiction, University of Pennsylvania School of Medicine

The Internet is a powerful resource for education, entertainment, and business. Unfortunately, it is also a haven for selling and buying all sorts of drugs without a prescription. Many "no prescription web sites" mislead potential customers into thinking they are legitimate by making false claims of legality. But buyer beware: It is illegal to possess certain medications in the United States without a valid prescription, and for several good reasons:

→ Many "no prescription web sites" ship counterfeit, expired, or simply bad drugs from countries that provide little or no oversight or control. In some cases, the web site will simply take your money and send nothing at all.

→ Of even greater concern are the web sites that ship drugs such as opioids (for example, Vicodin, codeine, and oxycodone), sedatives (such as Xanax and Valium), and stimulants (such as Ritalin and Adderall) without a prescription. These medications are potentially addictive and can easily be misused, with disastrous results. Just because a drug comes in the form of a pill doesn't mean it is safe.

→ Young people are particularly vulnerable to Internet-based drug dealing because they have grown up using the Internet and don't realize its risks. Somehow, professionally created web sites provide an illusion of safety. Sadly, there are several reports of young people who have died from drugs they bought over the Internet without a prescription.

Tips for parents

→ Look for unexpected credit card use. If unexpected charges appear on your credit card, call your credit card company and find out what is happening.

→ Know your child's online "friends." Just as you should know the friends your child spends time with, pay attention to where they go online, too. Question your child if they are visiting online pharmacies or web sites that promote drugs.

→ Look out for unexpected packages with unrecognized names. If unexpected packages arrive at your home addressed to your child or to unknown parties (that is, a name that you do not recognize), insist that your child open the package in your presence.

→ Get computer help. If you have reason to suspect that your child is using the computer to obtain drugs illegally, seek two kinds of professional help: 1. an addiction specialist to address the substance abuse problem; and 2. someone to secure your computer so you can ensure that it is used safely. In most communities, there are computer service companies that can help you set up controls over your computer (often called filtering or blocking software), or software programs that monitor which web sites are being visited.

→ For medications prescribed by a doctor, only use online pharmacies with the VIPPS certification. Web sites that have the VIPPS seal subscribe to safe online pharmacy practices and operate legitimately.

However, these medications work in the brain the same way that heroin does and can also lead to addiction when abused. Because prescription pain relievers can produce the same effects as heroin, particularly when snorted or injected, people addicted to these prescription drugs may switch to heroin to maintain their addiction. The consequences of prescription-painkiller abuse should not be underestimated.

Another substance showing up in youth surveys is over-the-counter cough medicine, particularly the kind that includes dextromethorphan—or DXM—as an ingredient. The 2006 Monitoring the Future Survey showed that 4 percent of eighth graders, 5 percent of tenth graders, and 7 percent of twelfth-grade students recently reported drinking cough syrup to get high. And they didn't have to do anything illegal to get it; it was right there in the medicine cabinet at home.

John Walters, the director of the White Office of National Drug Control Policy, recently issued an alert to parents: "Go to your medicine cabinet and take unused meds or prescriptions you're finished using and throw them away."

CYBER-DEALERS

The corner or schoolyard drug pusher seems to have been joined by the Internet. "There is a fair amount of illegal distribution of very powerful narcotics that have appropriate uses when properly prescribed," says Rosenbloom. "OxyContin, Vicodin. And when kids are surveyed about where they get them, it's from their parents' medicine cabinets, on the street, or via the Net."

While there are many legitimate online pharmacies, there are also numerous "rogue" pharmacies online. Just do an online search for oxycodone or methamphetamine, and watch how many sales sites pop up—and link you to others offering Percocet and Viagra, as well. Given that many of these sales sites are located offshore, it's difficult for the U.S. government to police them. And not having a credit card doesn't prevent teens from getting prescription drugs from these sites either; most will accept a money order or a cashier's check, forms of payment that are easy to obtain. Then the packages are delivered to a friend's house. "Eight to twelve tablets of Vicodin, one quarter to one-half tablet of OxyContin, are roughly as potent as one bag of heroin," warns Thomas McLellan, PhD, co-founder and CEO of the Treatment Research Institute in Philadelphia.

Eighty percent of the parents surveyed said they believed neither alcohol nor marijuana is available at parties their kids attend; 50 percent of the kids reported attending parties where both alcohol and drugs are easily available.

Nine out of ten kids are online these days, according to data from the Pew Internet & American Life Project, which also found that 56 percent of teens have more than one screen name. One of the reasons for this may be to create a fake identity to avoid detection by parents. Nearly half the kids surveyed in the Pew study reported that their parents know very little about what they do online.

PREVENTING DRUG ABUSE: THE ROLE OF SCHOOLS
Schools can play a constructive role in preventing your child's isolation or inactivity, and so can the extended community. What activities are offered after school and on weekends? If school sports or extracurricular activities are not an option, is there an open but supervised community center? Are there school-supervised peer counseling groups where a student can get a friendly, empathetic, but confidential hearing for a family or personal problem? Are teachers and guidance counselors easily accessible, are you accessible to them, and can you get your child's ongoing progress reports via e-mails or regularly scheduled meetings? As much as you need the teachers' support, they need yours as well. Make yourself known.

The reality is, most parents work—and often they're working at more than one job. That is doubly true for single parents. So, yes, constant vigilance is difficult, especially if it seems at the time that there's no problem; why expend all this effort and emotion in the absence of evidence that there's anything to worry about? Because the time to lay the groundwork, with both the kids and the parental "support team" of teachers, coaches, and even family doctors, is before trouble starts.

PREVENTING DRUG ABUSE: THE ROLE OF PARENTS

"The most important actor in a prevention program is an involved parent," says Rosenbloom. And the sooner that parent speaks up, the better—before a son or daughter drops out of high school or settles for a low-end/no-demand job. Before there's an unplanned pregnancy, or a sexually transmitted disease, or a wrecked car, or an arrest record for possession or sale of illegal substances. The earlier you recognize the problem, the easier it will be to treat it.

A 2006 survey by the National Center on Addiction and Substance Abuse at Columbia University found a significant disparity between what parents believe is going on with their kids and what is actually going on. Eighty percent of the parents surveyed said they believed neither alcohol nor marijuana is available at parties their kids attend; 50 percent of the kids reported attending parties where both alcohol and drugs are easily available. Parties are just one of the arenas where parents may underestimate their child's exposure to drugs and alcohol. Until recently, parents may have met all their children's friends. But many teens now are part of online communities that force parental monitoring to take on a whole new dimension. Now, more than ever, parents need to have clear and honest conversations with their teens.

We all hope we're getting the truth from our children, but if we're honest about our own adolescent years, we have to admit that sometimes, in a kid's mind, truth is relative. We can't be mind readers, and being a parent is hard enough without adding paranoia to the mix, but it is important to start the conversation early and keep it going. Keep it as simple as you can; the dialogue can grow more

Early Signs of Teenage Drug and Alcohol Use

Paula D. Riggs, MD

Associate professor, Department of Psychiatry, University of Colorado

1. Evidence of drugs or alcohol. The most obvious indication of drug or alcohol use are signs of intoxication, smelling alcohol or drugs on the breath or clothing, or finding alcohol, drugs, or drug paraphernalia, such as pipes or rolling papers, in your teenager's room, clothing, or car. Any one of these indicators is cause for a frank discussion.

2. Change in previous level of functioning. This can be somewhat less obvious but is often an earlier signal that there may be a problem. It's important for parents to be alert to any significant changes or decline in the following areas:

→ Change in school performance, such as a decline in grades, decreased motivation to complete assignments or be involved in school activities, skipping classes/truancy

→ Significant changes in sleep habits (sleeping much more or much less), level of activity, appetite (increased or decreased), or hygiene

→ Significant changes in behavior and/or mood, such as increased irritability, aggression, disregard for rules, mood swings, depression, expressing suicidal thoughts or behaviors

→ Decreased involvement in social activities, such as team sports or school-related activities, loss of interest in a favorite hobby

→ Association with a deviant peer group, gang involvement, legal problems

A significant change in mood, behavior, academic performance, or peer group does not necessarily mean your teenager is involved with drugs or alcohol. It does mean that a heart-to-heart, parent-child talk about concerns and problems is in order.

Don't feel that you have to handle everything alone. There are a growing number of clinical professionals with training and experience in evaluating and treating mental health and substance abuse problems in adolescents. This is important, because adolescents with substance abuse have a higher risk of having co-occurring mental health problems, such as depression or attention deficit-hyperactivity disorder (ADHD), compared with adolescents who are not using substances.

Will they just "grow out of it"?
Yes and no. While it is true that many teens simply grow out of problem behaviors that arise during the teenage years, many do not, and it's almost impossible to tell who will and who won't at the time problem behaviors begin. The important thing for parents to know is that they should take problems such as adolescent drug use seriously and seek appropriate support and treatment as soon as a problem is identified. They can help to ensure that their children will grow out of it, and flourish as happy and healthy individuals as they move into young adulthood.

sophisticated as the child gets older. Establish the rules for healthy behavior and responsibility early, and spell out the consequences for breaking those rules. And let your children know that this will be an ongoing conversation, from now until they're no longer living in your home.

Listen to what your kids have to say, even when it frightens or frustrates you. Stress how much you love them and offer to be a partner in the solutions and coping strategies

---

Teens who have five or more dinners a week with their families are less likely to try marijuana, smoke cigarettes, or drink alcohol.

---

you'll work out together. If and when the time comes to enforce the rules, do it—which is a very good reason for making consequences realistic, enforceable, and something you all can live with.

Talking with your children about drugs, however, is rarely easy. Perhaps the difficult and specific "Are you using or have you ever used?" conversation can wait until later, but a strong and consistent parental message about the dangers of putting brain-altering substances into a young body cannot. Baby-boomer parents, in particular, have acknowledged some awkwardness with the drugs-and-alcohol conversation. That generation's drug use has become the stuff of myth. (Although if everyone who claims to have been at Woodstock had actually been there, it's conceivable that the State of New York might have fallen into the ocean.) That said, what is a parent to do when the response from their child is, "But didn't you use?"

"The answer I give to that is, don't get pulled into telling your war stories," says Dennis. "You wouldn't let them have your car right now, either." What you did, and regret, is none of your child's business, and the world won't end if you say so. That said, don't be a hypocrite. Practice what you preach, or prepare to lose your argument.

The *Parents: The Anti-Drug* web site (www.theantidrug.com) has many helpful ideas about how to conduct The Conversation. It lists talking points, strategies, and even ways to rehearse. Another helpful web site is www.teen-drug-abuse.org, whose first piece of advice is "Educate yourself." Even in the absence of an immediate reason for concern, knowing the terminology and the issues is always a good idea.

Remember: you're not the first parent to fight this fight, you won't be the last, and you're not alone.

While there are known stressors that may lead kids to drug and alcohol abuse, there are also tactics and behaviors parents can use to head off that behavior. Here, for example, is something very simple: a 2006 study by the National Center for Addiction and Substance Abuse at Columbia University suggests that teens who have five or more dinners a week with their families are less likely to try marijuana, smoke cigarettes, or drink alcohol. So turn off the TV and remove everyone's iPod earbuds. Sit down together at the table and serve something up, even if it's only for a half an hour over a frozen dinner cooked in the microwave. It's the time that matters—and the connection.

When and if you suspect a problem does exist—slipping grades, secretive behavior, drug paraphernalia discovered in a backpack, accompanied by mood swings and unpredictable responses—don't panic (or, if that fails, fake not panicking). Voice your suspicions and concerns honestly. And don't ever confront a teen (or anyone else, for that matter) when it's clear that they are drunk or stoned or otherwise impaired; they can't hear you, they don't want to hear you, and in any case, they won't remember what you said. So, even if it means stifling your anger or fear and waiting until the clear light of the next day—wait.

If and when the conversation becomes a confrontation, the most important thing to remember is that the adult(s)

Adolescent Addiction

Michael L. Dennis, PhD

Senior research psychologist, Lighthouse Institute, Chestnut Health Systems

Five things you should know about adolescent addiction

1. About 90 percent of people with substance-abuse or dependence disorders started using under the age of 18 (half under the age of 15) and end up using for several decades. Still, the majority of people who have ever had substance disorders are now in recovery.

2. While most people who use alcohol or other drugs are able to stop on their own, the majority of those with dependence problems do not stop until they have gone to treatment three or four times over several years.

3. Going to treatment in the first decade of use typically reduces the time to enter recovery by more than half. However, only one in ten adolescents with abuse or dependence problems receive treatment, and only 10 percent of those access continuing care.

4. The majority of adolescents with substance disorders also have one or more co-occurring psychiatric problems (such as depression, anxiety, traumatic memories, self-mutilation, suicidal thoughts), behavioral problems (inattention, hyperactivity, conduct disorder), crime or violence problems, and/or have multiple sex partners or other HIV risks. Addressing these other problems is often a key part of successful treatment.

5. Relapse is common, particularly in the first ninety days after discharge. The presence or absence of recovery support through continuing care, self-help groups, recovery schools, and work with families is a key predictor of which adolescents can sustain early recovery.

Five things you should remember

1. Relapse is common. Most kids go to treatment two to four times before they are able to sustain recovery.

2. It is very important to learn to recognize the signs of relapse (spending time with using friends, breaking rules, staying out, inattention, anger, poor hygiene, declining grades) and get the adolescent back into treatment right away and back on the road to recovery.

3. Helping your adolescent to participate in continuing care and other recovery support services during the first ninety days after treatment (and, ideally, the first year) is key.

4. Most adolescents get outpatient treatment for two hours a week. Residential treatment is usually reserved for adolescents who are not making it in outpatient treatment or who have a home environment that makes stopping difficult.

5. While treatment is focused on getting people to stop, self-help groups, recovery schools, and other recovery support services are typically designed to help them stay in recovery. It is very important to try to put adolescents in follow-up programs that have other adolescents—not just adults.

Expert Advice

Why Adolescent Addiction Is Different

Thomas J. Crowley, MD *Director, Division of Substance Dependence, University of Colorado School of Medicine*

Elizabeth Whitmore, PhD *Associate professor of Psychiatry, University of Colorado School of Medicine*

Adolescent drug users are different from adults in many ways. Their drug and alcohol use often has different causes, and they have even more trouble seeing the future consequences of substance use. In treatment, adolescents must be approached differently than adults because of their unique developmental and psychiatric issues, differences in their values and belief systems, and environmental considerations (such as strong peer influences).

Adolescents generally have smaller body sizes, a lower tolerance for substances, and they do not have a fully developed brain, putting them at greater risk for abusing drugs and at greater risk for physical and other consequences related to their use. The use of substances may also negatively effect their mental and emotional development because substance use interferes with how people learn to handle situations and experiences.

Adolescents are also always part of a larger family unit, so family involvement plays a critical role in an adolescent's treatment and recovery.

Finally, unlike adults, very few adolescents attend treatment because they recognize they have a problem and are voluntarily seeking help. They are much more likely to be coerced to enter treatment by their parents, their school, and/or the court or social services system. While treatment does not need to be voluntary to be effective, special consideration must be given to these issues as part of the adolescent's treatment.

Although relatively few treatment programs are designed specifically for adolescents, these important differences demonstrate that adolescent treatment needs to be specifically tailored to the unique needs of adolescents and not just based on adult models of treatment.

in the room have to remain in charge—and that means no yelling. Try to stay calm and focused, even kind, and take a break when your fear or anger gets in the way. Walk around the block, come back, and start over again. Don't threaten, don't shout, and don't back down. If the rules and consequences have been clearly stated up to this point, your child will know exactly what's at stake and why.

The Center for Adolescent Substance Abuse Research has a tried-and-true system for setting up the conversation while attempting to gauge what kind of behavior your child might be engaged in. It is called the CRAFFT test (not to be confused with the CRAFT approach to getting a loved one into treatment; see page 158).

C Have you ever ridden in a CAR driven by someone (including yourself) who was high or had been using alcohol or drugs?
R Do you ever use alcohol or drugs to RELAX, feel better about yourself, or fit in?
A Do you ever use alcohol or drugs while you are ALONE?
F Do your family or FRIENDS ever tell you that you should cut down on your drinking or drug use?
F Do you ever FORGET things you did while using alcohol or drugs?
T Have you gotten into TROUBLE while you were using alcohol or drugs?

If you hear two or more yes answers, there may be a significant problem.

Once we get past our naïveté and denial, a parent's next response tends to be either "I've failed him" or "I'm going to kick him out of the house." In either case, it's a four-alarm fire and you need help. It is imperative not to let shame or anger prevent you from asking for help, even demanding it, from school guidance counselors, teachers, coaches, clergy, family doctors, and friends; from Al-Anon and Alateen, the family/friend support organizations; and from similar groups that support the families and loved ones of kids who are battling addiction. Remember: you're not the first parent to fight this fight, you won't be the last, and you're not alone.

FINDING TREATMENT

There are different treatment approaches for adolescent addiction than there are for adult addiction. Therefore, you should be wary of any addiction or medical professional who suggests a one-size-fits-all solution for your kid. Assessments differ; treatment needs to be matched to the needs of the individual. There are gender differences and differences in cultural mores or ethnicity as well, all of which may call for differences in treatment approach. For example, a 16-year-old high school boy who's been putting away a case of beer every night doesn't belong in an AA meeting filled with 50-year-old adults, some of them businessmen, some of them walking over from the homeless shelter. A 14-year-old girl, struggling with bulimia, as well as Internet-supplied oxycodone, needs to be in a different setting, with different treatment strategies, than does her mother's best friend who uses cocaine. In order to aid parents in finding help for their teens, Drug Strategies, a nonprofit research institute (www.drugstrategies.org), developed *Treating Teens: A Guide to Adolescent Drug Treatment.*

In treating adolescent addiction, the family may play a much larger role than it does in treating adults. Perhaps a custodial parent is still an actively using addict. What would that mean in terms of a teen's recovery and aftercare? What behaviors are siblings involved with, and how likely is it that they may need treatment and monitoring as well? What about families who see this as a discipline issue, or a matter of defiance? "The parent has to understand that there's been a change in the brain," says NIDA's Volkow. "The child isn't choosing the drug over love of the parent; the drug has taken over. It's not as simple as saying to a kid, 'don't do this.'"

Staff at treatment centers need to be trained and experienced in adolescent development, able to recognize and treat any co-occurring disorders, such as depression, ADHD, or thoughts of suicide. Adults usually show ample objective evidence of the effects of addiction and the need for a change of lifestyle when they come into treatment. Among young people entering treatment, the only evidence that damage has been done may be the disapproval of parents—

and many kids would argue that they're not particularly concerned with that, and, in fact, relish it.

The good news is, the very pliability of the adolescent brain, which leads to poor risk management and impulsive behavior in the first place, can also work in a kid's favor. "Our brain is what we call 'plastic,'" says Volkow. "In a young person, the degree of recovery is likely to be better than in a person in his forties or fifties, because as we grow older, we lose the ability of plastic recovery."

It may be difficult to believe while you're living through the ups and downs, the horrors and the reverses, but it does happen: they can heal.

Addiction Treatment for Adolescents: Advice for Parents

Mathea Falco, JD

President, Drug Strategies

Treatment specifically for teens is scarce. Although more than one million teens need drug treatment, only one in ten actually receives help. Why is adolescent treatment so hard to find? Lack of state and federal funding for treatment programs, as well as shrinking insurance benefits for drug treatment, are two major reasons. Without adequate insurance, many parents simply cannot afford to get the kind of help their children need.

When parents realize their children have substance problems and must find treatment, they often do not know where to turn. The family is frequently in a crisis situation, when decisions must be made quickly. Yet very little information is available about what parents should look for in choosing a program.

Key questions parents should ask a treatment program

Is your program specifically designed for teens? If so, how?

Most treatment programs are designed for adults, not teens. Even if programs say they treat teens, they may, in fact, just be including them in adult programs that have a few activities for younger people. Adolescents have unique challenges, such as relating to their families, dealing with peer groups, getting an education, and finding a job. They also are different developmentally than adults. Effective adolescent programs should address not only drug use problems, but also the many aspects of a teen's life.

What questions do you ask to determine the seriousness of the substance-abuse problem and whether my child will benefit from this particular program?

Good programs usually ask a brief set of initial questions to explore the severity of the youth's drug use: How long has the teen been using? Are they addicted? What other kinds of problems does the teen have? Are they involved in delinquent behavior? Answers to these questions will help a program decide if they can provide the kind of help needed. Once the teen is admitted to the program, the teen's problems will be examined in much greater depth. This kind of assessment should include a physical exam to determine if there are any medical conditions related to the substance abuse problem; a psychiatric exam to determine if there are mental health problems, such as depression, that must also be treated; a review of the teen's educational progress, including academic performance and learning disabilities; and a review of the teen's relationships with peers. Do they have friends? Are they involved in drugs? The program may also ask in-depth questions of the family about how well family members communicate, whether there are discipline problems, and whether there is a history of substance abuse within the family. The program will develop as complete a picture of the adolescent's problems as possible, so that the counselors can design a treatment plan to address them successfully.

How does the program involve the family in treatment?

Family involvement in the teen's treatment is critically important. Regardless of how well or badly the teen and the family relate to one another, parents are the dominant reality in the lives of most teens. Parents are also the major source of financial support, including medical insurance, if any. Most teens live at home, and their recovery will depend on how supportive the home environment will be in helping them build new lives free of alcohol and drug use. Recent studies of adolescents who stop using drugs report that parental involvement, new friends, and motivation are keys to success. Programs should encourage parents (or other caregivers) to participate in counseling, group meetings, drug education, and other activities. Families should also be asked to examine their own alcohol and drug use and to get treatment themselves when necessary. Programs should teach the family how to be more effective parents, including how to discipline children reasonably.

How does the program provide continuing care after treatment is completed?

The period after treatment is vitally important; most adolescents relapse in the first three months after treatment. However, continuing care services can greatly increase the likelihood of sustained recovery. Developing follow-up plans while the teen is still in treatment is important. Such plans create a structure for the teen and the teen's family, so that treatment gains continue. These plans may include relapse prevention training, referrals to community resources, and periodic check-ups by the program with the adolescent and family members. Twelve-step meetings can also be helpful for some teens in recovery, although finding twelve-step meetings specifically for teens can be difficult in some communities.

Unfortunately, many programs do not provide continuing care, and parents must try to support the teen's recovery as fully as possible. Parents should stay in close touch with their children every step of the way. Parents who believe their children can overcome their problems and be successful in school make a powerful difference.

What evidence do you have that this program is effective?

Very few programs have formal, scientific evaluations that measure their treatment success. However, even without such evaluations, other information can be helpful. For example, completing the entire course of treatment is closely related to success. Retention rate is an important indicator of whether a program is effective. How many teens drop out? How long do they stay in treatment? How many actually complete treatment? Other useful things to ask about are whether teens in the program show improvements in school performance (better attendance and grades) and family relationships (better communications, less aggressive behavior). How does the program monitor drug use among teens in treatment? Do they conduct drug tests? If so, how often do they test? What are the results? Good programs should have test results showing that teens in treatment are staying clean.

Residential Treatment for Adolescents

Mitchell S. Rosenthal, MD

President, Phoenix House

What to look for in a residential treatment program for teens

Suitability Is the program clearly designed for teens, and are there plenty of kids there the same age as yours? Ask about the program's treatment approach and methods, discipline, the behavioral problems of other youngsters there, daily activities, and how the program helps kids deal with the normal emotional stresses of adolescence.

Assessment Does the program carefully screen applicants to determine if it can provide the most appropriate treatment for your child? Ask about the criteria for admission, when admission is denied, and what the program does for youngsters who do not fit its profile.

Treatment length Treatment length depends upon individual need, but residential programs for most teens should generally last between three months and twelve.

Facility and amenities Is the setting homelike, or does it have an institutional character? Is the facility clean and well maintained? How many youngsters share a room? Is the food wholesome? Are there adequate recreational resources?

Education What educational services does the program provide? How will the program ensure that your child will not fall behind in school? What provisions are made for kids with special needs?

Holding power Since most youngsters who enter treatment programs fail to complete them, you need to know whether this program be able to engage your child in the treatment process. Is the mood of the program upbeat and positive? Do youngsters there seem comfortable with the program's demands?

Family involvement Family participation is essential, so make sure that you will be involved in the treatment process, that the program offers family support services, and that there will be an assigned staff member for you to contact. You should also feel free to ask to speak to parents of other adolescents who have participated in the program.

Staffing Is the program staff adequate in size and professional qualification? Is there a full- or part-time psychiatrist or other mental health professional on the treatment team?

Aftercare Because the danger of relapse is greatest in the first months following treatment, you need to know what provisions are made for continuing care, and whether they have support groups for youngsters leaving the program.

Effectiveness Few programs have long-term outcome studies, but you should be able to ask for some information on completion and subsequent behavior. How many youngsters who enter the program remain beyond three months and how many stay to the end? How many kids who completed treatment during the past year are drug-free, back in school, or are still involved with the program?

Ted TEXAS

After a failed stint at an outpatient program, Ted's parents sent him to the Phoenix Academy, a residential treatment program.

I started using around 14. I'd get up some mornings and say, "Man, today's gonna suck," and so I'd put a little vodka in my coffee just to get a buzz goin' and then I'd go and smoke my joint. I always had some weed in the morning. Some days if I had some prescription pills left over from the weekend, I'd pop a couple of those.

Before I came to the Phoenix Academy, I didn't really have much of a schedule besides, "Hey, let's go get messed up today." Boredom is a really big trigger. You're just sitting around the house feeling bored. You got a big sack of weed and a couple beers and you have a party right there.

I would always avoid confrontation. My parents would be yelling in my face, "You fucking blah-blah-blah-blah," and I'd just be sitting there saying, "Uh-huh," but thinking, *Thank God I got another gram stashed somewhere in my room.* Now they say as long as I'm open and I don't lie to them about shit then it'll be okay. There won't be any sort of heavy confrontation like that.

I know now that I can't live the life I wanna live with drugs in it. I know that if I do use drugs, if I decide to go down that pathway again, the things I wanna do in life aren't gonna come out the way I want them to. But I know if I stay sober, I'm more motivated. I have more of a drive to try and accomplish different things.

I'm very, very excited to get back into a home environment where I feel comfortable. But I'm also very scared. It's really sort of a dilemma that I have in my head every day. When I get out, what the fuck am I gonna do? Am I gonna be sober and hopefully live a good life and deal with all my shit without having drugs? Or am I gonna just go back to the same shit, which I really don't wanna do? I don't know what the hell's gonna happen.

JOE

Treatment: The Worst Thing You Can Do Is Nothing

I have been in after-hours clubs where there were guns and drugs on every table, and I was never afraid of walking in. But when I first walked into rehab, I had never been so scared in all my life. JOE, RECOVERING ADDICT

How, exactly, do we know when addiction has taken hold? What are the signs and symptoms that tell us it is time to do something? The time to take action is as soon as abuse is detected, preferably before drugs or alcohol cause recurring problems in our lives. The key words to remember in determining when to act are *continued use despite negative consequences or recurring problems*. What kind of problems? Here is a general but by no means all-inclusive list:

Changes in patterns of drinking or drug use Strong desire or sense of compulsion to drink or use drugs; difficulties in controlling use in terms of when to start, when to stop, and how much is ingested; increased tolerance, as evidenced by the need to drink or use more in order to get high or intoxicated; desire to cut down or control use, often combined with unsuccessful attempts to do so.

Relationship problems Fights and disagreements at home; deteriorating relationships with family members, friends, employers, co-workers, teachers, coaches; giving up old friendships; holding grudges and resentments that prevent reconciliation.

Personality changes Gradual or abrupt changes in personality, including dramatic or unusual mood swings, depression, irritability, aggressive behavior, suicide threats or attempts, anxiety, insomnia, defiance, paranoia, apathy, progressive neglect of important social, occupational, or recreational activities.

Problems at work or at school Numerous sick days, gradual decline or rapid deterioration in performance or grades, employer/teacher complaints about attitude or performance.

Legal problems Arrests for driving under the influence, burglary, assault; in adolescents, arrests for truancy, shoplifting, minor-in-possession (MIP) or minor-in-consumption (MIC) charges; probation or parole violations.

Physical symptoms Headaches, loss of memory or blackouts, morning nausea, indigestion, unexplained seizures, head injuries.

Withdrawal symptoms Ranging from subtle early-stage symptoms (anxiety, irritability, nervousness, nausea, insomnia, gastrointestinal distress, loss of appetite) to more obvious and undeniable later-stage symptoms (blackouts, uncontrollable tremors, seizures, hallucinations, mental confusion).

GETTING TREATMENT: WHERE TO START

When an addict is ready to get treatment, there are a few options that the individual or family should consider. It's worth discussing with your doctor concerns you may have about drug use behavior. They may not have all the answers you need, but primary care physicians can be a good resource. "You want to be screened by a physician," says Kathleen Brady, current president of the American Academy of Addiction Psychiatry. "You then take your cue from the physician." Be cautioned, however, that they are often not trained in diagnosing or treating addiction and may not be aware of the addiction treatment resources that are available. Thomas McLellan of the Treatment Research Institute warns, "Medical schools have not taught

AUDIT
(Alcohol Use Disorder Identification Test)

The AUDIT is a brief self-report test that screens for both at-risk drinking (heavy drinking alone) and alcohol abuse and dependence (heavy drinking that interferes with life or causes significant distress). This is a screening test, and positive results suggest that assessment by a health professional is needed. The AUDIT does not make diagnoses. Higher scores indicate more severe problems and more urgency to seek help.

Please note: "Alcohol" includes beer, wine, liquor, or any other alcoholic beverage.

1. How often do you have a drink containing alcohol?
   (0) never (1) monthly (2) 2 to 4 times a month
   (3) 2 to 3 times a week (4) 4 or more times a week

2. How many drinks containing alcohol do you have on a typical day when you are drinking?
   (0) 1 to 2 (1) 3 or 4 (2) 5 or 6 (3) 7 to 9
   (4) 10 or more

3. How often do you have six or more drinks on one occasion?
   (0) never (1) less than monthly (2) monthly
   (3) weekly (4) daily or almost daily

4. How often during the last year have you found that you were unable to stop drinking once you started?
   (0) never (1) less than monthly (2) monthly
   (3) weekly (4) daily or almost daily

5. How often during the last year have you failed to do what was normally expected of you because of drinking?
   (0) never (1) less than monthly (2) monthly
   (3) weekly (4) daily or almost daily

6. How often during the last year have you needed a drink first thing in the morning to get yourself going after a heavy drinking session?
   (0) never (1) less than monthly (2) monthly
   (3) weekly (4) daily or almost daily

7. How often during the last year have you felt guilt or remorse after drinking?
   (0) never (1) less than monthly (2) monthly
   (3) weekly (4) daily or almost daily

8. How often during the last year have you been unable to remember what happened the night before because of drinking?
   (0) never (1) less than monthly (2) monthly
   (3) weekly (4) daily or almost daily

9. Have you or someone else been injured as the result of your drinking?
   (0) no (2) yes, but not in the last year
   (4) yes, during the last year

10. Has a friend, relative, doctor, or other heath worker been concerned about your drinking or suggested you cut down?
    (0) no (2) yes, but not in the last year
    (4) yes, during the last year

Total score

A score of three or less indicates that your drinking is not exceeding the limits for healthy adults.

Scores between four and seven suggest that you should examine your drinking and its effects on your life, and that you may wish to quit or cut down on your drinking.

A score above eight is a positive test, indicating that unhealthy alcohol use is occurring. Higher scores indicate more serious problems. A score of sixteen or more strongly suggests that professional help should be sought.

SOURCE: AUDIT WAS DEVELOPED BY THE WORLD HEALTH ORGANIZATION.

DAST-20
(Drug Abuse Screening Test-20)

The DAST-20 is a widely used test that can help assess whether you or a loved one has a drug problem. The test should take about five minutes to complete.

The following questions concern information about your potential involvement with drugs, not including alcoholic beverages, during the past twelve months. Carefully read each statement and decide if your answer is yes or no. Then check the appropriate box beside the question.

In the statements, "abuse" refers to the use of prescribed or over-the-counter drugs in excess of the directions, and any nonmedical use of drugs.

Please answer every question. If you have difficulty with a statement, choose the response that is mostly right.

These questions refer to the past twelve months.

Check your responses

1. Have you used drugs other than those required for medical reasons? ☐ YES ☐ NO
2. Have you abused prescription drugs? ☐ YES ☐ NO
3. Do you abuse more than one drug at a time? ☐ YES ☐ NO
4. Can you get through the week without using drugs? ☐ YES ☐ NO
5. Are you always able to stop using drugs when you want to? ☐ YES ☐ NO
6. Have you had blackouts or flashbacks as a result of drug use? ☐ YES ☐ NO
7. Do you ever feel bad or guilty about your drug use? ☐ YES ☐ NO
8. Does your spouse (or parents) ever complain about your involvement with drugs? ☐ YES ☐ NO
9. Has drug abuse created problems between you and your spouse or your parents? ☐ YES ☐ NO
10. Have you lost friends because of your use of drugs? ☐ YES ☐ NO
11. Have you neglected your family because of your use of drugs? ☐ YES ☐ NO
12. Have you been in trouble at work because of drug abuse? ☐ YES ☐ NO
13. Have you lost a job because of drug abuse? ☐ YES ☐ NO
14. Have you gotten into fights when under the influence of drugs? ☐ YES ☐ NO
15. Have you engaged in illegal activities in order to obtain drugs? ☐ YES ☐ NO
16. Have you been arrested for possession of illegal drugs? ☐ YES ☐ NO
17. Have you ever experienced withdrawal symptoms (felt sick) when you stopped taking drugs? ☐ YES ☐ NO
18. Have you had medical problems as a result of your drug use (for example, memory loss, hepatitis, convulsions, bleeding)? ☐ YES ☐ NO
19. Have you gone to anyone for help for a drug problem? ☐ YES ☐ NO
20. Have you been involved in a treatment program specifically related to drug use? ☐ YES ☐ NO

Your score

The quiz is scored by allocating one point to each "yes" answer—except for questions 4 and 5, where one point is allocated for each "no" answer—and totaling the responses.

A score of six to ten points indicates a moderate drug problem.

A score of eleven to fifteen points suggests a substantial drug problem.

A score of sixteen or more points indicates a severe drug problem, and follow-up evaluations by a professional are recommended.

addiction. Nursing schools are just now starting to teach about addiction. The people who are relied upon for information often do not know what to do, or when to do it, or what the resources are."

In addition to physicians, another important resource is addiction doctors (see sidebar) who have been trained in assessment. Professionals who have experience with addiction are more likely to be able to diagnose addiction, and these experts will then have the best advice about how to proceed. They may be found at (or you can often get referrals from) hospitals, medical and mental-health clinics, rehabilitation programs, and other treatment programs, such as halfway houses and outpatient programs. Further, the federal government's agency dedicated to facilitating recovery for addicts, the Substance Abuse and Mental Health Services Administration, offers a web site (www.findtreatment.samhsa.gov) that can assist in identifying area providers. This web site does not, however, assess the quality of care these providers offer, and therefore, it should serve as a place from which to start your search, rather than a referral service. Finally, specialists who routinely refer addicts for help may include counselors at school or the workplace, hospitals, county or state health services, or social-service agencies. Addicts or their families often do not have the benefit of time or the emotional energy to do a thorough search of all of the options available. Ideally, this is a time to call on friends and other family members to help in the search for resources. Contacting family physicians, gynecologists, or other regularly seen specialists can be useful for quick assessments of local inpatient and outpatient programs. Many experts advise people to call as many reputable sources as possible to check and double-check programs, therapists, or other specialists before choosing a place to go for an assessment. (Similarly, they recommend seeking second and third opinions if an assessment leads to a recommendation of a treatment plan.)

"One of the issues about alcohol and drug treatment, and the quality and standards of treatment, is that it's still a relatively young field. And so, standards of care are emerging," says David Rosenbloom of Join Together. "And it

Finding an Addiction Doctor

Navigating the healthcare system can be difficult, especially when trying to find a qualified addiction specialist. There are two national organizations that specialize in addiction medicine: The American Society of Addiction Medicine and The American Academy of Addiction Psychiatry. They are good resources when looking for a Board-certified doctor with addiction experience.

The American Society of Addiction Medicine is an association of physicians dedicated to improving the treatment of alcoholism and other addictions. ASAM-certified doctors have passed a six-hour examination in addiction medicine, as well as met the high standards of qualification. You can find more information about ASAM at www.asam.org.

The American Academy of Addiction Psychiatry is a professional organization dedicated to promoting accessibility to quality treatment for addiction. The membership consists of psychiatrists who work with addiction in their practices, faculty at various academic institutions, nonpsychiatrist professionals who are making a contribution to the field of addiction psychiatry, residents, and medical students. Their web site has an online patient referral database. You can find more information about the AAAP at www.aaap.org.

Although heavy drinking is common—about 30 percent of Americans drink enough to be considered at risk for health and mental problems even if they do not have them now. Doctors often have trouble recognizing patients who need help. Only about 10 percent of patients with alcohol dependence receive the quality of care from professional treatment services that the National Institute on Alcohol Abuse and Alcoholism (NIAAA) recommends.

Primary caregivers, whether doctors, nurses, or psychologists, are often the weak link in the healthcare chain. "Their training just doesn't prepare them very well," says the NIAAA's Mark Willenbring. All doctors get some instruction for dealing with substance-abuse problems, but few are trained in-depth. "That's just the way med school is," Willenbring says.

To help those without specialty training, NIAAA publishes a guide for medical professionals who could detect at-risk drinking and alcoholism as part of routine physical or mental healthcare. About 140,000 copies of *Helping Patients Who Drink Too Much: A Clinician's Guide* were mailed to healthcare providers since the guide was revised in 2005. The guide focuses on one critical question: how many times in the past year have you had five (for men) or four (for women) or more drinks in a day? Studies have shown that heavy drinking (drinking more than those quantities) is associated with physical, mental, and social problems.

Doctors can use the NIAAA guidelines to determine whether they can address the drinking themselves or whether more in-depth evaluation is necessary. At the very least, caregivers can advise patients to cut back or stop drinking and help set up a plan (tracking drinks, managing high-risk situations, and so on) to help. Studies have shown that these brief interventions from doctors can reduce drinking levels for at-risk patients.

In addition, new medications and brief behavioral approaches enable primary care doctors to treat mild to moderate cases of alcohol dependence in their office. Patients may be referred for treatment if they have more severe dependence, do not respond to initial approaches, or have other conditions that complicate management. In this way, treatment for alcohol dependence may come to resemble that for asthma or depression.

Unfortunately, the healthcare system has not really worked out how to address behavioral disorders such as addiction very well, and most providers today are unaware of these new treatments. "I think it is going to take a generation to figure out how to do it," says Willenbring.

is hard—just as with the rest of the medical care system—it's really hard for people to figure out what's good, and what's bad care."

"We took my 17-year-old daughter, who is addicted to marijuana and who also suffers from severe anxiety and depression, to a local chemical dependency clinic for an assessment," says one mother. "The intern assigned to her case concluded that she suffered from severe depression and referred her to a mental health hospital for further assessments. But when I called to set up an appointment, the hospital told me I had to contact our county's Crisis Response Unit. I called them only to be told that my daughter didn't fit the criteria for referral. So now we're back at square one, except that my daughter is angry and withdrawn and says the whole system is so messed up that she can't trust anyone."

ASSESSING FOR CO-OCCURRING DISORDERS

Addiction is often accompanied by other illnesses, in particular mental health disorders. It is not always clear if the mental health problem is driving the drug abuse, if it is a result of the drug abuse, or if they share a common cause.

"Co-occurring mental disorders and drug addiction appear to be the rule rather than the exception," says NIDA's Nora Volkow. It is undeniable that many addicts use drugs to treat, or at least attempt to treat, their mental health conditions. In many cases, co-occurring mental illnesses are never diagnosed because they were masked by drug use. It is crucial to recognize that addiction treatments probably won't work unless these other illnesses are treated, too. According to SAMHSA's 2004 National Survey on Drug Use and Health, 4.6 million individuals in the United States suffer directly from co-occurring mental and substance use disorders, yet only a small percentage receive treatment that addresses both disorders. Many receive no treatment at all, and others may receive misguided advice that delays or undermines effective treatment.

A thorough assessment should consider if an addict has any of a wide range of co-occurring mental illnesses,

On Cure

Thomas McLellan, PhD

Co-Founder and CEO, Treatment Research Institute

"Elimination of desire to use alcohol and drugs" is not listed as an expected result of rehabilitation. This is important to understand. There is no available therapy, program, medication, or surgical procedure that is able to remove this recurrent desire or craving for alcohol and other drugs.

It is also important to understand that even very effective rehabilitation care is rarely enough to resolve an addiction. A more reasonable expectation is that rehabilitation will teach people what they must be prepared to do in order to manage and contain their addiction—in the same way individuals with diabetes or hypertension must learn to manage their lives and control their illness.

including depression, bipolar disorder, schizophrenia, or ADHD. "It's really critical if someone has an addictive disorder and anxiety or depression or some other psychiatric disorder that the treatment is aimed at all of the problems the patient is experiencing," explains Brady. "By the time an individual reaches professional attention with multiple disorders, you're not going to simply treat the anxiety and depression and see the addiction melt away. That just won't happen. Both disorders need to be addressed aggressively."

Neurological testing may be part of this initial assessment process. Depending on the results of the initial screening, additional assessments may be needed to uncover a history of trauma, sexual abuse, physical or emotional abuse, eating disorders, ADHD, self-mutilation, or suicidal thoughts or acts, among others. Referral to the appropriate treatment program depends on the accuracy of the assessment process.

WHAT EXACTLY IS TREATMENT?

It is best to think of addiction treatment as a continuum of care with three separate stages. Each stage has a different function in the larger picture of care. These are:

→ **Detoxification/stabilization**
→ **Rehabilitation**
→ **Continuing care**

DETOXIFICATION/STABILIZATION

"Detoxification is the initial stage that allows a person to get clean," Volkow says. "But that's just the beginning of the road. The rest is what we're going to call recovery—that process by which the person who has been addicted is reintegrated into society without the need of drugs."

Following a period of heavy and sustained alcohol or drug use, most individuals will develop significant withdrawal symptoms. While some of these problems can resolve with just rest, the use of drugs such as alcohol, opiates (heroin, oxycodone, Vicodin, and others) and tranquilizers (Valium, Xanax, and others) usually requires medically supervised detoxification or stabilization.

Settings of care Almost always in hospitals or other residential facilities where medical care is available.

Components of care Medication reduces the severity of withdrawal symptoms.

Duration of care Usually three to five days; more severe cases require a few more days.

Appropriate results of care Effective detoxification will remove drugs from the patient's system and begin the process of recovery by engaging the patient into some form of continued rehabilitative care.

REHABILITATION

Rehabilitation is appropriate for patients who are no longer suffering from the acute physical or emotional effects of recent substance abuse.

Rehabilitation care typically offers an array of treatment components to help address the many health and social problems associated with substance abuse. Medications can help reduce cravings for drugs and symptoms of co-occurring medical or emotional illness. Individual, group, and family therapy is helpful to assist with understanding the specific issues that may have led to the addiction—issues that patients will confront again following treatment. Assistance and guidance in developing a new, drug-free lifestyle is also an important part of rehabilitation.

Settings of care Most rehabilitative care for addiction occurs in specialty "programs" that include the components just described. If an individual is abusing substances in the context of a life situation that has gotten so out of control that they cannot become sober while living in it—even with treatment—they should seek residential rehabilitation. Most other, less severe forms of drug and alcohol abuse can be rehabilitated in outpatient settings that provide essentially the same components of care.

Components of care The components of rehabilitative care are typically delivered in a coordinated effort to bring about total abstinence from all drugs and alcohol. "Once an individual loses control of their substance use to the point of addiction, very few can regain controlled use of alcohol or drugs," says McLellan.

FAQ: Which Treatment Should I Pursue?

Thomas McLellan, PhD

Co-founder and CEO, Treatment Research Institute

Happily, there are an increasing number of options to treat alcohol and other drug addictions. Perhaps the best way to consider these options is to consider the nature and severity of the addiction problem. Here is a series of typical cases to consider.

I am not sure I have a substance-use problem.
Perhaps you have found yourself drinking or using more than you intended, or you have had an accident or social problem associated with your alcohol or drug use.

→ **Option 1: Try to reduce or quit yourself.** In the case of alcohol, there are guidelines that might help you. Drinking more than five drinks in a day, fifteen in a week if you are a man; or more than four drinks in a day, eight in a week if you are a woman, is considered "heavy drinking." If many of your friends drink this much, this may make it more difficult for you to drink less and still be around them.

There are drink-reducing strategies, such as having a glass of water or soda between alcoholic drinks, or taking only the amount of cash that you wish to spend at a bar and not using credit cards. Other strategies include deciding to drink only on planned days and at certain time periods. The Internet offers many other reduction strategies.

Regardless of your strategy, keep the alcohol guidelines in mind—and be honest. If you find you cannot keep within the rules you set for yourself, you may need additional help.

→ **Option 2: See a physician.** Ask about medications to aid in the reduction of drinking. There are now three medications that can be prescribed by a physician that can help you limit your drinking (see pages 142–145). Unfortunately, there are no FDA-approved medications available to help reduce marijuana, cocaine, or methamphetamine use.

I have a substance-use problem but I don't want to go into a "program."
Assuming your level of alcohol and drug use is not out of control, you might want some help that will preserve your confidentiality.

→ **Option 1: See a psychiatrist, psychologist, or counselor in private practice.** Many people go to private, office-based therapists for a variety of personal problems. Licensed and appropriately trained therapists may help you not only reduce your substance use but also resolve additional personal, relationship, and emotional problems. If you feel you need a medication to help deal with some of these problems, it is best to choose a psychiatrist, as they are trained physicians who can prescribe medications.

It is important to seek therapists who have experience and specific training in alcohol and drug issues. You can find this information on the Internet and in the telephone directory. Once you do make contact with a prospective therapist, it is important to ask directly about training and experience in substance-abuse treatment, and about methods of treatment. Unless a potential therapist has a plan for directly addressing and monitoring the substance use problem, it would be wise to make a different choice.

→ **Option 2: See a member of the clergy.** Many people value spiritual and religious counsel in their daily lives. Clergy who have been trained for counseling in matters involving drugs and alcohol can be located through the Internet. Again, there should be a plan to directly address the substance use and an agreement to pursue a more intensive option if results are not satisfactory.

→ **Option 3: Try Alcoholics Anonymous.** AA is the most widely available form of intervention and care for alcoholism. It is anonymous and free, and it meets at virtually all times of the day at many locations. It might be wise to go to an AA meeting even if you think this is not for you. You will meet people who will be glad to give you advice and suggestions from their own experiences, and you can hear from them about treatment options. It may not be for you, but AA could give you some valuable information and it won't cost a thing.

→ **Option 4: If your problem is with opiates (heroin, methadone, Vicodin, OxyContin, etc.), see a specialty physician who is trained and licensed to prescribe buprenorphine (Suboxone or Subutex).** This is a relatively new medication for treating opiate dependence and is very effective at reducing craving and use. This treatment will also likely involve counseling in addition to the medication, but this, too, can be provided in a confidential setting.

(continued on next page)

(continued from previous page)

I have a substance-abuse problem that I cannot control by myself.
If self-management efforts have not worked, it may be time to seek specialty care.
Consider the following questions as you make your decisions.

→ **Do you need detoxification or stabilization?** If your use of various substances
has really gotten out of control; you have used significant amounts of various
substances for extended periods of time; or if you have used significant amounts
of alcohol or opiates (heroin, methadone, OxyContin, etc.), you may need a period
of medical care to help you safely stop using.

Yes: Call a detoxification center and arrange for an appointment. Sometimes detox
can be conducted for outpatients, but most cases require hospitalization for three
to five days. Following stabilization and evaluation, you will have other treatment
options, as described below.

No (or if you have completed detoxification): Do you think you have to get
away from your living arrangements to get control of your substance abuse?

If yes: You may want to consider a period of rehabilitation care (usually twenty-
one to thirty days) in a residential program. With persistence, you can get your
insurance company to pay for at least part of the cost (about $15,000 to $25,000).

If no: You may do well in an outpatient program. Insurance will often pay most
or all of this cost (approximately $100 to $200 per week).

→ **Do you have an opiate problem and abstinence-oriented treatments have failed?**
Consider methadone or buprenorphine maintenance. Because of federal regulations,
methadone can only be prescribed in methadone-maintenance programs.
Buprenorphine (Suboxone or Subutex) can be prescribed either by a methadone
maintenance program or by a specially licensed physician in the office or clinic.

Quality Issues
Good rehabilitation treatment programs employ qualified and well-trained staff, and offer
a range of treatment components (medications, therapies, and services) that address the
problems of their patients. Better treatment programs have more quantity and better quality of the following components:

→ Therapies and therapists
→ Medications
→ Family involvement

→ Social services
→ Urine drug screening
→ Continuing care

Duration of care Most residential rehabilitation programs last from twenty-one to thirty days and involve full-time programming. Outpatient rehabilitation programs are typically sixty to ninety days long, and patients spend between two and eight hours a day in the program, two to five days a week.

Appropriate results of care Effective rehabilitation will sustain the elimination of alcohol and other drug use, improve health and social functioning, and engage the patient in continuing care, personal therapy, mutual help groups, and other healthy lifestyle changes.

CONTINUING CARE

Continuing care refers to the period following rehabilitation when addicts gradually assume control over the combination of support and monitoring services they need to maintain long-term recovery.

The first three to six months following addiction treatment is the period when recovering addicts are most vulnerable to relapse. Consequently, continuing-care services are designed to monitor the emotional health of recovering individuals, remind them of their commitments to lifestyle changes, and support their needs as they attempt the difficult job of living their former lives with resolve and a new perspective.

Settings of care All continuing care occurs in a community setting to assist individuals in adjusting to their day-to-day lives.

Components of care The components of continuing care are very similar to those in rehabilitative care, but they typically occur less frequently. Individual, group, and family therapy sessions are important and may be scheduled monthly or more often. Some rehabilitation programs offer telephone contact with former counselors.

Duration of care Most continuing-care programs continue for six to twelve months following completion of rehabilitation. Telephone calls last between ten and thirty minutes, depending on the needs of the individual. They usually take place twice a week during the first month, gradually decreasing to once a month over time.

What to Know about Treating Alcoholism

Mark Willenbring, MD

Director, Treatment and Recovery Research Division, NIAAA

Recent medical advances in the treatment of alcoholism suggest that effective treatment may soon become much easier to obtain. The first treatments for alcoholism involved group counseling and referral to community support groups, and only took place in specialized treatment centers. Although this type of treatment is effective and necessary for some people, researchers have developed new behavioral treatments ("talk therapy") and new medications that can be delivered in many locations.

Results from Combining Medications and Behavioral Interventions for Alcoholism (the COMBINE study) found that naltrexone, when combined with as few as nine brief counseling sessions from a doctor or nurse, was as effective as up to twenty sessions of specialized alcohol counseling. The best news of all was that most people improved a lot and many were able to stop drinking completely. Patients now have more choices and health professionals have more tools to help them.

Five things to know about alcoholism

1. Alcohol dependence is a common, diagnosable medical condition. Almost one in ten people in the United States experience alcohol dependence at some time during their lives. Alcohol dependence occurs in both sexes, in all ethnic and racial groups, and in people from all walks of life. It develops when someone drinks too much, too often. If you are a woman, drinking more than four drinks a day—five drinks a day if you are a man—increases health risks, including your risk for alcohol dependence.

2. Alcohol dependence usually starts in the late teens or early twenties, yet most people don't seek help until fifteen to twenty years later. Earlier treatment is more successful and results in far less destruction to individuals and their families. Seek help if you keep going over your limit, can't quit or cut down on your own, continue drinking in spite of emotional, physical, or social problems caused by drinking, or find that your friends or family are expressing concern. You don't have to wait for a crisis.

3. Only about one in ten people with alcohol dependence ever receives professional treatment. Recent research suggests that newer medications offer effective treatment for alcohol dependence, when combined with a brief period of counseling by a health professional. This means that many more people can receive treatment from their regular doctor. Specialized alcohol counseling also works well, and all approaches (twelve-step, cognitive, motivational) are about equally effective. Some people will need more intensive programs.

4. Whatever treatment you receive, the most important thing is to stick with it. The longer you stay in treatment, the more likely you are to succeed. If you have a relapse, recognize that alcohol dependence is a chronic disease and try to get back on track as quickly as possible. If you are taking medication for alcohol dependence, be sure to take it as prescribed.

Do not discontinue it even if you don't notice feeling any different. You know the medicine is working if you are not drinking or if you are drinking much less.

5. Twelve-step and other support programs really do work! Recovering people who attend groups regularly do better than those who do not. If you are taking medication for alcohol dependence, don't worry about whether it is a "crutch." Medication can improve recovery rates by 20 to 40 percent in the first three months after you stop drinking. Also, it's fine to combine medication and support groups or alcohol counseling.

Five questions to ask your doctor

First, do some homework on the Internet or at the library. It helps if you know something about what kinds of treatments are available and what kind you might want (counseling, medications, etc.). Take this information with you when you see your doctor.

1. Let your doctor know why you are concerned about your drinking. Ask whether they think you have alcohol dependence. If you drink a lot nearly every day, be sure to say so, because you may need treatment for withdrawal (sweating, tremors, anxiety, insomnia); quitting suddenly without treatment for withdrawal can be dangerous. Don't be afraid to ask for such treatment.

2. Ask your doctor if they prescribe medications for alcohol dependence, such as naltrexone (tablets or monthly injections) or acamprosate. These medications correct abnormalities in the brain caused by alcoholism and make it easier to quit. They are not addictive, nor do they make you sick when you drink. If you would like to try one of them, tell your doctor.

3. Find out whether you have any evidence of organ damage, such as liver disease, due to heavy drinking. Ask your doctor to order appropriate tests to find out. If you have organ damage, ask whether it will get better if you quit drinking and what might happen if you do not.

4. Be sure to mention if you are feeling depressed, suicidal, or anxious. If you are experiencing one or more of these feelings, ask your doctor whether additional treatment would be helpful. One example might be an antidepressant medication. Many people with alcohol dependence also have depression or anxiety.

5. If you would like a referral to a specialist, ask for one. You are more likely to stick with a treatment that you like. Since there are several proven ways to help people recover (such as different counseling approaches, medications, and support groups), you can select one that has the most appeal for you.

Appropriate results of care The goals of continuing care are exactly those of rehabilitation. Effective continuing care will help a recovering individual self-manage the recurrent occasions of temptation and craving and, just as important, develop an enjoyable, fulfilling life.

The special role of AA For the past sixty years, the most common (and often the only) form of continuing care has been Alcoholics Anonymous (AA) and the various other mutual assistance groups (Smart Recovery, Narcotics Anonymous, etc.). There are many different types of AA and mutual help groups in most cities. Many have a strong spiritual component. Some permit smoking during the meetings. Some are reserved for particular groups of recovering people (e.g. physicians, nurses, lawyers, athletes), while the majority are open to all. It is wise for an individual to try several different meetings prior to deciding upon the value of AA participation in recovery.

QUALITY AND EFFECTIVENESS

Treatment comes in a bewildering array of options, including private and public, inpatient and outpatient, hospital-based and outside a hospital, long-term and short-term, medical and nonmedical, intensive and less intensive, and, most significant of all, effective and ineffective. Finding your way through the maze of options may seem overwhelming, but the task becomes more manageable if you stay focused on that essential word—*effective*.

Research has demonstrated the effectiveness of specific types of treatment for specific addictions. In treating alcoholism, motivational enhancement, cognitive behavioral therapy, and twelve-step approaches all have about the same rate of good outcomes. For adolescents who are dependent on marijuana and alcohol, motivational, family, and cognitive-behavioral approaches all have similar outcomes.

The specific technique is less important than the quality of the program and its staff. Perhaps the most important thing to keep in mind is that good treatment techniques share certain characteristics:

→ an empathic, engaging approach
→ skillful, well-trained therapists

Expert Advice

What Is Evidence-Based Treatment?

Kathleen Brady, MD, PhD

President, American Academy of Addiction Psychiatry

Evidence-based treatment is treatment that has been proven to work through rigorous scientific studies. Evidence-based treatment is particularly important in the addictions field because many myths and personal biases have infiltrated the treatment area and are often accepted without question. For example, the notion that an individual needs to reach "rock bottom" before they can benefit from treatment is absolutely wrong. Data shows that individuals who have more psychosocial support and economic stability—who have not lost their jobs or families—will have a much better outcome in treatment compared with those who enter treatment without a strong social network to support their recovery.

Important questions to ask when evaluating treatment services

→ What kind of treatments do you use and how do they work? (Cognitive behavioral therapy, contingency management, twelve-step facilitation, family therapy, etc.)

→ Are there well-controlled studies that support the treatments used in your program?

→ How do you monitor the quality and success of your program? Do you follow up with patients to see how they are doing?

Co-occurring disorders

Substance use disorders often co-occur with mood, anxiety and other psychiatric disorders. Careful assessment and treatment of co-occurring disorders is critical to maximizing the chances of success in treatment. If both disorders are not treated, the chances of recovery are poor. Individuals suffering from untreated depression or anxiety in addition to addiction are very likely to continue with their drinking or drug use. Treatment of mood and anxiety disorders can improve their chance of recovery from addictions.

Important questions to ask about treatment services

→ Do you have a psychiatrist on your treatment staff?

→ Is every patient routinely assessed for psychiatric disorders?

→ Do you provide specific medication and psychosocial treatment for anxiety, mood, and other psychiatric disorders?

The role of addiction psychiatry

Addiction psychiatry focuses on understanding, preventing, and treating individuals with addictions. It is the only medical subspecialty focused on addictions, and is recognized by the American Board of Medical Examiners. Because Board-certified addiction psychiatrists are physicians, they have specific expertise in the use of medications in the treatment of addictions. Because they are psychiatrists, they have special expertise in the recognition and treatment of co-occurring psychiatric disorders in individuals with addictions.

→ integration of addiction and mental health treatment (and sometimes medical treatment)

→ use of evidence-based practices, including medications where indicated. (For opioid dependence—heroin, morphine, OxyContin—in adults lasting a year or more, maintenance on either methadone or buprenorphine has been demonstrated to be more effective than abstinence-based programs.)

Studies show that only a minority of addicted persons will maintain complete abstinence during the first year of recovery. The exact number depends a lot on the substance involved, as well as co-occurring disorders and social support. As with all chronic diseases (such as heart disease, diabetes, and asthma), a relapse must be viewed not as a sign of treatment failure but as an indication that a higher intensity of care or different treatment approaches may be necessary.

OTHER CONSIDERATIONS WHEN CHOOSING TREATMENT

Treatment matching The treatment plan should match the severity of the addicted person's physical, emotional, and behavioral problems. Factors that should be considered include the patient's readiness and willingness to change, the potential for relapse, and the stability and safety of the home and living environment. Less intensive treatment (outpatient treatment several times a week, for example) may be effective for an employed individual whose home life is stable and who does not suffer from any co-occurring disorders; but that same treatment may be wholly inadequate and therefore ineffective for an adolescent with a co-occurring mental health problem or a disabled elderly patient addicted to prescription drugs.

Co-occurring disorders When addiction and mental disorders co-exist, they both should be considered primary, and treatment for the co-occurring disorder should take place at the same time. Patients with more severe problems generally have a more difficult time maintaining abstinence. Effective treatment must be tailored to the individual's specific history and needs. Length of treatment often needs to be extended to increase the individual's chances of long-term recovery.

People with undiagnosed and untreated mental health problems often turn to alcohol or other drugs as a way of self-medicating anxiety, depression, insecurity, loneliness, or fear. While alcohol and other drugs may temporarily alleviate certain distressing symptoms, they inevitably and invariably make the mental health problem worse in the long run, intensifying the original symptoms and

The treatment plan should match the severity of the addicted person's physical, emotional, and behavioral problems.

creating serious and potentially life-threatening problems. At the same time, chronic or heavy use of drugs or alcohol affects the brain's ability to function normally and can cause depression, anxiety, panic attacks, irritability, paranoia, and suicidal thoughts. The general rule is that it is much more difficult to recover from either disorder if they aren't both treated.

However, many programs do not adequately identify or treat any but the most serious mental disorders. Many programs will advertise that they are dual diagnosis, but the devil is in the details. Is a psychiatrist on staff? What kind of screening for mental health disorders is done, and by whom? What are their qualifications? Unfortunately, for many people a well-staffed program capable of managing both mental and addictive illness may not be available. In that case, it is often up to the addict and their family members to make sure that any mental illness is assessed and treated.

Developmentally appropriate As discussed in Chapter 3, adolescents have unique physical and emotional developmental issues that must be addressed in treatment. Programs that focus specifically on adolescents will be able to provide teens addicted to drugs with an appropriate support system and will be able to tailor the treatment to types of day-to-day stressors that are unique to this population. Similarly, older individuals also have special needs, and elder-specific programs may be more acceptable and have better outcomes.

Qualified staff Treatment staff must be knowledgeable about substance-abuse disorders, co-occurring mental, emotional, and behavior disorders, and co-occurring physical disorders, especially HIV/AIDS and hepatitis. Staff members in adolescent treatment programs need to understand the unique developmental needs of addicted youth. Older individuals with addiction often need active management of medical conditions, especially insomnia and pain, in order to fully recover.

Gender and cultural differences Prevention, treatment, and recovery support programs must also be designed to reflect general and cultural differences in patterns of drug use, development of problems, obstacles to treatment, likelihood of relapse, and pathways to long-term recovery.

Level of care Behavioral treatment ranges from once-weekly outpatient therapy to residential therapy for several weeks or months. Perhaps most common is an intensive outpatient program, described earlier. It involves six or more hours per week for several weeks, followed by less intensive continuing care. Residential care may be necessary when it is not possible to stabilize the addiction on an outpatient basis. Hospital treatment is usually reserved for severe cases of withdrawal, or when there is a severe co-occurring mental disorder that must be stabilized.

Sometimes issues related to an addict's family may influence the decision whether to choose an inpatient or outpatient program. Says Michael Dennis of the Chestnut Health Systems, "If an addict's family is distraught and out of control, all of his friends are using, and his environment is out of control, you may have to consider residential treatment. If the family is able to participate and there's a stable environment, and there are friends who aren't involved in drugs, then I would tend to look at an outpatient program."

Therapeutic communities (TCs) Originally designed to treat hardcore addicts, TCs are highly structured, drug-free residential programs that rely heavily on peer influence to shape attitudes, perceptions, and behaviors. Some programs take a tough-love approach, others function as modified boot camps, and still others offer daily Bible study and emphasize moral and ethical development. Personal accountability and the values of honesty, hard work, community, and service to others are essential elements of all therapeutic communities. Research on the effectiveness of therapeutic communities shows that they offer some advantages for certain addicts, such as cocaine addicts with complex problems, but do not offer any advantage for others, such as most alcoholics or opioid addicts.

MEDICATION THERAPIES

For decades, researchers investigated medications that make drinking and drug use less pleasurable and that reduce the intense physical cravings that can lead to relapse. But it has been the growth of neuroscience research that has led to significant advances in the development of new medications capable of regulating specific neurotransmitters or receptors involved in addiction.

"Recent research has made a great deal of progress in understanding what's going on in the brain with addiction, and using brain imaging, we can actually see what's happening in the brain," explains Charles O'Brien, MD, PhD, director of the Center for Studies of Addiction at the Philadelphia VA Medical Center, University of Pennsylvania School of Medicine, and one of the nation's leading experts on addiction medications. "We can see which parts of the brain are activated. And this is helping us to develop new medications for nicotine, alcohol, cocaine, and methamphetamines."

To date, there are currently no medications approved for the treatment of cocaine, marijuana, or methamphetamines. There are, however, effective medications available for treating alcohol and opioid dependence. In the case of opioid dependence in adults lasting more than a year, opiate replacement therapy is much more effective than other approaches. There is also a medication that blocks the effect of opioids (an antagonist) that may be helpful in some circumstances. Many of these medications (except

How to Select a Good Treatment Provider

Thomas McLellan, PhD

Co-founder and CEO, Treatment Research Institute

Providers of addiction treatment span a wide range of backgrounds, approaches, and methods. It is useful to consider each type of care provider relative to the problems you may have.

Physicians

There are many types of physicians, but only a few are likely to have training or experience in addiction. A greater proportion of psychiatrists than other physicians have received specialty training in addiction.

→ **Is a physician right for me?** If you have a nicotine, alcohol, or opiate-use problem, it is likely that medications will be an important part of your addiction treatment. If physical problems, such as pain, or psychiatric problems, such as depression or anxiety, are complicating your addiction problem, your treatment will very likely benefit from appropriate medications. In these cases, a trained and experienced physician can be very helpful. You can find listings of physicians with this type of training in most state medical directories, from your insurance provider, or from the American Society of Addiction Medicine (see page 123).

Therapists

Therapists use the power of clinical discussion to help addicted individuals get insight into the causes of their addiction, recognize and prepare for the situations that may trigger relapse, and develop a lifestyle that will be rewarding without alcohol and other drugs. Good therapy is not simply interested listening; it requires sophisticated techniques that, when done properly, can be very effective.

→ **Counseling vs. therapy** There is a difference between counseling and therapy. In general, counseling focuses on the here and now and offers advice and direction in solving daily problems. Counselors may come from many professional backgrounds, but good counselors have received formal training in counseling—particularly group counseling.

Therapy is generally more sophisticated than counseling and focuses on issues involving personal development and forming and maintaining relationships. A background in psychiatry, psychology, clinical social work, or family systems is usually a prerequisite for training as a therapist. But again, regardless of background there is always a need for formal instruction and training in the particular therapy techniques that deal with addiction.

→ **Is a therapist right for me?** The more severe your substance use and the more complex your additional social and relationship problems, the greater the likelihood that you will need a professional therapist. The only way to find out if a therapist or counselor is right for you is to have a few sessions—at least three. By that point, you should feel a bond with the therapist, feel that your problems are being heard and understood, and feel that the therapist has the interest and ability to help you figure things out. If you do not feel this way, you should find another therapist.

Rehab programs

Most rehabilitative care for addiction occurs in programs that are dedicated to this specialty. Residential programs lasting between twenty-one and thirty days are most appropriate for patients whose substance use or life situation has spiraled out of control. Outpatient programs that typically last thirty to ninety days and require participation from two to eight hours a day for two to five days a week are suitable for individuals who have a reasonably supportive living situation.

All programs—whether residential or outpatient—have group and individual counseling. Many programs now offer medications for addiction and psychiatric problems. Some of the better programs offer social services to help gain better employment, deal with pending legal problems, improve parenting and marital relationships, and even obtain drug-free housing. Better programs have more structure in their curriculum, better trained and supervised therapists and counselors, individualized treatment plans, monitoring of alcohol and drug use during treatment, and continuing care after discharge.

→ **Is a rehab program right for me?** If you have not had success in your efforts to control your substance use on your own, or with help from others, it is likely that a rehab program will be more appropriate. Virtually all programs work to bring about total abstinence from alcohol and all other drugs, so if this is not what you want, a program may not suit you. On the other hand, if you have tried and failed in many ways to control your substance use without quitting, abstinence may be the most appropriate treatment goal for you.

for methadone) may be prescribed by doctors who are not necessarily addiction specialists. When you are looking for a program, ask whether treatments and medications based on solid research are routinely used when appropriate.

There is reason for excitement about the effectiveness of maintenance medications for patients in some circumstances—as long as the medications are used in conjunction with effective behavioral therapies as an adjunct to treatment. These medications are not cures for addiction, but, as part of a treatment and recovery program that includes education, individual and group counseling, and social support networks, they can be effective. "One of the things that's most important for people to understand here is that the medicines won't do the work for you. You've got to work at this," says the NIAAA's Willenbring. "What it can do is make it easier to do the right thing. It can make it easier to achieve your goals." O'Brien agrees, "There's no medication that I can ever conceive of, even in the future, that will take away the need for the struggle, the hard work that's required in psychotherapy, family therapy, group therapy, whatever. But the medications will get better and better at helping the person to control these extreme compulsions to go back and use drugs."

MEDICATIONS FOR ALCOHOL DEPENDENCE
For alcoholics, the following FDA-approved medications currently offer the most promise in controlling cravings and preventing a relapse.

Disulfiram (Antabuse), first introduced for use in treating alcoholism in the late 1940s, interferes with the metabolism of alcohol, leading to a buildup of the highly toxic substance called acetaldehyde. If an alcoholic drinks while taking disulfiram, acetaldehyde accumulates in the bloodstream, producing an extremely unpleasant reaction with symptoms such as flushing, violent headaches, nausea, vomiting, sweating, extreme thirst, chest pain, heart palpitations, difficulty breathing, abnormally rapid heart rate, weakness, blurred vision, and mental confusion. As long as recovering alcoholics continue to take the medication daily, they know they can't drink without suffering great discomfort and potentially life-threatening side effects.

Only 13% of those with alcohol dependence are being treated with medication that is proven to be effective.

Naltrexone (Trexan, ReVia, Depade, Vivitrol, Vivitrex) is a narcotic antagonist that blocks opiate effects and helps prevent relapse to alcohol abuse. Originally used with heroin addicts in recovery, naltrexone was approved by the FDA in 1994 for use with alcoholics. Numerous studies confirm naltrexone's effectiveness in blocking the pleasurable effects of alcohol and reducing cravings in alcoholics. Naltrexone appears to be especially successful in treating alcoholics with a strong family history of alcoholism, high levels of craving, and motivation to take the drug. Long-term (nine-month) treatment is more effective than a short-term (three-month) program.

"We can see which parts of the brain are activated. And this is helping us to develop new medications," O'Brien says.

Acamprosate (Campral) has a similar structure to GABA (gamma-aminobutyric acid), one of the brain's most widely distributed neurotransmitters and a key chemical involved in alcohol addiction. GABA helps quiet the brain cells, decreasing brain activity. Acamprosate's primary activity is to inhibit the glutamate channel, an excitatory neurotransmitter channel. This action is thought to weaken acute and long-term withdrawal symptoms in alcoholics.

Acamprosate, which is believed to restore the normal neurotransmitter balance in the brain, is indicated for maintaining sobriety in alcohol-dependent patients who are abstinent when the medical therapy is started. The drug is considered safe for use in patients with liver disease and when used in combination with commonly prescribed medications, including antidepressants, anxiolytics (anxiety-reducing drugs), and nonopioid painkillers. Experts agree that treatment with acamprosate, as with any medical therapy, should be part of a comprehensive management program that includes psychosocial and spiritual supports such as ongoing addiction therapy, psychological counseling, outpatient programs, and twelve-step groups.

Both naltrexone and acamprosate are considered safe and effective as adjunctive therapies for alcohol dependence in adults. Acamprosate appears to be especially useful in a therapeutic approach targeted at achieving abstinence, whereas naltrexone may be more effective in programs geared to controlling consumption.

MEDICATIONS FOR OPIATE DEPENDENCE

The following FDA-approved medications show the most promise in treating opiate addicts.

Methadone, a synthetic narcotic developed in Germany during World War II, was approved by the FDA in 1972 for the treatment of heroin addicts and other opiate-dependent patients. Methadone blocks the high associated with opiate use and reduces the cravings for the drug. While patients remain dependent on methadone, they are freed from the compulsive, uncontrolled, and harmful behaviors associated with heroin use. Numerous research studies confirm that when heroin and other opiate-addicted individuals are treated with methadone, health and productivity improve significantly, while criminal activity, needle sharing, and risky sexual activity decrease.

Buprenorphine (Suboxone, Subutex) is the first major narcotic medication approved by the FDA for treatment of opioid addiction (heroin, morphine, and prescription opioids, including oxycodone) in the last two decades. The drug, which is taken as a pill that dissolves under the tongue, weakens the effects of the opiates, is less likely to cause overdose, and produces a lower level of physical dependence than methadone. Subutex has been approved for treatment in a doctor's office, as has Suboxone, a buprenorphine formulation that includes the opiate antagonist naloxone. An advantage of buprenorphine is that it can be distributed out of a regular pharmacy.

Research has shown that many opiate addicts, especially

Replacement Therapy for Opiate Addiction

Scott Farnum, MS, MPA

Department Head of Pharmacological Therapies, Hill Health Center

Important things to know about methadone

→ Methadone enables people to function normally by stopping withdrawal symptoms, eliminating the craving for opiates, blocking opiate-induced euphoria, correcting the neurochemical abnormalities in the brain caused by opiate addiction, and allowing the brain to heal.

→ Methadone maintenance is the most effective treatment we currently have for opiate addiction.

→ Methadone is the most cost-effective treatment for opiate addiction.

→ Participation in a methadone treatment program significantly reduces a person's risk of HIV and hepatitis C infection.

→ Methadone is the most widely used treatment for opiate addiction in the United States.

Important things to know about buprenorphine

→ The use of buprenorphine enables people to function normally by stopping withdrawal symptoms, eliminating the craving for opiates, blocking opiate-induced euphoria, correcting the neurochemical abnormalities in the brain caused by opiate addiction, and allowing the brain to heal.

→ Buprenorphine can be prescribed at the office of your personal physician. Patients may receive up to thirty days of the medication at a time once they are stable.

→ Buprenorphine has very few side effects.

→ Buprenorphine can be prescribed for young people with shorter histories of addiction, allowing intervention early in the addictive cycle.

→ Buprenorphine is a safe medication with a low risk of overdose.

→ Buprenorphine is less tightly regulated than methadone, making it more like other prescription drugs. This allows people to adapt the medication more easily into their lifestyles and reduces the negative attitudes often associated with methadone.

Important things for friends and family members to know about replacement therapy

→ Replacement therapy is not short term; your loved one will need to remain on the medication for years in order for it to be effective.

→ Patients receiving methadone will need to be present at the program every day, although as they become more stable the daily visits may be only a few minutes long.

→ Methadone patients can earn the ability to take home some doses of medication over time if they stop using illegal drugs and do well in treatment.

→ Patients on replacement therapy, particularly methadone, may encounter travel restrictions, making visiting family or taking vacations difficult.

→ Methadone and buprenorphine are treatments for opiate addiction and will not stop the abuse of other drugs.

→ Replacement therapy is not a magic bullet. Patients usually have to participate in counseling, self-help groups, or other forms of treatment to recover fully.

→ There are side effects to methadone, such as sedation, sweating, constipation, and weight gain, that usually go away after a person has been on the medication for a short time.

Important questions to ask your replacement therapy treatment provider

→ What are the risks and benefits to me of methadone and buprenorphine, and how will you know if one of these medications is best for me?

→ What are your program rules for continuation in treatment if I should relapse or be unable to stop my drug use?

→ Will I have input into a treatment plan that addresses my needs as an individual?

→ What happens if I become unable to pay for treatment?

→ Do you have referral relationships with specialty care providers if I need treatment for HIV or hepatitis C, or become pregnant?

those who are more functional and may be working, have a hard time with all of the rigors and time-of-day limits imposed by traditional methadone maintenance programs, and thus may keep using heroin rather than seek treatment. Buprenorphine helps overcome those issues. As with methadone, also a narcotic medication, the potential exists for misuse, so careful medical supervision is essential.

PROMISING NEW MEDICATIONS

Some medications show promise but have not yet established a track record or received FDA approval for use with particular addictions.

Baclofen (Kemstro, Lioresal), a medication used to treat muscle spasms in people with multiple sclerosis, acts through GABA receptors to inhibit the release of dopamine, thus reducing the desire for cocaine. When combined with counseling, baclofen seems to be most successful with chronic, heavy users of cocaine.

Immunotherapy (treatment with antibodies, like a vaccination) has the potential to deactivate alcohol and other drugs but has not been approved for this use. Cocaine and nicotine vaccines are currently in clinical trials.

Nalmefene is an opioid antagonist—it neutralizes or counteracts the effects of opiates. In preliminary studies, it appears to reduce cravings and prevent relapse in alcohol-dependent patients.

Topiramate (Topamax), an anticonvulsant used to treat seizure disorders, works through several mechanisms (including GABA and glutamate) to decrease abnormal activity in the brain. In clinical trials, topiramate helps prevent relapse to alcohol, opiate, and cocaine addiction, and preliminary research indicates that the drug may be useful with nicotine-addicted patients as well.

Disulfiram (Antabuse), according to recent studies, has helped cocaine-addicted individuals in early recovery significantly reduce cocaine use with no adverse side effects.

Despite groundbreaking advances and FDA-approved medications, not all programs offer these treatments, even though research is clear that they work. "They feel a medication is like a drug, and what they say is if you're started on a medication and you've already been addicted to a drug, you'll become addicted to the medication," says NIDA's Volkow. "My perspective is, we have a situation like heart disease. And in diseases—whether it's something like cancer, or whether it's addiction—you want to do an aggressive intervention that increases the likelihood of helping the person. If that involves a strong behavioral intervention, a twelve-step program, and medications, why not? Why limit it? If we're speaking of drug addiction as a disease, then we cannot have it both ways. In a disease, there are medications that can help."

BEHAVIORAL THERAPIES

Behavioral therapies are a component of all substance-abuse treatment. They focus on changing the thinking that underlies our emotional reactions and leads to self-defeating behaviors. Clinical studies have proven their effectiveness, and behavioral therapies are currently the only treatments available for addiction to stimulants and marijuana.

"Everybody should receive some sort of talk therapy for their addictions," says Brady. "Whether that goes hand-in-hand with medications is a decision that needs to be made case by case." Changing behavior patterns is the basic goal of all the behavioral therapies, but methods and strategies differ from one approach to another.

Here are five behavioral therapies that have been shown to be effective in treating addiction.

Cognitive behavioral therapy Cognitive behavioral therapy is a structured, focused, short-term approach (twelve to sixteen sessions lasting approximately twelve weeks) that occurs in two basic stages. The first is functional analysis, in which the therapist focuses on helping patients identify thoughts, feelings, and situations that may lead to drug use.

The second is skills training, in which the patient learns (or relearns) effective, individualized strategies to avoid high-risk situations and cope more effectively with these situations by developing healthier skills and habits. Treatment generally takes place in an outpatient setting, helping patients practice new skills and approaches in the context of their daily lives.

Behavioral Therapies in the Treatment of Addiction

Richard A. Rawson, PhD

Associate director, Integrated Substance Abuse Programs, UCLA

Among the most important ingredients in addiction treatment is deciding which counseling or talk therapy approaches are used. A number of behavioral therapies offer the best assistance for successfully treating individuals with drug and alcohol disorders, and are frequently used together with medications. The techniques focus on helping drug and alcohol users change the way they live their lives (their behavior) so they can successfully stop using alcohol and drugs and develop healthy, productive lives.

What is good addiction counseling?

Counselors and therapists who provide treatment for addicted individuals and their families need special training in behavioral treatments for addiction. It is important for counselors and therapists to teach their addicted patients about addiction, encourage them to make changes in their lives, praise them when they make progress, and support them when they run into problems. There are several specific behavioral counseling approaches that improve treatment success.

→ **Improve motivation for recovery**
  Many, if not most, addicted individuals resist entering addiction treatment. They are ambivalent about stopping their alcohol and drug use. It is as if part of them wants to stop their substance use and part of them wants to continue using. Motivational interviewing and motivational enhancement therapy are techniques that help addicted individuals recognize the damage that drug and alcohol use is doing to their lives, encourage them to stop using, and support positive steps toward recovery.

→ **Teach skills for stopping drug and alcohol use and avoiding relapse**
  Once people become dependent on drugs or alcohol, they truly don't know how to stop their use and avoid relapse. Cognitive behavioral therapy (sometimes called relapse prevention) teaches patients why they crave drugs or alcohol and how to cope with craving; how to avoid the people, places, and things connected to drugs or alcohol; how to cope with difficult feelings that can trigger relapse; and how to prevent a minor slip from becoming a major relapse.

→ **Use positive incentives to encourage treatment participation and reward progress**
  Addiction recovery takes time. Longer stays in treatment produce greater success. Changing friends, habits, and lifestyle is difficult. Incentives, such as small prizes (movie tickets, gift certificates, restaurant coupons) can promote behavior changes and provide positive reinforcement for treatment progress. When patients make progress in treatment (for example, thirty sober days or perfect attendance at treatment sessions), these small motivational bonuses can help encourage and reward these accomplishments.

→ **Involve family members in treatment activities**
Family members who are well-informed about addiction and who participate in treatment activities can greatly improve the success of treatment for the addicted individual. Family therapy and couples therapy provide appropriate help and support for involving family members in the recovery process.

→ **Encourage participation in recovery support groups**
Alcoholics Anonymous (AA) and other twelve-step groups (Narcotics Anonymous, Cocaine Anonymous, etc.) can be extremely valuable support systems for recovering individuals. In addition, there are counseling approaches, called twelve-step facilitation therapy, that help teach patients about the value of twelve-step programs and encourage meeting attendance.

Stimulant addiction: a special case

The behavioral therapies just described are important in the treatment of all drug and alcohol dependence disorders. However, their use with individuals addicted to stimulants (cocaine and methamphetamine) is especially important. At the present time, there are no medications that have been proven to be useful for stimulant addiction. Two outpatient treatment approaches that combine many of the strategies described (the Community Reinforcement Approach and the MATRIX Model) have been shown to be effective in treating individuals who are addicted to cocaine or methamphetamine.

Three questions to ask when choosing a therapist or counselor and type of therapy

1. Does the therapist/counselor have a professional license or certification? Psychiatrists, psychologists, social workers, marriage and family therapists, and certified addictions counselors are the main categories of qualified professional practitioners.

2. Has the therapist or counselor received special training in the use of effective behavioral therapies? Asking a therapist or counselor if they have had training in cognitive behavioral therapy, motivational enhancement therapy, family therapy, or the other approaches specially developed for addiction is an important first step. Just as medical doctors need special training to treat complex diseases, therapists and counselors need to be trained in addiction treatment.

3. Is urine testing and breath alcohol testing used as a part of treatment? In addiction treatment, testing is an essential tool. Testing is needed to monitor treatment progress in the same way blood tests are needed to monitor high cholesterol or blood sugar levels. Testing should not be used as a way of catching patients or as a basis for punishing drug or alcohol use. Rather, it is an invaluable tool in documenting treatment progress and recognizing when treatment plans should be modified.

Medications for Treating Drug and Alcohol Dependence

Depressants	MEDICATION	FDA-APPROVED	ACTION
Alcohol	Disulfiram (Antabuse)	Approved 1949	Inhibits intermediate metabolism of alcohol, causing a build-up of acetaldelhyde and a reaction of flushing, sweating, nausea, and chest pain if a patient drinks alcohol.
	Naltrexone (ReVia, Vivitrol)	Approved 1994 (Vivitrol was approved in 2005)	Blocks opioid receptors, resulting in reduced craving and reward in response to drinking alcohol.
	Acamprosate (Campral)	Approved 2004	Appears to modulate/normalize alcohol-disrupted brain activity, particularly in the GABA and glutamate neurotransmitter systems. Acamprosate has not been shown to work in people who have not stopped drinking alcohol.
	Topiramate (Topamax)	In clinical trials	Anti-epileptic medication that works through multiple brain systems, including GABA and glutamate. In clinical trials, found to reduce alcohol cravings.
Benzodiazepine (BZD, Xanax, Valium, Ativan, Klonopin)	There are no medications available to treat benzodiazepine addiction. Behavioral treatments are the most effective.		

Stimulants			
Cocaine	There are currently no medications approved to treat stimulant addiction. Promising new medications are in clinical trials. Behavioral treatments are the most effective.		
Methamphetamine	There are currently no medications approved to treat stimulant addiction. Promising new medications are in clinical trials. Behavioral treatments are the most effective.		
Amphetamines	There are currently no medications approved to treat stimulant addiction. Promising new medications are in clinical trials. Behavioral treatments are the most effective.		
Methylphenidate (Ritalin)	There are currently no medications approved to treat stimulant addiction. Promising new medications are in clinical trials. Behavioral treatments are the most effective.		

Opiates	MEDICATION	FDA-APPROVED	ACTION
Heroin, prescription painkillers (oxycodone, OxyContin, Percocet, Percodan)	Methadone	Approved 1973	A synthetic opiate that stabilizes the level of opiates in the bloodstream (prevents withdrawal and craving), but doesn't produce a comparable euphoria or high.
	Buprenorphine (Suboxone, Subutex)	Approved 2002	Opioid partial-agonist that, like methadone, stabilizes the level of opiates in the bloodstream, but doesn't produce a comparable high. There is less risk of addiction, overdose, and can be prescribed in the privacy of a doctor's office.
	Naltrexone (ReVia)	Approved 1985	Provides complete blockade of opioid receptors. Provides no narcotic effect. Cravings for narcotics may continue during treatment.

Inhalants

Aerosols, plastic cement, nail polish remover, lighter fluid, hair spray, insecticides, and cleaning solvents	There are no medications available to treat inhalant addiction. Behavioral treatments are the most effective.

Hallucinogens

LSD	There are no medications available to treat LSD abuse. Behavioral treatments are the most effective.
MDMA (Ecstasy)	There are no medications available to treat MDMA abuse. Behavioral treatments are the most effective.
Ketamine Hydrochloride	There are no medications available to treat ketamine abuse. Behavioral treatments are the most effective.
Phencyclidine (PCP)	There are no medications available to treat phencyclidine abuse. Behavioral treatments are the most effective.

Cannabis

Marijuana	There are no medications available to treat marijuana addiction. Behavioral treatments are the most effective.

Motivational enhancement therapy Internal motivation is the focus for this counseling approach, which seeks to change behavior through strategies designed to increase a patient's desire to engage in treatment and stop drug use. In this approach, the therapist asks open-ended questions (generally, questions that cannot be answered with a "yes" or a "no," such as, "What's been happening since the last time we met?"); offers motivation to change and the ability to explore and resolve ambivalent thoughts or feelings; practices reflective listening, mirroring back to the patient what they have expressed in an empathic, nonjudgmental manner; and offers summaries, a specialized form of reflective listening that communicates the therapist's interest in the client, calls attention to important elements in the discussion, and allows for a shift in attention or direction.

Contingency management/community-based incentives Research shows that the opportunity to win rewards worth as little as $1 can help motivate patients to stay in treatment and remain drug-free. Incentives might include simple affirmations ("good job"), bus tokens, snacks, or a pass to an ice-skating rink. "Reinforcing abstinence helps keep patients interested in attending treatment for longer periods, which can facilitate behavioral changes to keep them off drugs for the long haul," says Nancy Petry, PhD, associate scientific director of the University of Connecticut School of Medicine's Alcohol Research Center. "Incentive programs, including low-cost ones, add excitement and additional reasons to attend substance abuse treatment. Many substance abusers are ambivalent about treatment, and rewards may help them stay involved in counseling." Further, Maxine Stitzer, PhD, professor of behavioral biology at The Johns Hopkins University School of Medicine offers, "The idea of catching people being good and rewarding the behavior can infuse addiction treatment with a positive outlook and reinvigorate patients and counselors."

Therapy for adolescents Individual or group sessions focus on helping addicted young people avoid situations associated with drug use, recognize and change thoughts, feelings, and plans that lead to drug use, and enlist the support of family members and significant others to assist with therapy assignments and reinforce desired behaviors.

No single method is appropriate or effective for treating all individuals.

The success of this therapy is largely dependent on the involvement of family members in therapy and on rewarding abstinence, as verified by random urinalysis.

In multidimensional family therapy for adolescents, family, peers, and community are the focus. This therapy recognizes the need to address all aspects of the adolescent's life in treatment and long-term recovery. The adolescent meets individually with a therapist to acquire the decision-making, problem-solving, and negotiation skills needed to deal with life stresses and accurately communicate thoughts and feelings. Family members meet with the therapist in separate sessions that focus on helping parents examine their parenting style and working with family members to develop positive approaches for influencing the addicted adolescent's behavior. Treatment takes place in the clinic, at home, or with family members at the court or juvenile justice center, school, church, or other community locations.

FAMILY INVOLVEMENT

Family involvement in treatment increases the addict's chances for a successful, long-term recovery. Certain interventions, such as behavioral marital therapy, have been shown to improve the outcome in cases of alcohol dependence. For adolescents in rehabilitation, treating the whole family is a core precept. Family members require special attention as they deal with their own emotions and seek to understand what has happened to their addicted loved one and to the family as a whole. Educational lectures and discussions, individual family therapy sessions, and group therapy sessions that include the addicted person help to resolve feelings of guilt and shame and release family members from self-destructive patterns of behavior.

Family treatment is complicated. "In many cases, addicts have alienated their families," says Richard Rawson of the Integrated Substance Abuse Programs at UCLA. "Many families feel betrayed. They are mad at the addicted person, and yet now they are asked to help in their treatment."

In treatment, the family learns that an addict's behavior "doesn't mean that they don't care for their family very much," says NIDA's Volkow. "It's just that the motivation to procure the drug becomes much more powerful than the motivation to be responsive to their family." Only one thing matters to a using addict: using. "It is the equivalent to the signal to seek food and eat it when you are starving," she explains. "It's so powerful that it's almost like a survival signal."

Understanding the facts about this brain disease and learning what they can do to help both the addicted person and themselves can be healing for the family and the addict. "All family members are affected by the particular problems of even just one member," says Jeanette Friedman, director of adolescent services at Caron Foundation of New York. "Resentments on the part of family members who feel neglected, often for years, make family work essential to the emotional health and survival of everyone involved."

WHAT IF THEY DON'T WANT HELP?
Sometimes, people with substance-abuse problems will ask for help. They know they have serious problems and they desperately want to change their lives. But frequently, people with untreated addictions falsely believe that they can control their drug or alcohol use. That's why it may be tempting to take a hands-off approach to the problem, hoping that your relative or friend's drug or alcohol problem will just go away—that he or she is just going through a phase and will get better with time. Or you may decide that treatment won't help because your addicted friend or relative doesn't want to make a change. But both of these beliefs are myths that can lead to more severe addiction and to greater family disruption. Addiction is a progressive disorder—it gets worse over time. The sooner a person receives treatment for addiction, the greater the chances for long-term recovery.

"Intervention" is an umbrella term used to describe a number of strategies designed to help addicted people before alcohol and other drugs destroy their relationships, careers, physical health, and mental stability. No matter what strategy is used, however, we need to emphasize that intervention is not confrontation.

"Brief intervention" is a term that has come to mean a combination of alcohol- or other drug-screening questions, followed by a brief discussion of the results. Brief interventions, by doctors or other healthcare professionals in an office or an emergency room, can be extremely effective in motivating addicted people to seek help (see page 124).

Whenever a crisis occurs—a suicide attempt, an emergency room admission for a drug overdose, an arrest for drunk driving, or a minor-in-consumption or minor-in-possession charge—the opportunity exists for family members or caring professionals to intervene. In a crisis intervention, the trick is to focus on the individual's drinking or drug use as the underlying cause of the emergency and take steps to help the individual get into appropriate treatment as quickly as possible.

Conventional wisdom has taught us that a confrontational intervention is necessary to get a loved one into treatment. Aggressive approaches are sometimes successful, but they may not be best suited to a particular situation. Intervention methods have been refined in recent years. A newer approach, called Community Reinforcement and Family Training, or CRAFT, relies on a gentler, more supportive method (see opposite).

And so we come to have hope—not in the abstract sense of "someday, maybe, things will change," but in the here-and-now understanding that effective treatment for addiction exists, and it works. Numerous scientific studies show that treatment for addiction is just as effective as treatments for other chronic, relapsing diseases, such as diabetes, asthma, and hypertension, and relapse rates are similar for all four diseases.

Millions of recovering alcoholics who are now productive members of our society—our friends, our neighbors, our family members—offer living proof of the fact that treatment works and recovery is a common reality. The challenge before us is to ensure that high-quality, evidence-based treatment is available to everyone who needs it, and not just to those who can afford it or who have insurance policies that cover it.

The CRAFT Model: An Alternative to Intervention

Robert J. Meyers, PhD

Research associate professor of psychology, University of New Mexico

If you have a substance-abusing loved one who refuses treatment, the CRAFT model (Community Reinforcement and Family Training) may be able to help. CRAFT teaches the use of healthy rewards to encourage positive behaviors. Plus, it focuses on helping both the substance abuser and their family.

One goal of CRAFT is to teach you how to encourage a substance abuser to reduce use and enter treatment. The other goal is to help you enhance your own quality of life. This nonconfrontational approach teaches you how to figure out the best times and strategies to make small but powerful changes. And it will show you how to do so in a way that reduces relationship conflict. You can teach yourself CRAFT techniques using the book *Get Your Loved One Sober.*

Five things to know about coping with a loved one's unhealthy behavior

1. Your love has power. Research has shown that family members can successfully learn techniques to draw their substance-abusing loved ones into treatment.

2. You are not alone. As isolated as you may feel as you cope with your loved one's substance abuse, the fact is that you are not alone. At this very moment, millions of families are suffering from problems just like yours. Although knowing that others suffer certainly doesn't lessen your pain, you may take hope from knowing that many have resolved their problems and learned to live more satisfying lives.

3. You can catch more flies with honey than with vinegar. Just as it is easier to attract flies with sweet honey than with sour vinegar, it is easier to get your loved one to listen to loving words than to criticism. Choose the honey alternative to nagging and threatening, and help your loved one move toward sobriety by talking about what you do like about them and what positive changes please you.

4. You have as many tries as you want. Relationships are a process. They exist over time. One event or discussion rarely defines an entire relationship, so the truth is that you have as many tries at improving your relationship as you wish to take. As you develop better ways to interact with your loved one, take heart when things go well, but do not be overly discouraged when they go poorly. The next word, the next day, the next interaction gives you another chance to make a positive change.

5. You can live a happier life whether or not your loved one sobers up. In a perfect world, you will successfully encourage your loved one to get clean. In the real world, this often happens, but sometimes it does not. Whether or not your loved one's lifestyle improves, you can enhance yours. Learning to take care of yourself, regardless of your loved one's behavior, is important.

(continued on next page)

(continued from previous page)

Five things to remember

1. You have alternatives. No matter the nature of the problem, it can only go one of three ways: it can get worse, it can stay the same, or it can get better. Odds are that if you change nothing, your loved one's drinking or drug use will continue to get worse, or at best stay the same. On the other hand, if you choose to learn alternatives to nagging, pleading, and threatening, you can help resolve the problem.

2. Small steps carry you long distances. Although it may sometimes feel like right now is not soon enough for change to happen, small steps can make a huge difference in relationships. As you plan those steps, think about when the best time is to make your move and what small change would be most likely to have a positive outcome. Keep your own safety, and those for whom you are responsible, at the forefront of your mind. Small, carefully timed changes will carry you the furthest.

3. Emotions are fluid. When you are frustrated, hurt, angry, and exhausted, remember that these feelings are responses to current situations. When you change the way you interact with your loved one, the situations will change, and so will your feelings. As you develop more effective ways of addressing your loved one's substance abuse, your emotional pain will gradually change into feelings of confidence and hope.

4. Asking for help is a good thing. Humans are communal beings. We thrive best when we work together and share our experiences and our abilities. As you strive to enhance the quality of your life and help your loved one, turn to the people who love you and turn to the people who have learned to deal with similar problems. Ask for help, accept help, and breathe a sigh of relief as things get better.

5. Patience pays. Family problems usually do not develop overnight and seldom go away in a single day. Take small steps and remind yourself that change takes time. If you patiently invest that time, your efforts will be rewarded with a happier future.

The sooner
an addict gets
into treatment,
the better.

NIDA Principles of Effective Drug-Abuse Treatment

Because addiction has so many dimensions and disrupts so many aspects of an individual's life, treatment is never simple. Drug-addiction treatment must help the individual stop using drugs and maintain a drug-free lifestyle while achieving productive functioning in the family, at work, and in society. Of course, not all drug-abuse treatment is equally effective. But research has revealed a set of overarching principles that characterize the most effective drug-addiction treatments and their implementation.

1. No single treatment is appropriate for all individuals. Matching treatment settings, interventions, and services to each individual's particular problems and needs is critical to their ultimate success in returning to productive functioning in the family, workplace, and society.

2. Treatment needs to be readily available. Because individuals who are addicted to drugs may be uncertain about entering treatment, taking advantage of opportunities when they are ready for treatment is crucial. Potential treatment opportunities can be lost if treatment is not immediately available or is not readily accessible.

3. Effective treatment attends to the multiple needs of the individual, not just their drug use. To be effective, treatment must address the individual's drug use and any associated medical, psychological, social, vocational, and legal problems.

4. An individual's treatment and services plan must be assessed continually and modified as necessary to ensure that the plan meets the person's changing needs. A patient may require varying combinations of services and treatment components during the course of treatment and recovery. In addition to counseling or psychotherapy, a patient may require medication, other medical services, family therapy, parenting instruction, vocational rehabilitation, and social and legal services. It is critical that the treatment approach be appropriate to the individual's age, gender, ethnicity, and culture.

5. Remaining in treatment for an adequate period of time is critical for treatment to be effective. The appropriate duration for each individual depends on their problems and needs. Research indicates that for most patients, the threshold of significant improvement is reached at about three months in treatment. After this, additional treatment can produce further progress toward recovery. Because people often leave treatment prematurely, programs should include strategies to engage and keep patients in treatment.

6. Counseling (individual and group) and other behavioral therapies are critical components of effective treatment for addiction. In therapy, patients address issues of motivation, build skills to resist drug use, replace drug-using activities with constructive and rewarding nondrug-using activities, and improve problem-solving abilities. Behavioral therapy also facilitates interpersonal relationships and the individual's ability to function in their family and their community.

7. Medications are an important element of treatment for many patients, especially when combined with counseling and other behavioral therapies. Methadone and buprenorphine are very effective in helping individuals addicted to heroin or other opiates stabilize their lives and reduce their illegal drug use. Naltrexone is also an effective medication for some opiate addicts and some patients with co-occurring alcohol dependence. For patients with mental disorders, both behavioral treatments and medications can be critically important.

8. Addicted or drug-abusing individuals with co-occurring mental disorders should have both disorders treated in an integrated way. Because addictive disorders and mental disorders often occur in the same individual, patients presenting for either condition should be assessed and treated for the co-occurrence of the other type of disorder.

9. Medical detoxification is only the first stage of addiction treatment and by itself does little to change long-term drug use. Medical detoxification safely manages the acute physical symptoms of withdrawal associated with stopping drug use. While detoxification alone is rarely sufficient to help addicts achieve long-term abstinence, for some individuals it is a strongly indicated precursor to effective drug addiction treatment.

10. Treatment does not need to be voluntary to be effective. Strong motivation can facilitate the treatment process. Sanctions or enticements in the family, the workplace, or the criminal justice system can significantly increase both treatment entry and retention rates and the success of drug treatment interventions.

11. Possible drug use during treatment must be monitored continuously. Lapses into drug use can occur during treatment. The objective monitoring of a patient's drug and alcohol use during treatment, such as through urinalysis or other tests, can help the patient withstand urges to use drugs. Such monitoring also can provide early evidence of drug use so that the individual's treatment plan can be adjusted. Feedback to patients who test positive for drug use is an important element of monitoring.

12. Treatment programs should provide assessment for HIV/AIDS, hepatitis B and C, tuberculosis, and other infectious diseases, and counseling to help patients modify or change behaviors that place themselves or others at risk of infection. Counseling can help patients avoid high-risk behavior. Counseling can also help people who are already infected manage their illness.

13. Recovery from drug addiction can be a long-term process, and it frequently requires multiple instances of treatment. As with other chronic illnesses, relapses can occur during or following successful treatment. Addicted individuals may require prolonged treatment and multiple instances of treatment to achieve long-term abstinence and fully restored functioning. Participation in self-help support programs during and following treatment is often helpful in maintaining abstinence.

Lisa MISSOURI

Lisa is a working mother who has struggled with addiction for years.

For the past twenty or twenty-five years, I've struggled off and on with addictions to different prescription medications. About three years ago, some friends of mine had some meth. And they asked, "Do you wanna try it?" And I said, "Sure." I don't know what I was thinking. But from the first time I smoked it, I just loved it. Meth gave me energy; it made me feel like I could get everything done. I needed to take care of my kids. I needed to clean the house. I needed to go to work. There's so much stuff that I had to get done, and if I smoked meth, I was able to do everything and do it right and still feel good and have energy.

I can remember a time using drugs when it was fun. I was gettin' high with my friends and runnin' dope all around town and going to the casinos all night. But it doesn't last. For the life of me I can't remember when it happened, but there came a point when it wasn't fun anymore. I woke up one morning and just realized that my whole life was consumed by the methamphetamine.

I could not go to sleep at night unless I had a pipe with meth in it to get me up the next morning. I mean, literally, I couldn't and I wouldn't. It consumed my whole life. At first I was able to afford it. Then I started selling it so that I could have more to supply my habit. Then I was pawning everything I owned. My relationship was going in the toilet because of the drugs and the lying. And my family was pulling away because they didn't know what to do.

If I had any advice for a family out there who wants to help their children or spouses or brothers and sisters who have a drug problem, it is don't do anything at all. In other words, if their electricity's gonna get shut off, don't turn it on for them. My mother did that for me. She loves me so much, and I know I've put her through so much. She would give me the money to pay my bills or she would buy groceries. And she would always say, "Lisa, I'm not doing this anymore. You've got to stop what you're doing. You've got to." But as long as somebody's there picking up the slack for you, you have no reason to stop. And you won't.

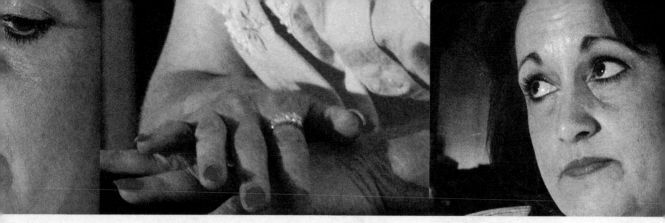

I have a grown son named Rob who educated himself on addictions. He finally went to my mom and said, "Grandma, if we want Mom to get well, we've got to start telling her 'No!'" And when my mom started telling me "No," there was no one there to bail me out, I went to a treatment center and successfully completed it. It's changed my life. I mean completely.

When I was about to be released from treatment, my mom called and said, "Rob said you can't go back to the house. I'm letting Rob run everything because he knows what's going on. And we've decided you can't." I was totally devastated. I could not believe she had said that. I remember I got off the phone and I was just crying hysterically. I felt like my family had finally had enough. I felt like what my mom was saying to me was, "We don't want you around anymore. We're done with you."

I talked to some other people who were in recovery. I told them what had happened. One of the guys said, "Lisa, I just heard you tell about a son who loves his mother so much and about a mother who loves her daughter so much that they are willing to do anything for you. They just want you to be okay and be well." And when he told me that, it was like all of a sudden it was different. It was like, "Yeah, you're right. They really do." The times I've been through treatment and gone back to that house, I started using again. I know my mom telling me no and not letting me go back to that house was hard for her. I know it was a very hard decision for her because she does love me.

In my whole adult life I've had somebody—whether it be a husband or my mother—to pick up the slack when I got behind. Somebody was always there to bail me out. Nobody's there to bail me out anymore. I gotta do things right. But it's good. I like this feeling of independence. I do it on my own.

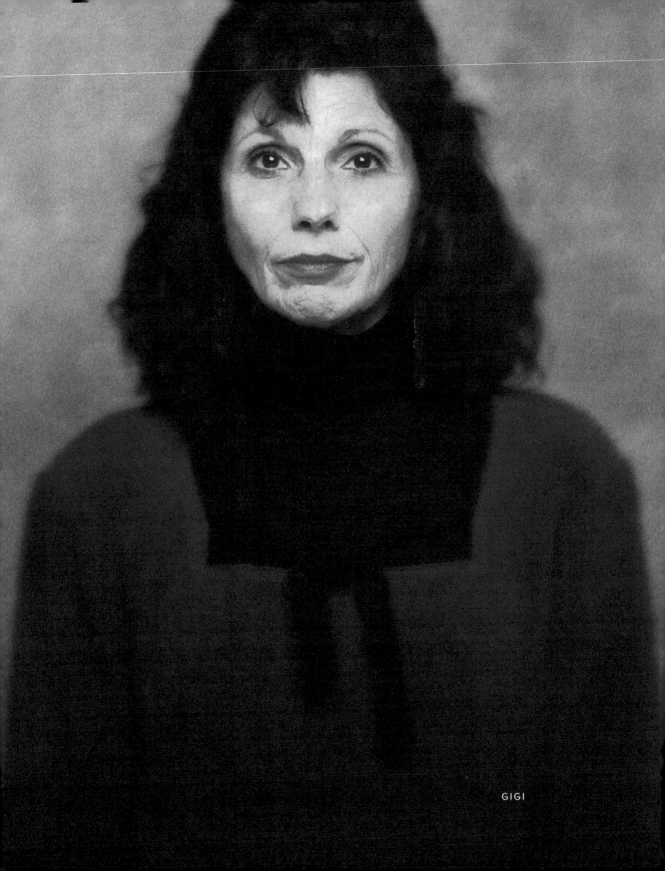

GIGI

A Broken System: The Tangled Economics of Treatment

This thing is so deceitful, it's so cunning, and it's so baffling. It's my security blanket, for now. And that's why I need to go out and get the help. Because alcohol should not be a security blanket. GIGI, RECOVERING ALCOHOLIC

Every day, people get sober. Every day, lives are saved. If you aren't convinced, sit in on an Alcoholics Anonymous or Narcotics Anonymous meeting. Listen.

"That was ten years ago," a girl in her mid-twenties says at a meeting in Nashville, describing the time she woke up in an alley. On heroin, she had been repeatedly raped. She had multiple fractures and a concussion. "I have stayed sober since then. My life now is a blessing." She describes the appreciation she has for her family and friends. She describes a better life than she ever dreamed possible.

A boy who was captain of his high school football team in Phoenix—whose life collapsed when he became addicted to meth—says, "My last relapse landed me in jail. Thank God, because I wound up in rehab. Now I'm back in school. I've got friends, a good relationship with my parents. I love my life." In the room, fellow addicts applaud. They understand what it feels like to say "I love my life" after experiencing long periods of hating it.

How does one get there? It's a cliché, but virtually everyone who gets and stays sober says the same thing: They do it one day at a time. They have many stories about what led to their sobriety. At the beginning, most of them were confused about where to go for help. Family and friends—and friends of friends, and school and work counselors, and psychologists, and law enforcement officers, and medical doctors, and every other variety of expert—have their own opinions about what will work. Many of these opinions are strident, and many are contradictory. Addicts are advised to go to AA, traditional and alternative therapies, intensive outpatient psychotherapy, traditional and alternative inpatient and outpatient rehabs, detoxes, and hospitals, and short-term and long-term programs—never mind boot camps, wilderness programs, and the like.

BARRIERS TO TREATMENT: THERE IS NO ROADMAP

Many people begin by checking the Internet. A Google search for "drug and alcohol addiction treatment" results in more than one million hits. One program promises to "End Opiate Addiction Now." There are listings for Christian-based, "rational," "revolutionary," and holistic treatments. One web site promises: "End heroin addiction forever." Another: "We find the right rehab for your loved one." Still more: "We will help you take the first step toward a better life," and "Our drug rehab is the most effective drug and alcohol rehabilitation program available today. Seventy-six percent of our graduates *happily* choose to remain drug free and become productive members of society."

For anyone who has ever had to obtain addiction treatment for themselves or a loved one, there are numerous obstacles and unlimited frustrations. Knowing that treatment is the only way to recovery may, in and of itself, energize you to persevere. Or, you may only need to know that you are not alone. The system, while it can work and it does work, is flawed, but the outcome—sobriety—is a goal worth fighting for, and so is the life of your loved one.

In Boise, Idaho, a young boy named Jack, while a high school student, had been frequently cautioned by his mother, Charlotte—an alcoholic and addict in recovery for more than twenty years—who told him that chances are he had the gene that gives people a predisposition to addiction. "It runs in our family," she would say. "Both sides; from both your father and me. We can't drink casually like some people. We can't do drugs. Please, stay away from them. They can destroy you."

Knowing that treatment is the only way to recovery may, in and of itself, energize you to persevere. Or, you may only need to know that you are not alone. The system, while it can work and it does work, is flawed, but the outcome—sobriety—is a goal worth fighting for, and so is the life of your loved one.

Jack was an exceptionally bright, handsome, and popular boy. How often do we hear people who become addicted described like that—bright, handsome, successful, charming—the last people on earth you would ever expect this to happen to? In spite of the warnings, he began drinking. "It's just everywhere," his mother says. "Everywhere he went—to parties, to friends' houses, to clubs. It was probably inevitable that he would drink. And kids don't believe it, but drinking does lead to drugs, at least most of the time." For Jack, it led to cocaine and OxyContin. "He spun out of control," Charlotte says. Jack eventually discovered what he would describe as "the magic combination"—heroin and cocaine together, the potent and dangerous mix known as a speedball. Charlotte found out how far it had gone when Jack finally called and asked for help. He was desperate. Charlotte says, "I was frantic to find him help."

Over 18 and no longer in school, Jack wasn't covered by his mother's health insurance and had no insurance of his own. After making many, many telephone calls, Charlotte learned that without insurance there were no options—not one. In the entire state of Idaho there were just a handful of what were called "indigent beds" in the state's very few rehab centers. She never thought of her son as indigent, but she would have taken one of those spots. Except none were available.

Jack detoxed at home. Charlotte sat with him. "It was a nightmare," she says. "You never want to see your child in that much pain." He got through it and said he would never use again. Soon, he moved across the country to Seattle— "away from his dealers and friends, away from the drug scene out here"—promising his mother, "I'll be okay." She was excited to see him when he was coming home to visit for Thanksgiving in 2004.

He never showed up. Later Charlotte learned that instead of coming home, he went to his dealer's. That night he shot up, overdosed, and died. At 23. "Without money or insurance, we never found a treatment program that would take him," his mother says. "He never had the help he needed."

Yes, there are grim stories, but many have happier endings. Across the country, on the West Coast near San Diego, Jeanne*, a 32-year-old teacher, shakily confessed to a friend that she was in trouble. Her drug use had, she says, "gone way out of control." It began casually. She snorted cocaine occasionally, "on weekends just to loosen up and party." Not now. "I've been using it every day," she confided, "first thing. I need it to get through the day." She choked on her words and continued, "I never understood what it meant to be addicted to something. I thought drug addicts were homeless and derelicts and criminals. Like— "

She looked at her friend and immediately felt self-conscious. Jeanne had chosen this friend to confide in because her former boyfriend was an addict. He wound up in jail, but not before her friend tried to help him get sober. Three or four times.

This friend said, "Rehab's a waste of time and money." Instead, she told her about a new treatment for cocaine

Since the advent of managed care, the duration of inpatient treatment has declined significantly.

Before you commit to a program, keep a few things in mind.

→ Avoid treatment programs that aren't evidence-based—those whose methods are not supported by science. If the advertised approach is different from what's commonly believed in the field, challenge the treatment center staff to present convincing evidence of their program's efficacy.

→ Know who you're dealing with. Investigate. Do some research on the counselors and doctors at the center and seek anecdotal advice from previous and current patients. If possible, visit the treatment facility before committing—glossy photos and pretty web sites are no substitute for firsthand experience.

→ Quick-fix therapies are seductive because of their optimism and savings, but they may not deliver what's promised. Be suspicious of a program that promises to drain the addict of desire for drugs or alcohol in two days with heavy medication. Patients in such programs may be putting their health at risk without gaining the essential supportive tools to help them through a devastating relapse.

→ If you are resistant to religion or uncomfortable with spirituality, avoid programs that ask patients to find the strength for their recovery in a higher power.

addiction—what she called "anti-addiction drugs"—offered at a clinic in Los Angeles. "It takes a month and works miracles," she said. But when Jeanne asked another friend—an alcoholic in recovery—he told her to go into rehab. "There's no shortcut," he insisted. Jeanne's sister said she just needed some time away and recommended a meditation retreat. She asked her family physician, who prescribed sedatives. She filled the prescription, but ignored the other advice. One evening, high on the pills and cocaine, she ran a red light and was stopped by a police officer who administered a sobriety test. She failed. The officer searched her and her car and discovered two grams of cocaine. Arrested, Jeanne spent the night in jail and later, in court, pleaded no contest to possession and DUI charges. She no longer had a choice about treatment: a judge mandated a rehab program. That was seven years ago. "I never expected to be able to say this," she said recently. "But what at the time seemed like the worst thing that could ever happen to me was the best—a gift. To anyone out there who is struggling with alcoholism and addiction, I would tell them, 'At first, yeah, it's really hard, but it gets easier. I promise.' Not only that, but at the start of the process of recovery, the rewards of a better life may seem impossible to imagine. Once you choose to face your problem and treat it, however, everything in your life can improve. You can have the life you always dreamed of. I do."

BARRIERS TO TREATMENT:
A LACK OF RELIABLE INFORMATION

Facing any health crisis is daunting, but with addiction it can feel overwhelming—or impossible. "Help is out there, but addicts and their families have to navigate a system that is fraught with snake-oil salesmen, charlatans, unproved treatments, and contradictory and inadequate advice," says Richard Rawson, PhD, associate director of the Integrated Substance Abuse Programs at the University of California at Los Angeles. "There are often financial constraints. Insurance, when someone has it, is often limited; it may not cover adequate addiction treatments. It's often worse for those without insurance."

The system is complex and confusing, and meanwhile

addicts, when they finally are ready for treatment, are usually in no condition to wade through the thicket of choices. Their families, when they are involved, usually aren't in much better shape. "The addict and his family are in a state of panic and desperation," Rawson explains. "They are at their most vulnerable. And yet, in this debilitated condition they must try to make a broken system work. At its best, it's bewildering. At its worst, it's a nightmare. There is no roadmap."

"At the start of the process of recovery, the rewards of a better life may seem impossible to imagine. Once you choose to face your problem and treat it, however, everything in your life can improve."

Given the misinformation and uncertainty, how do you decide on a course of action? Often, addicts aren't ready to go into treatment unless there's a crisis—a disaster. So how do you decide *quickly*—quickly and at a time when you are under enormous stress?

The experts offer some general cautionary advice. Not all treatments are the same. It is important to consider the quality of the treatment in identifying the right treatment for you or your loved ones.

Poorly developed treatments may do little more than briefly interrupt periods of substance abuse. Gantt Galloway, a scientist in the Addiction Pharmacology Research Laboratory at the California Pacific Medical Center Research Institute, says, "addicts are probably more likely to abandon poorly constructed treatments and we will have missed what otherwise could be an opportunity to start an addict on the path that leads to recovery." Also, "some ineffective treatments may be harmful because they may turn an addict off to the idea that they can be helped," he says.

Most experts warn you to stay away from programs that

offer easy solutions or miracle cures. Addiction is a chronic and progressive disease. Walter Ling, MD, director of the UCLA program, says, "I would distrust anyone who says they can cure addiction."

There also appears to be strong evidence for avoiding some boot camps or similar programs. While they may have helped some addicts stop using drugs, many experts say programs with militaristic regimens that badger patients—especially those that use harsh discipline—don't work for most addicts and may, in fact, be harmful.

"The only treatments that have been proven to be effective involve a comprehensive program of rehabilitation and recovery. For some addictions, specific medications have been shown to help, but there are no shortcuts."

The U.S. Bureau of Prisons closed its fourteen-year-old boot camp program, calling it "a failed concept." A U.S. Department of Justice study documented physical abuse by guards and inadequate care for attendees at some boot camps. The study concluded that the camps were "not only ineffective, but harmful." Since 1983, thirty-five children have died in boot camps. And thousands of people attending these camps have been injured—many at the hands of counselors. "There are no studies that show that these tactics treat addiction, and they may be psychologically damaging," says Rawson. "They could lead to increased drug use because patients could become more alienated, angry, or depressed."

Some treatment programs for alcoholism and drug addiction increase their success rates with the judicious and carefully monitored use of medications, as discussed in Chapter 4. However, some widely publicized programs rely on combinations of medications whose efficacy has not been proven in controlled studies. In addition to their warnings about boot camps, many specialists advise caution about treatments that use untested combinations of medications. "Everyone would like an easy answer—a medication or series of medications that cures addiction," says Rawson. "Unfortunately, the only treatments that have been proven to be effective involve a comprehensive program of rehabilitation and recovery. For some addictions, specific medications have been shown to help, but there are no shortcuts."

To choose a good program, it is important to do your homework. Unfortunately, there is no independent *Consumer Reports* for rehab centers. There is no central place for you to go to get reliable statistics on how well one program works compared to another. In fact, few reliable statistics on success rates exist because there haven't been many controlled studies of specific treatment centers. Many don't systematically follow up with former patients. As such, claims of success rates may not be entirely reliable.

Maybe one day there will be a central database with reliable statistics for rehab options in every community. It would be an invaluable public service. Whether it was compiled and monitored by a government or nongovernmental agency, if it was independent—that is, if it did not take advertising from or rely on funding from the treatment programs themselves—it would be a godsend for addicts and their families. Given the enormous need, it's unfortunate that such a database does not exist. The lack of such a clearinghouse for information leaves addicts and their families vulnerable. Thomas McLellan, MD, CEO of Treatment Research Institute, agrees, "This is a real problem in our field. The lack of information in a timely fashion that contributes to some of the crisis."

BARRIERS TO TREATMENT: ECONOMICS
Rehab programs range in price from free to more than $50,000 a month. Some experts recommend a minimum of three months of inpatient treatment, followed by outpatient programs and other aftercare measured in

many months, so high-end programs can cost a fortune. When treatments involve medication, the cost is higher. The drug Suboxone, for example, which has been effective in curtailing cravings in heroin addicts, costs as much as $180 a month.

"Help is out there, but there are enormous obstacles to getting good treatment. As a result, we are losing people who could be helped. We wouldn't allow this if it were any other disease."

The amount of money that is spent, however, is no guarantee of success. Even extremely expensive and highly renowned programs cannot guarantee results. In fact, the prognosis for a patient who goes through them may be no better than it is for a patient who completes a good community-based, public program that costs the addict nothing—if the patient is motivated and the treatment fits them.

The range in the cost of treatment raises the question: what are you getting for tens of thousands of dollars a month? One drug and alcohol counselor compares it to expensive private versus public colleges. "The professors are just as good, but the classes are smaller and there's a better film club," he says. It's no secret that in America, no matter what the health problem, money can buy excellent care. But some expensive rehabs may simply offer better food and fancier rooms or spa-like additions such as massage, swimming pools, and acupuncture.

Despite no guarantees of success, some high-end centers with comprehensive treatment programs may include—for patients with co-occurring disorders—regular and frequent visits with therapists, psychologists, or psychiatrists, plus state-of-the-art addiction treatments. "The high-end programs have a variety of treatment options and experienced people in charge of those options," says McLellan. "It means it's more likely that they will find something that works for you. In addition, they are good about teaching someone to understand that their addiction is a lifelong condition requiring consistent efforts, including AA for most people." These may be worth considering—if you can afford it.

If.

It is not uncommon to hear families say that they have used every penny they have saved—mortgaged homes, drained retirement accounts and college funds—trying to treat their own or a loved one's addiction. The high cost of effective healthcare for addiction and alcoholism is of enormous concern for people who aren't covered by insurance—and, as it turns out, many who are.

NINE OUT OF TEN DON'T GET
THE TREATMENT THEY NEED

Ashley had thick, long, blond hair and luminous blue eyes and was, her mother, Roberta Lojak, says, "a blessing from the day she was born. A special child. She never got into trouble. She did well in school—was in a program for gifted and talented students. She was kind and helpful around the house. She had a job and worked hard. She came home when she was supposed to come home. We were very close."

The family lived twenty miles north of Pittsburgh in a quiet community. At age 17, when she was a high school senior, Ashley began experimenting with drugs. "She changed her friends," her mother says, "and became different."

Roberta suspected Ashley was using and confronted her, but her daughter denied it. Roberta worried incessantly. She talked to Ashley, but it didn't seem to do any good. Then Roberta found drug paraphernalia in Ashley's car. Finally Ashley admitted that she was using Ecstasy and heroin.

"I pleaded with her to stop," Roberta says. "At first she said it was no big deal. It wasn't a problem. She was just experimenting. She could stop on her own."

When she didn't, or couldn't, Roberta finally intervened. Along with her ex-husband, Ashley's father, Roberta took Ashley to programs in and around Pittsburgh, but no one

Who Pays for Treatment?

Mady Chalk, PhD

Director, Center for Performance-Based Policy, Treatment Research Institute

Generally, treatment is paid for by private health insurance, by public insurance such as Medicaid and Medicare, or, for those without any insurance, their treatment provider is reimbursed by public "block grant" funds that are a combination of federal and state dollars, or they self-pay for treatment.

Below are five essential things you should know before going to a treatment program.

1. Am I insured? What are my health insurance benefits? What are the deductibles, co-pays, annual and lifetime limits of my benefits?
Often health insurance has rather severe limits on what type of treatment services it will reimburse. Health insurance typically has higher co-pays for treatment of substance use disorders than it does for other types of medical care, and usually there will be a limit on how many days and how many times in the course of a year treatment will be covered.

Typically, insurance pays for a limited number of outpatient sessions (generally thirty) and a very limited number of inpatient hospital or residential treatment days per year. Many insurers also impose lifetime limits on the amount of care covered by the policy and caps on the number of times you can be treated for substance use and addiction. Providers often discharge people after health insurers deem treatment "not medically necessary" or after the patients have exhausted the number of treatment days or sessions the insurance company will reimburse.

Insurers often use nurse practitioners to make decisions about access to and continuation of treatment. This "management" of continuing care often means that the treatment program must get permission every ten sessions or, for inpatients, every three days, to continue treatment services. Some treatment organizations find this requirement a nuisance, but if they do not comply, reimbursement will be stopped and it may be necessary to discharge the patient.

2. What are the criteria my health insurance company will use to decide if it will allow admission to treatment and if it will pay for the treatment?
Often, when you call the insurance company's 800 number to get permission to access services, there will be a nurse-practitioner at the other end. The nurse-practitioner uses what is called "medical or clinical necessity criteria" to decide whether and in what settings (inpatient, residential, outpatient) the insurer will pay for treatment services. Although we know that there are other criteria that should be applied in making decisions about coverage, at present health insurance companies use only medical necessity criteria. If your insurance does not think these criteria are met, you may be denied access to some treatment services. Gaining access to hospital inpatient care is generally very difficult.

There are no specific or consistent criteria for approval. The standards used to determine if an individual is eligible to receive care vary. The medical necessity criteria used to deny access treatment often will not be revealed, though a few insurance companies have posted their criteria.

It is very important that you insist that your insurance pay for a full clinical assessment that identifies all of the physical and psychological problems that need to be addressed by treatment and by other services, such as child care, educational/vocational services, and the like. Ask whether these services will be included as part of treatment or whether they have to be paid for separately.

3. If Medicaid is paying for my or my child's treatment services, what do I need to know about the treatment provider I want to use?

Even if you qualify for Medicaid by reason of income or disability, that does not mean that all treatment settings will be available to you. Treatment providers must be certified as "Medicaid-eligible" to provide treatment services and receive Medicaid reimbursement. Medicaid limits the types of services and settings it will reimburse. Before you or your child enters treatment you must ask what services will be reimbursed. Medicaid is considered a state program, so what services are paid for and which treatment programs are identified as "Medicaid eligible" differs by state. Be aware that a diagnosis of substance abuse does *not* qualify as a disability.

4. Will someone coordinate the care that is being reimbursed? Who? Where are they located and how do I reach them?

Private health insurers and Medicaid will often identify someone, often a nurse-practitioner, to coordinate or "manage" the care provided. It is very important to know who that person is and to communicate with them directly. Care managers also may be used to track whether a patient is moving through levels of care.

If there is no care manager, demand that the insurance agency provide one. Health insurance companies are contracted to provide and pay for this service. If the care manager is inadequate, go to the manager or insurer's supervisor to request better care management.

5. If I use my health insurance, who else will know of my or my child's problem? Will the record follow me or them? For how long?

Health insurance privacy protection is ensured by the federal privacy laws HIPAA and 42 CFR Part 2 (which is specific to substance-use privacy protection). However, under some conditions it may be very important for other professionals to know about a child or adolescent's substance-use treatment history and current treatments. Information and guidance are available for every parent about how to handle the issue of privacy. It is also true that there are conditions under which no privacy protections exist. For example, if the police suspect that a crime has been committed involving drugs or alcohol they are permitted to access treatment records of any clinician, including therapy notes.

Why People Don't Seek Treatment

20.9 million people need treatment for addiction. Only a fraction get it.

94.4%
DID NOT FEEL THEY
NEEDED TREATMENT

4.1%
FELT LIKE THEY NEEDED TREATMENT
AND DID MAKE AN EFFORT

1.4%
FELT LIKE THEY NEEDED TREATMENT
AND DID NOT MAKE AN EFFORT

SOURCE: SAMHSA, 2005 NATIONAL SURVEY ON DRUG USE AND HEALTH

would admit her. "She didn't meet their criteria," Roberta says. "They weren't convinced she had a serious problem."

But things got worse. Roberta finally got Ashley into a three-day-a-week outpatient program and her daughter seemed to get a little better. "But then the people in the program said they were going to discharge her," Roberta says. "They told me I should save my benefits for later down the road."

Roberta had health insurance for her family through her employer. Like many insurance plans, hers had extremely limited benefits for drug and alcohol addiction treatment. "Most insurance plans discriminate against addiction and alcoholism," says U.S. Congressman Jim Ramstad, who represents Minnesota's third district. "A lot of plans cover seven days of detox. Well, the medical experts know that effective treatment requires months of care. Would you tell a cancer patient, 'We'll pay for seven days of treatment and then you're on your own?'"

Ramstad and a colleague, Congressman Patrick Kennedy, have sponsored a bill that, if passed and signed into law, would require insurance companies to offer the same types of coverage for addiction as they offer for other serious medical conditions. For now, however, "When it comes to treatment for alcoholism and addiction, most insurance companies have barriers to people in health plans, such as higher co-payments, higher deductibles, and limited treatment stays," Ramstad says. "Or, in many cases, there's no effective coverage whatsoever."

Ashley's drug use continued and she finally told Roberta she needed help. In a letter to her mother, she wrote, "I don't want to turn out like some of my friends—I don't want to be some dopehead. I haven't seen anything in this world so far and I want to."

Finally, Roberta found an inpatient program that would take Ashley. She provided the family's insurance information and Roberta was told that Ashley was approved for admission "at least for twenty-eight days but probably longer." "I took her out there," Roberta says. "She was admitted. I was hopeful that Ashley would finally get the help she needed."

Reasons Why Those Who Seek Treatment Don't Get It

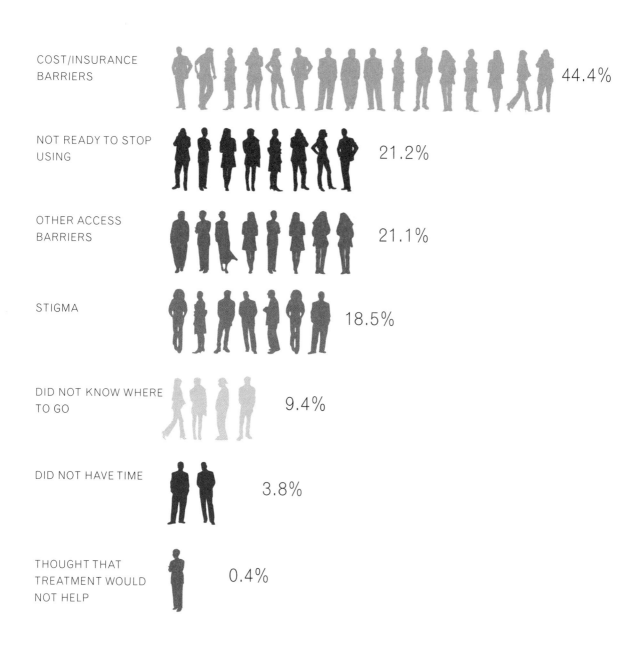

COST/INSURANCE BARRIERS — 44.4%

NOT READY TO STOP USING — 21.2%

OTHER ACCESS BARRIERS — 21.1%

STIGMA — 18.5%

DID NOT KNOW WHERE TO GO — 9.4%

DID NOT HAVE TIME — 3.8%

THOUGHT THAT TREATMENT WOULD NOT HELP — 0.4%

SOURCE: SAMHSA, 2005 NATIONAL SURVEY ON DRUG USE AND HEALTH

How to Fight the Stigma of Addiction

David Rosenbloom, PhD

Director, Join Together

Stigma is one of the meanest and most difficult aspects of addiction, because it makes it harder for individuals and families to deal with their problems and get the help they need. Stigma is the reason there is so much social and legal discrimination against people with addictions. In many ways, hiding an addiction problem is the rational thing to do because seeking help can mean losing your job and medical insurance, or even losing your child when a social service agency declares you an unfit parent because you have an alcohol or drug problem.

The stress of stigma often causes other medical and social problems for addicted individuals and their families. This is especially true when an adolescent has an alcohol or drug problem. Teens often hide the problem from their parents in part because of fear generated by stigma. When parents find out about the abuse problem, the stigma of society makes them feel guilty and somehow negligent. Both illness and family dysfunction explode. When that happens, it is even harder for parents to fight for the care and resources their child urgently needs from a social and medical system that blames the family and the child.

We may not be able to change the way society feels about people with alcohol and drug problems overnight, but we can end the legal discrimination that both causes and reinforces this stigma. Here are five things you can do to fight the stigma of addiction.

→ **Demand equal medical insurance coverage for alcohol and drug treatment.**
Almost all private or public health insurance and managed care policies still provide no or unequal coverage for alcohol and drug treatment. Repeated studies have shown that adding this coverage does not raise premiums, in part because it eliminates or reduces many of the covered medical illnesses that are caused by untreated alcohol and drug problems. Many managed care plans say they cover alcohol and drug treatment, but their case managers almost never approve the amount of care a person needs to actually get and stay better. Research shows that results really start to improve after a person has received three months of some form of treatment, most commonly outpatient counseling. In the world of managed care today, this minimal standard of good care is almost never approved.

→ **Tell your congressperson and senators to stop punishing babies for the past problems of their mothers.**
It is hard to believe, but current federal law bans mothers with past drug convictions from participation in the Food Stamp Program and the Women, Infants, and Children Nutrition Program. More than 135,000 babies have suffered from this law in recent years.

(continued on next page)

(continued from previous page)

→ **Tell your state lawmakers to remove the legal barriers that prevent recovering alcoholics and drug addicts from getting jobs.**

The American concept of justice is supposed to be that if you break a law, get arrested and convicted, and do your time, you should then be able to resume your life. That does not happen today for people with alcohol and drug convictions. State laws and regulations keep on punishing them, often making it impossible for them to get jobs. For example, many state or local licensing regulations for jobs such as barbers, construction workers, and even restaurant workers ban those with nonviolent drug or alcohol felony convictions from applying. In some states, employers have easy access to criminal records that are supposed to be confidential, making it very easy for them to avoid hiring anyone with a past problem. This continuous punishment condemns many—mostly young male minorities—to wasted lives. Research has shown that recovering individuals who don't have jobs are significantly more likely to relapse and to commit new crimes than similar individuals who do hold jobs.

→ **Give more than just lip service to the reality that addiction is a disease, not a character weakness.**

A recent poll showed that 80 percent of Americans think there is discrimination against recovering people in the workforce. But more than a quarter of those polled said they themselves would be reluctant to hire someone in long-term recovery. Large-scale social change often starts with small individual steps, even when they take us out of our personal comfort zone.

→ **Be an advocate for an individual or family with an addiction problem.**

Until you have actually been there, it is impossible to describe how hard it is for a family or individual to get access to quality and medically appropriate alcohol or drug treatment. At this most vulnerable time, any setback is likely to send a person with a drug or alcohol problem right back to the bottle or pills. They will feel guilty and scared. They will need an advocate, someone to stand next to them, to ask the right questions, to insist on the appropriate insurance coverage, and to make sure there is a treatment plan that makes sense. They will need someone who will say no to a suggestion that the patient come back in three weeks for an assessment, and who will insist on timely action. A mother and father who are fighting with their insurance company for their child's care will need someone on their side who will stand up to a managed care clerk. You can be that person.

A week later, someone from the program called and told Roberta that Ashley was being released because the family's insurance would not cover more time in the program. Roberta was stunned. "I said, 'I know she's not ready to come home,' but they told me, 'I'm sorry, but you have to come pick her up.'" Roberta asked to speak to a supervisor, but that person also said no. "I was told, 'When the insurance is declined, there's nothing we can do.'" The program cost $600 a day.

"Addiction is America's number-one public health crisis. Last year, 150,000 Americans died as a direct result of chemical addiction. Treatment center doors were slammed shut on the faces of people who came in for help because they couldn't afford to pay. In some cases they had no insurance. In many, their insurance was inadequate."

Roberta drove to pick Ashley up. Back home, she frantically searched for another place to send her daughter. She finally found one—a much less expensive outpatient program. In the morning, Roberta went in to wake Ashley to help her get ready to go to the first day of treatment. She entered her daughter's bedroom. Ashley's fingers and lips were blue. "I tried to do CPR on my daughter," Roberta says. "But she was already dead."

She may never know for sure, but Roberta suspects that drugs were delivered during the night through Ashley's bedroom window. Two weeks after her daughter died, Roberta received a letter from the insurance company. It said she had the right to appeal the company's decision to end Ashley's treatment.

Annie CALIFORNIA

Annie used heroin daily. She is in recovery.

I have a younger brother who died of a heroin overdose two years ago. I was so mad that he got into it at all. I thought he was so stupid. How could he even do drugs like that?

When I started doing heroin I had it under control—or so I thought, because I went from drinking to doing it. It sounds so stupid, but it made my life more controlled. If you drink, your actions are more accountable. You smell like alcohol. People know you're drinking. You get a drunk-driving charge. You can't pick your son up from school. You can't drink in the morning without people knowing.

Heroin is a very sneaky drug. You can do anything you want. You can go anywhere. You can function and no one has any idea at all. At first I thought, *Am I really getting away with this? People don't know?* And they don't. No one has a clue. I know it's not a good thing. But it still amazes me that people just don't know.

At first I was only sniffing. I never shot up at all. I didn't cross that line and I felt safe. When I came out here, I hadn't even touched heroin because I found doctors that I could get pills from. But then this guy I know moved out here. He had been shooting heroin for probably fifteen years, and when he got here he was like, "Oh, you gotta try this shit, Annie. It's so good."

No one makes you do anything. I take full responsibility. So I tried shooting it for the first time. And it was incredible. I started doing that over a year ago. It's so much cheaper. I'll get my own prescription of OxyContin and I'll sell those and make some money to pay my bills and to give my son anything he wants. It's like this crazy little system that I think has been working great, but it's like a house of cards. It's gonna break.

I'm thinking, *I gotta think of a Plan B.* I don't know how I'm gonna get out of it yet. I haven't figured that out. But I definitely will. I'm at a

point where I need to make the change and do something different because my arms are gross. I have sores. It's terrible. No one wants to walk around like that. You're always worried someone's gonna see it. No one should have to worry about that. It's really humiliating.

Getting high doesn't interfere with my son as far as infringing on his time with me and my responsibility of taking care of him, because I always put him 100 percent first. I make sure I walk him to school, pick him up from school. He plays every sport. I've been involved with everything with the school. He's in the high-honors classes. He's an awesome kid. He has no idea at all.

And there's nothing amiss or out of place for him to suspect anything. Nothing bad has happened. My fridge is stocked. My cabinets are stocked. Which makes it so stupid because it shouldn't be this easy. It's like I wish it wasn't. I really do. I wish something would change.

I totally think I can stop this on my own. I got in it on my own and I think I'm gonna get the hell out of it on my own. I'm fearful of seeking help because I don't want someone taking my son away from me. And that is the first thing they'd wanna do. And that wouldn't be very helpful to me. It would send me over the edge.

I do heroin because I like to be high and escape. It's terrible how good it can make you feel. It's different than any other feeling. It's not the same kind of feeling as love; like my love for my children. It's nothing at all like that. But it's something that you have to have and you can't go without once you have it. And I wish I never did it. I'm just someone being controlled by a drug. That's it. It's pretty shitty. I don't have any right to get high. I have the responsibility of that son of mine and I have no right to get high.

"It is unconscionable," Ramstad says. "Every day people are dying." According to the Substance Abuse and Mental Health Service Administration (SAMHSA), 22.2 million Americans are addicted to drugs and alcohol, but nine out of ten fail to get the treatment they need. Various studies throughout the country have shown that the number-one obstacle to treatment is cost. Ramstad says, "This is America's number-one public health crisis. Last year, 150,000 Americans died as a direct result of chemical addiction. Two-hundred-seventy-five thousand Americans were denied access to treatment. Treatment center doors were slammed shut on the faces of people who came in for help because they couldn't afford to pay. In some cases they had no insurance. In many, their insurance was inadequate."

"The system is failing," says Eric Goplerud, director of Ensuring Solutions to Alcohol Problems, which reviews state insurance policies for the Department of Health Policy at George Washington University in Washington, DC. "Help is out there, but there are enormous obstacles to getting good treatment. As a result, we are losing people who could be helped. We wouldn't allow this if it were any other disease."

BARRIERS TO TREATMENT:
THE STIGMA OF ADDICTION

Why aren't we doing a better job of helping individuals and their families? Most of it has to do with the stigma of addiction, the experts say. "A lot of people think the taboo of addiction and treatment is gone when the Mel Gibsons and Robin Williamses step up," according to Rick Pine, president of the Livengrin Foundation, a substance-abuse treatment center in Bensalem, Pennsylvania. "But to everyday folks, there's still a barrier to climb over. It's still something people are afraid to talk about."

One reason is the shame associated with addiction. In spite of the fact that addiction is a disease—and in spite of the conclusions of the American Medical Association, the World Health Organization, and doctors and researchers worldwide—there remains a notion, whether it is expressed overtly or hidden, that addicts are to be blamed for their own suffering. They are viewed by some as weak

Employee Assistance Is Cost-Effective

Samuel B. Bacharach, PhD

Director, Smithers Institute for Alcohol-Related Workplace Studies, Cornell University

Employers often ask if workplace intervention is worth it. In fact, Employee Assistance Programs (EAPs) spring from the understanding that by helping employees better manage their personal problems, employers will be able to enhance employee productivity.

Federal data estimate that in 2002 (the most recent year for which data are available), alcohol and drug use cost U.S. employers more than $128.6 billion in lost productivity, and an additional $15.8 billion in substance use–related employee healthcare costs, typically covered by employer-paid insurance premiums. Much of the lost productivity stems from an increased rate of absenteeism and tardiness among workers with substance-use problems. Alcoholism alone causes 500 million lost workdays annually. One major automaker reports that substance-using employees average forty days of sick leave annually versus five days for non-using employees.

Alcohol and other drug problems also take their toll on productivity in the form of industrial accidents and fatalities. Up to 40 percent of industrial fatalities can be linked to alcohol use, and 47 percent of all industrial injuries are attributed to substance use.

All of these side effects from employee substance use add up to enormous costs. But EAPs and Members Assistance Programs (MAPs) are major cost savers. One study has shown that a successful on-site EAP or MAP can cost as little as $30 per employee annually. In an analysis of the effectiveness of the MAP of a large construction union in New York City, we found that the union-based aftercare service (weekly AA-type group sessions led by the MAP director) played a significant role in lowering relapse rates and paid insurance claims.

In short, the workplace matters. In the case of helping employees beat drug and alcohol addiction, it matters a lot.

and amoral. According to a 2001 national survey titled "The Face of Recovery," one-quarter of people in recovery reported they had been denied a job or promotion or had trouble getting insurance, and four in ten said they experienced shame or social embarrassment.

These experiences are supported by the findings of focus groups conducted by Goplerud's organization with corporate executives to discuss coverage for substance-abuse treatment in their company-sponsored health plans. "Most of them knew about the research that has identified the biological factors associated with addiction, but they still weren't sure they wanted to pay for what they still consider bad behavior."

Stigmatization has led to relatively meager insurance coverage for the treatment of addiction, compared with what is available for most other diseases. In addition, when many cities, counties, and states are in the midst of budget crises, it has led to cuts in addiction treatment from public health systems. "When it comes to the availability of accessible addiction treatments, we are way behind where we should be—and where we could be," says Galloway. "We need more research into treatments and, meanwhile, existing treatments must be accessible to everyone who needs them. For now, addicts and their families must work extremely hard to find appropriate and accessible treatments. Sometimes it feels like a miracle that people get well."

Another reason addicts are stigmatized is that people don't understand that treatment, although it takes time and may involve relapse, actually works. "I still don't think the general public believes that an addict or alcoholic ever gets well," Phillip Valentine, executive director of Connecticut Community for Addiction Recovery, told *The Capital Times* of Hartford. "Many, many people have long-term, sustained sobriety and you may not know about it. We need to put a face on recovery so people won't be so afraid or fearful or angry at it. It's not a hopeless condition."

Whatever the reasons behind the stigma, the implications are dramatic. Goplerud says there are laws in a handful of states that require insurers to treat addiction as a chronic disease, like diabetes or cancer; these states include

How to Fight Addiction Discrimination

Paul N. Samuels, JD

Director and president, Legal Action Center

You don't have to live with discrimination—you can act to stop or remedy it! Consider these options:

Informal resolution

You many want to try to talk to the person who you believe has discriminated against you, and ask why that person took the action that you believe is discriminatory. This may accomplish two things. Getting the person to admit that the action was taken because of your drug or alcohol history will help you prove a claim if you decide to resort to formal legal proceedings. It may also give you an opportunity to sit down and discuss the matter, stress your qualifications, and determine if the matter can be resolved informally.

Administrative appeals (sometimes)

If you believe a government agency (such as a public employer or occupational licensing agency, public housing agency, or government benefits program) discriminated against you, you may have the right to challenge the action in an administrative appeal to that agency or another one designated to hear such appeals. Always check if there is a deadline for appealing this way.

Formal legal challenges—charging a violation of the federal antidiscrimination laws that protect people from disability-based discrimination, such as the Americans with Disabilities Act

If you believe you have been or are being discriminated against because of your history of addiction in violation of these federal laws, you can challenge the violation of your rights. You may be able to get those charged with the discrimination to correct their actions and policies, compensate you, or give you other relief.

→ Discrimination complaint—with federal (or state) agency. You may file a complaint with the Office of Civil Rights of the federal agency(s) with power to investigate and remedy violations of the disability discrimination laws. In many states, these complaints may be filed with the state human rights agency. You do not need a lawyer to do this, and it can be faster and easier than a lawsuit and get you the same remedies.

Do not sleep on your rights!

The deadline for filing these administrative complaints can be as soon as 180 days after the discriminatory act—or even sooner, with federal employers, so always check.

→ Discrimination lawsuit—in federal or state court. In most (but not all) cases, you may also file a lawsuit in federal or state court, in addition to or instead of filing an administrative complaint. Deadlines vary from one to three years.

Connecticut, Delaware, Indiana, Kentucky, Minnesota, New Jersey, Vermont, and Virginia. However, in Arizona, Idaho, Iowa, Oklahoma, and Wyoming, insurers aren't required to pay for treatment or recovery programs. In the rest of the nation, coverage is minimal. "If you need the extended treatment recommended for a good chance at recovery, you're out of luck," says Ramstad.

And rather than expanding, Goplerud says, "Coverage for addiction and alcoholism is actually eroding." He says insurance companies today pay roughly 25 percent of all claims related to alcohol and drug addiction treatment and recovery expenses, down from a third in 1991. Another problem, Goplerud says, is that thirty-two states still enforce statutes enacted in 1947—the Uniform Accident and Sickness Policy Provision Laws—that allow insurance companies to refuse payment to hospital emergency rooms if alcohol or drugs were involved in the problem that brought you there. So they don't jeopardize being paid for their services, many hospitals instruct ER doctors not to diagnose or treat alcoholism or addiction, only the injury. Goplerud says, "It's a missed opportunity to help millions of people."

Ramstad and Kennedy are pushing the insurance coverage parity bill at the federal level. Meanwhile, Goplerud and others are trying to convince companies to invest in treatment—"If not because it's the right thing to do, because it will save them money," he says. On his organization's web site, a calculator compares the losses due to untreated addiction to the savings a company would realize if its insurance provider did cover treatment. "When you see the figures, it's a no-brainer," Goplerud says. "You save money in missed days of work plus extra healthcare costs, including ER visits and hospital days."

Ramstad says, "We have all the empirical data to show that we save money if we treat addictions." He cites a RAND Corporation study that showed the average health insurance premium increase attributable to full treatment would be less than one-half of 1 percent. He continues, "In addition, we know that for every person who's treated, we actually treat four people, which is the average number of people who are directly impacted by one person's addiction.

We can save marriages, save families, save careers. Treating addiction makes good economic sense and good social sense. Eighty percent or more of all [prison] inmates are there because of drugs and alcohol. Think of the results of that: all the children whose fathers and mothers are incarcerated. Studies show that for every dollar spent on addiction treatment, we save seven to twelve dollars in direct primary health care costs as well as costs associated with criminal justice and social services. Other than ignorance and prejudice, there's no reason not to fix this."

FINDING A TREATMENT PROVIDER

Experts suggest calling reputable sources—physicians, drug and alcohol counselors, school health counselors, research and other hospitals. In addition, *Treating Teens: A Guide to Adolescent Drug Programs* lists 144 adolescent treatment programs across the country. It is available at www.drugstrategies.org. For referrals to psychiatrists who specialize in addiction, the American Academy of Addiction Psychiatry web site (www.aaap.org) lists licensed practitioners throughout the country. It is also worth checking with state mental health organizations to find out if, and how, treatment centers are licensed or accredited. "These seals of approval are no guarantee it's a good program, but it's a place to start," says TRI's McLellan.

As outlined in the previous chapter, medical assessment is the first step in determining whether a person needs treatment and, if so, what type. Often, managed withdrawal is next. Experts in assessment and detoxification can often recommend good programs; they routinely send their patients to them. Word of mouth—personal referrals—can be useful, too, but it's important to know that what works for one addict may not work for another. Personal recommendations shouldn't replace professional ones.

In addition to consulting professionals, most experts advise people to research programs to learn what they offer. As a general rule, the experts advise people to look for programs that offer evidence-based cognitive and behavioral therapies, medication therapies for alcohol or opiate dependence, individual and group therapies, education about addiction, family programs if that is appropriate, and relapse prevention counseling. Once again, if a patient has co-occurring disorders, the program should include treatment for addiction as well as the other illness. Look for addiction psychiatrists and doctors who are ASAM-certified.

If you're fortunate, your consultations and research will direct you to the best place for treatment.

GETTING ADDICTION TREATMENT: EMPLOYEE ASSISTANCE PROGRAMS

Some employee assistance programs (EAPs) cover addiction treatment, Goplerud says, but currently most are extremely limited. Many offer a few sessions with a therapist or a brief detox, which isn't enough to help most people. In addition, there are disincentives for employees to use the help that is available. "In some companies, people still can be fired for admitting they have a problem with drugs or alcohol," he says.

On the other hand, there are some trailblazing companies with what Goplerud calls "enlightened policies"— comprehensive plans that cover treatment for alcoholism and addiction. He cites Quad Graphics, a private commercial printing company based in Milwaukee, and Kimberly-Clark, the hygiene-products maker. In addition to some individual companies sprinkled throughout the country, some labor organizations have addressed the problem for their members.

One is the Steamfitters Union, Local 638 in New York, which was frustrated by the restrictions of its insurance plan when it came to coverage for alcoholism and addiction. "Everyone knew the steamfitters," says Don Perks, director of the union's EAP. "We were the hardest workers and the biggest drinkers."

Many union members were alcoholics and addicts, Perks says, but it was a culture in which such problems were hidden. "We decided to bring it out of the closet," he says. "We decided to face it for what it was: a disaster that was destroying families, destroying lives."

The union's insurance premiums were sharply rising and it had great trouble finding insurance for its members that adequately covered addiction treatment. It decided on a radical change. The union worked with addiction special-

Expert Advice

Challenging Your Insurance Company

Deb Beck, MS

President, Drug and Alcohol Services Providers Organization of Pennsylvania

Forty-three states require commercial, group health insurance plans, including managed care plans, to provide coverage for addiction treatment. The states without such laws are Arizona, Georgia, Idaho, Indiana, Iowa, Oklahoma, and Wyoming. (Visit www.natlalliance.org to check your state law.) Group health insurance plans are required to comply with state laws and any additional coverage that employers may request. However, health plans have a financial incentive to deny treatment and to misinterpret the requirements of employers and state laws.

→ **Check your addiction treatment coverage in your employee benefit handbook.**
Ask your employer for help, if appropriate. Your employer can override the decision of the health plan or managed-care company.

→ **Ask for the assistance of the state insurance department, state health department, and the office of the attorney general.**
These state offices are responsible for enforcing the addiction treatment laws. Speak up!

→ **Ask your local state legislator to intervene.**
Legislators appropriate funding to the state offices listed above and expect the laws they pass to be enforced.

→ **Ask addiction treatment facilities for help while you fight the health plan.**
Limited alternative funding is sometimes available. If you are serious about challenging the insurer, the treatment program will usually stand by you.

→ **Use treatment facilities that will help you.**
Programs that will start treatment immediately—while you challenge the health plan—understand the seriousness of the illness.

→ **Be prepared to hold your health plan accountable and expect to challenge them.**
Be sure to document all interactions.

NEVER DELAY TREATMENT WHILE YOU FIGHT YOUR INSURER!

ists to create a treatment program that would become a model in the United States and would allow the union, not the insurance company, to determine what is covered. Now any member of the Steamfitters Union, Local 638 with a problem with drug addiction or alcoholism is covered for a full range of treatments. First, they are counseled and assessed. If they are in need of treatment, the union arranges for members to be picked up and driven to a hospital for detox. After detox, they are picked up from the hospital and driven to a thirty-day inpatient rehab program. If a counselor or doctor prescribes more time, the union—not an insurance company representative—extends the program. The union then provides long-term aftercare and continuing care. Fourteen hundred union members have been through the program since it began in 1986. Perks says the union has studied the impact of its program: "We're saving money," he says. "And we're saving lives."

Unfortunately, the Steamfitters Union and other companies with good coverage are the exception. That, says Ramstad, "is a national disgrace." It's a personal crusade for Ramstad, cochair of the Addiction Treatment and Recovery Caucus. He is a recovering alcoholic who's been sober for two and a half decades. In 1981, Ramstad woke up in a jail cell in South Dakota. He had been arrested for disorderly conduct while in an alcoholic blackout. "I was able to get help," he says. "But many people can't."

GETTING ADDICTION TREATMENT: INSURANCE

If you have insurance, the first step is to see what's covered. Some plans pay almost nothing. Most pay for detox—but there is usually a cap on the number of days or instances. Some insurance programs cover thirty days of inpatient treatment—but often that depends upon whether a fourth party, the managed-care company, agrees that it is "medically necessary."

Ultimately, one should be aggressive with insurance companies. And persistent. Often insurance companies will say no, but they may change their decisions upon appeal. It's always worth asking if programs have sliding fee scales; many do. Some have grants. Ask them.

GETTING TREATMENT WITHOUT INSURANCE

There are also options for those who do not have health insurance that covers substance abuse or mental health services. In some cities, there are free or almost free community-based treatment programs in hospitals and clinics. In some communities there are treatment facilities run by St. Vincent De Paul, the Salvation Army, and similar organizations. In addition, Medicaid covers some treatment costs for low-income patients. In 2007, the Centers for Medicare and Medicaid services announced that for the first time, they will pay for alcohol and drug screening and brief intervention.

To find free programs, you should call local and state health services and clinics and religious and community-based organizations. If they don't offer free services, they may know who does. You can also check research hospitals in your area to see if they have ongoing clinical trials and need volunteers. "Many different clinical research trials are underway across the nation, and new treatment interventions—behavioral or medications—may be available in a location close to you," says Anna Rose Childress of the Philadelphia VA Medical Center at the University of Pennsylvania School of Medicine. "Research treatments are usually available at no cost, since they are supported by research grants." A list of clinical treatment trials for addiction/relapse prevention supported by the National Institutes of Health can be found at www.clinicaltrials.gov.

If free programs aren't available in your community, try looking in nearby communities. "There are treatments out there," Galloway says. "They aren't easy to find, but the price for not finding treatment is always higher."

Clearly, there are hurdles to getting treated. The programs are often overcrowded, with long waiting lists. But, says Ling, "Addicts need to be treated when they are ready to be treated. If they have to wait a month or two or three, they may change their minds. We can easily lose them. They can die."

Not surprisingly, the public systems are overburdened. "Yes, there are community mental health and substance abuse agencies in most cities that offer publicly funded treatment programs," Goplerud says. "But generally they

The Benefits of Drug Courts

Douglas B. Marlowe, JD, PhD

Director, Division on Law and Ethics Research, Treatment Research Institute

Drug courts serve certain people who have been charged with a misdemeanor or felony offense that is either drug-related or was committed to support a drug habit. Participants in drug courts avoid criminal prosecution or imprisonment in exchange for completing an intensive regimen of treatment and supervisory services.

Clients must participate in needed treatment sessions and submit urine samples that are tested for drugs on a random weekly basis. Clients also appear frequently before the judge to review their progress in treatment. The judge may administer positive rewards for doing well or negative sanctions for doing poorly. Rewards may include praise, small gifts, and certificates of recognition. Sanctions may include a verbal scolding, written homework assignments, fines, community service, or even a few days in jail. Graduation leads to the ultimate reward: either the criminal charges are dropped or the sentence is considerably reduced in length or harshness.

Research indicates that clients in drug courts receive more treatment services, closer monitoring, and more certain and immediate consequences for their behaviors than individuals in most other types of criminal justice programs. They also engage in less drug use during treatment and have lower re-arrest rates for up to three years after their arrest. Largely because of this success, there are now more than 1,750 drug courts in the United States and its territories. There are also more than eight hundred other types of "problem-solving courts" that are similar to drug courts, but focus on other issues such as driving while impaired (DWI), mental illness, juvenile delinquency, or domestic violence. Unfortunately, despite their impressive growth, drug courts still serve less than 5 to 10 percent of the people who need them, according to estimates. Nearly two-thirds of local counties do not have a drug court, and many that do can handle only a relatively small number of people.

Five things to ask about drug courts

1. Am I or my loved one eligible?
In some jurisdictions, drug courts are only open to individuals charged with simple possession or use of drugs. Other jurisdictions may admit people charged with drug dealing, theft, or property crimes, but only if a significant drug problem led to the criminal activity. Individuals charged with violent crimes are rarely eligible.

2. How do I access these programs?

The prosecutor makes the initial decision about whether to consider an individual for drug court. The final decision is then made by the judge after reviewing all of the pertinent information, including clinical assessment results and the individual's past criminal record. In some counties, all individuals charged with eligible crimes are routinely screened by the prosecution. In others, the matter may need to be specifically brought to the prosecutor's or judge's attention. This requires defense attorneys to be knowledgeable about the available options and how and when to make a request.

3. What rights must I or my loved one give up? What are the penalties for poor performance?

Just like in a plea bargain, the client must waive certain rights to participate, such as the right to a trial. They must also give consent for treatment-related information to be shared with the court and prosecution, and to be subjected to certain types of sanctions for infractions without the benefit of a full trial or due process hearing. Nonattendance in treatment, continued drug use, or a poor attitude can earn punitive sanctions from the court that gradually increase in magnitude. Eventually, these sanctions can become quite restrictive and may include brief intervals of jail or placement in a residential treatment setting. Failure to complete the program results in sentencing on the original charge; the client might not receive credit for time served in the program. Indeed, he or she might receive a stiffer sentence than would otherwise been have imposed because of the demonstrated inability or unwillingness to improve. It is important to consider this before deciding whether to participate.

4. Are all programs created equal?

Like all treatment programs, the quality of care can vary considerably. Some drug courts have a wide array of treatment services available to them, whereas others may have relatively little to offer. This can be a particular challenge in rural or poor communities. In addition, some drug court judges may be very patient and lenient with clients, whereas others may be unduly harsh. Defense attorneys often have a good sense of the quality of various programs.

5. How do I find a drug court in my county?

The National Association of Drug Court Professionals (NADCP) maintains a list of drug courts and other problem-solving courts in every state and territory in the United States as well as a list of primary contact persons for each jurisdiction. In addition, the BJA Drug Court Clearinghouse at American University maintains a list of drug courts organized by state and county.

Treatment Centers by State

WA 6,287,759 pop.

OR 3,641,056 pop.

MT 935,670 pop.

ND 636,677 pop.

MN 5,132,799 pop.

ID 1,429,096 pop.

SD 775,933 pop.

WI 5,536,201

WY 509,294 pop.

IA 2,966,334 pop.

NV 2,414,807 pop.

IL 12,76

UT 2,469,585 pop.

CO 4,665,177 pop.

NE 1,758,787 pop.

CA 36,132,147 pop.

KS 2,744,687 pop.

MO 5,800,310 pop.

AZ 5,939,292 pop.

NM 1,928,384 pop.

OK 3,547,884 pop.

AR 2,779,154 pop.

HI 1,275,194 pop.

TX 22,859,968 pop.

LA 4,534,628 pop.

AK 663,661 pop.

Number of Treatment Facilities

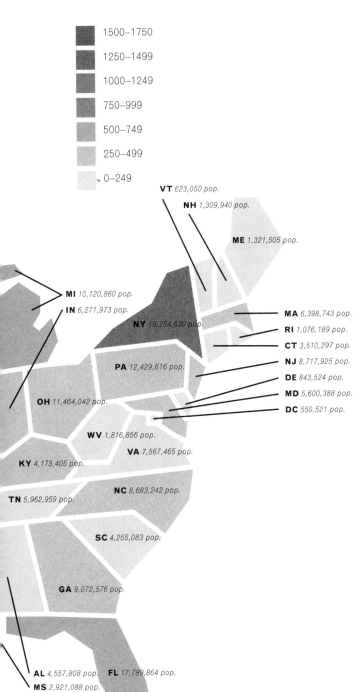

⬛	1500–1750
⬛	1250–1499
⬛	1000–1249
⬛	750–999
⬛	500–749
⬛	250–499
⬛	0–249

VT 623,050 pop.
NH 1,309,940 pop.
ME 1,321,505 pop.
MI 10,120,860 pop.
IN 6,271,973 pop.
NY 19,254,630 pop.
MA 6,398,743 pop.
RI 1,076,189 pop.
CT 3,510,297 pop.
PA 12,429,616 pop.
NJ 8,717,925 pop.
DE 843,524 pop.
MD 5,600,388 pop.
OH 11,464,042 pop.
DC 550,521 pop.
WV 1,816,856 pop.
VA 7,567,465 pop.
KY 4,173,405 pop.
NC 8,683,242 pop.
TN 5,962,959 pop.
SC 4,255,083 pop.
GA 9,072,576 pop.
AL 4,557,808 pop.
FL 17,789,864 pop.
MS 2,921,088 pop.

Number of Drug Courts by State

ALABAMA	28
ALASKA	10
ARIZONA	35
ARKANSAS	31
CALIFORNIA	160
COLORADO	24
CONNECTICUT	3
DELAWARE	14
DISTRICT OF COLUMBIA	4
FLORIDA	95
GEORGIA	41
HAWAII	11
IDAHO	38
ILLINOIS	26
INDIANA	28
IOWA	10
KANSAS	6
KENTUCKY	52
LOUISIANA	46
MAINE	15
MARYLAND	30
MASSACHUSETTS	28
MICHIGAN	65
MINNESOTA	17
MISSISSIPPI	15
MISSOURI	119
MONTANA	13
NEBRASKA	12
NEVADA	38
NEW HAMPSHIRE	7
NEW JERSEY	26
NEW MEXICO	33
NEW YORK	164
NORTH CAROLINA	38
NORTH DAKOTA	7
OHIO	70
OKLAHOMA	53
OREGON	32
PENNSYLVANIA	21
RHODE ISLAND	8
SOUTH CAROLINA	22
SOUTH DAKOTA	4
TENNESSEE	28
TEXAS	52
UTAH	28
VERMONT	4
VIRGINIA	28
WASHINGTON	43
WEST VIRGINIA	3
WISCONSIN	13
WYOMING	25

have to do triage first. They have to take people who are under court supervision and are mandated to be in treatment. And they take people who are absolute train wrecks, because they have to."

Ironically, more than one expert says, as Goplerud put it, "If you have no insurance, the way to get the intensive substance abuse treatment that you need is to commit a crime." He says he's only half joking. In many states, drug courts and criminal justice programs send nonviolent felons with alcohol or drug problems into treatment that is paid for by the state or a municipality (see pages 198–199).

"Of course, sobriety is difficult under the most ideal circumstances, and no one has those," says Rawson. "It may not be easy to find help, especially affordable help, but it is out there. You must do everything you can to get into treatment. If it's for a loved one, you must try everything you can to get them into treatment. Every day, people are being treated. Every day, lives are saved. If addicts trying to get well are as tenacious in their search for treatment as they were in their search for drugs, they will find it. Do not give up. Work tirelessly to find the treatment you need."

In 2006, Joan Ward, the mother from Cranberry Township, Pennsylvania, testified before the Pennsylvania state legislature about the paucity of affordable addiction treatment in America. Her son was addicted to drugs. She tried to find treatment, but was unsuccessful. He is currently in jail. Ward spoke gravely, with an unwavering voice, her hands folded in front of her. "We can build a better system," she concluded, "or we can continue to bury our children."

The longer an addict stays in treatment, the greater the chance treatment will be effective.

ALEC

Recovery: It Really *Is* One Day at a Time

I feel good. Occasionally, I'll look at a glass of wine and want to taste it, especially if it's really expensive. But basically what's happened to me is that I feel good about myself again. I can work out. I can still tap dance. I can still dance. ALEC, RECOVERING ALCOHOLIC

"I'm Sarah and I'm an addict and alcoholic."

The line was familiar. It is a standard yet profound admission that is heard every day and every night in countless twelve-step meetings throughout the country and the rest of the world.

Sarah told her story: "I started drinking as a teenager. We drank a lot of beer. I didn't think it was a big deal. At first it wasn't. But in college, drinking led to drugs. Cocaine was my thing. Cocaine was . . . cocaine was it for me. I loved it."

Sarah had short, nearly white blond hair. She wore blocky glasses, a plain white blouse, and a beige skirt. She pushed her glasses up onto the bridge of her nose.

"After a while, I couldn't afford to buy coke, so I started dealing. I sold to an undercover cop, a narc. The next thing I knew, I was in jail and they told me I had one phone call. Like in the movies. I called my mother."

Sarah began crying.

Relapse: Part of a Chronic Disease

Nora D. Volkow, MD

Director, National Institute on Drug Abuse

Despite the availability of many forms of effective treatment for addiction, the problem of relapse remains the major challenge to achieving sustained recovery. People trying to recover from drug abuse and addiction are often doing so with altered brains, strong drug-related memories, and diminished impulse control. Accompanied by intense drug cravings, these brain changes can leave people vulnerable to relapse even after years of being abstinent. Relapse to drug abuse happens at rates similar to the relapse rates for other well-known chronic medical illnesses like diabetes, hypertension, and asthma.

How is relapse to drug abuse similar to what happens with other chronic diseases?

Just as an asthma attack can be triggered by smoke, or a person with diabetes can have a reaction if they eat too much sugar, a drug addict can be "triggered" to return to drug use.

With other chronic diseases, relapse serves as a signal for returning to treatment. The same response is necessary with drug addiction.

As a chronic, recurring illness, addiction may require repeated treatments until abstinence is achieved. Like other diseases, drug addiction can be effectively treated and managed, leading to a healthy and productive life.

To achieve long-term recovery, treatment must address specific, individual patient needs and must take the whole person into account. For it is not enough simply to get a person off drugs; the many changes that have occurred—physical, social, psychological—must also be addressed to help people stay off drugs, for good.

"'Mom,' I said, 'you're not going to believe where I am.'" She wiped her tears on her sleeve. "As far as my mom knew, I was a happy sophomore on the volleyball team studying pre-med. I had a boyfriend—a football star also in pre-med. I got good grades—honor roll. I thought I might become a pediatrician. I loved children. My mom used to tell me that I'd make a good mother. But I said, 'I'm in jail, Mom. I'm in trouble. I'm on drugs.' My mom had no idea. She nearly had a nervous breakdown."

Sarah described what happened next. Rehab. Then relapse. Rehab again. Then relapse. She dropped out of school. Her boyfriend disappeared. She said her life then was about only one thing: "Cocaine in the morning, cocaine in the afternoon, cocaine at night, and all night. Then one day I smoked some coke and I was with some people, and we shot up some smack, too. I still don't remember what happened, but the next thing I knew I woke up in a hospital. They said I was lucky to be alive. I called my mom again..." Sarah looked toward the back of the room. "Well," she continued, "my mom came and she couldn't stop crying."

The room was still. Only the ticking of a fan. Sarah cried harder. So did a woman in the back row.

"I knew I had to get sober or I would die, and so I went back into rehab and this time I did everything they told me. I knew I would get sober and stay sober, and I did. For six years. I gave up on being a doctor, but I was working, and had a boyfriend, and we were going to be married. It took about two years before my mother forgave me for almost killing myself, but she did. We were close. We had lunch once a week and went on walks and . . .

"After six years I thought I'd licked my addiction. I thought, *I messed up as a kid, but that's all over.* Well, I went to a party and someone gave me a joint. I don't have to tell you what happened. Pretty soon I was using again. I was using everything I could get my hands on. I made excuses so I wouldn't have to see my mother. But she came over one day—it was my birthday—and she brought me a present. I didn't answer the door, but she had a key to my apartment. She came inside to leave me a present—later I learned that it was a sweater and bouquet of flowers—and she found me there. I was there unconscious. I'd OD'ed again. She felt for a pulse and there wasn't one." Sarah wept, but stopped herself. "My mom called 911. Later she told me she was hysterical when the emergency team came and worked to resuscitate me. They had to restrain her. She was screaming at them, 'You have to save my baby! Please, God, please.'

"At the hospital, a doctor said I was lucky to be alive. I *was* lucky to be alive. It was the second time I was told that. But I didn't feel lucky. I felt like shit. I couldn't believe I had relapsed. I swore I would never use again and there I was. I relapsed. I wanted to die. My mother came in to see me, and I couldn't look at her. I said I wanted to die, and she looked at me with an expression that scared the hell out of me. She said, 'I can't take this anymore. If you want to kill yourself, go ahead.' She left. I cried out, 'Mom, no!' But she kept going."

Sarah cried more but managed to say, "That was five years ago. I didn't see her for five years. I'm five years sober. Today. She's here tonight with me." Sarah cried uncontrollably. Her mother in the back row of the meeting cried, too. Looking only at her mother in the back of the room, Sarah said, "Thanks, Mom." She said, "I love you, Mom."

THE REALITY OF RELAPSE

Relapse is heartbreaking for addicts. It is heartbreaking for those who care about them. Relapse can be devastating. Recovering from relapse is likely, but nonetheless, every relapse comes with the possibility of death. "There are psychological and biological reasons that relapse sometimes is fatal," says Tom McLellan, PhD, co-founder of Philadelphia's Treatment Research Institute. "A biological reason is their previous use probably built up slowly to a high level of tolerance and adaptation. Without slowly building up again, they easily can do too much and overdose. The psychological reason is what is called the 'abstinence violation effect'—the despair and defeat an addict feels when they leave an abstinent lifestyle. They may feel that they don't want to come back from a relapse."

Even if they survive it, relapse can be devastating. It can feel like the ultimate defeat. An addict thinks, *I blew it.* Their family often blames them. But is it their fault? "Yes it is and no it isn't," says Walter Ling, MD, director of the UCLA program. "It is not their fault but it is their fault. That is, it's unanswerable and ultimately it's irrelevant. The bottom and relevant line is that we—addicts, their families, healthcare professionals, researchers—all have the same goal: keep people sober. Let's focus on that instead of these circular, unanswerable arguments. They relapse and, if they survive, they then have the opportunity to get sober again."

The experts now know that it can and often does take relapse—often more than one—for someone to stay sober.

When dealing with addiction, one learns to live with the counterintuitive notion that while the decision to take the drug is a choice, once it is back in the addict's system, the brain is altered and the disease takes over. "At that point, voluntary behavior becomes a compulsive behavior as a result of the changes to the brain," says Richard Rawson, also of the UCLA program. "The disease makes them do terrible things, but it doesn't make them terrible people. At the same time, it doesn't mean they are not responsible for bad things they may do." These are the contradictions inherent in addiction.

Relapse is high-risk, but nonetheless, the experts now know that it can and often does take relapse—often more than one—for someone to stay sober. "All the data say that the more times you keep trying, you increase your likelihood of that success being more sustained. And that is really, really important," explains Anna Rose Childress of the Center for Studies of Addiction.

RELAPSE IS NOT INEVITABLE
For addicts and their families, it may feel overwhelming to imagine years, if not decades, of a cycle of recovery interrupted by relapse stopped by a new period of recovery followed by yet another relapse. But the horror stories

Jason OREGON

Jason is a husband and father of two. He has made repeated attempts to stop drinking.

I drink a lot. Every waking hour involves me drinking. And it affects my family. There was one time when I was trying to quit and I was standing with my daughter, drinking a soda. She looked at me and she cried, "Dad, what are you doing?" And I said, "I'm drinking a soda." And she said, "You don't drink soda. That's not a beer. You need a beer." And she tried to go get me a beer. It was a realization that I've already had thousands of times: I'm not a good dad.

I'm the bad guy here. I got mad at my wife for writing me a message: "Jason—We love you and want you healthy! DON'T DRINK!" The message is awesome. And I feel bad about getting mad that Sherry would write me a loving message like this. I know the family cares, but I'm trying my hardest not to drink, and she's throwing this at me? I confronted her for writing it. I said, "Look. I don't need another message." But there it is. And the whole thing really sucks, for me to be such a selfish person that I can't acknowledge somebody doing this. I can't say, "I am so glad that you're doing this for me."

Poor Sherry and my poor kids; they don't know if it's gonna be a nice daddy today, or if it's gonna be a bad daddy today. And the whole point is, we never know. Is this gonna be a good day or a bad day? A bad day is Jason yelling, Jason upset. Whether or not there's something wrong, Jason's gonna find something that's wrong. And I usually get really angry. Where does that anger come from? It comes from me being sorry for myself because I can't solve my own problems.

I feel like alcohol is my best friend. And that's the hardest part of quitting, because I drink all the time. The craving for alcohol doesn't go away. Let's say tonight I decide to give it up and tomorrow I'm not gonna drink. It's an easy thought if I'm still drunk. But tomorrow when I wake up, it's like there's a sense of loss, a sense of grief. It's like, *Oh fuck, well, now I can't drink.*

I've been trying to quit drinking for a long time. I feel hopeless about the whole thing. I don't think I can quit. I want to. I think it is willpower that's stopping me. I've done AA; I've been through treatment centers, but they really didn't

do much for me. They told me exactly what is wrong with me. They showed me things that I could have learned in a science or health class. But they didn't teach me how to stay off drugs and alcohol. That might have been their main function, but that's not what I got out of it.

The second time I relapsed, I was riding a bus to work. I didn't have any thoughts of drinking. I had twenty minutes before I had to be at work. And I was like, *What am I gonna do with twenty minutes?* I remember this very clearly now. I got off the bus, ran into a convenience store, grabbed

I feel like alcohol is my best friend. And that's the hardest part of quitting, because I drink all the time. The craving for alcohol doesn't go away.

The first time I came out of treatment was an absolute failure. I don't even know how it happened. I was sober. I was done with drinking. Everything was a-okay. And then one day I walked into a store. I don't even know why I was in the store. And I bought a couple of the forty-ouncers that I used to drink. That's how fast it happened. It was like a snap of the finger. That was it.

a 32, and drank it. And then I thought, *Okay, I've still got fifteen minutes, I'll get one more.* Every time I bought a beer, I ran behind some buildings into the woods to drink it. I couldn't stop. By the time I was done, I was drunk. I hadn't had a drink in six months. And I called work and said, "Well, I can't make it."

aren't meant to discourage or to make the task of recovery seem overwhelming. Instead, they are meant to present a lesson inherent in this picture: one should remain hyper-vigilant, because the specter of relapse is always present for most addicts.

Still, the fact that time and mistakes are part of the process may terrify some addicts and their families. Worse, this data may suggest to some that relapse is inevitable. It is not inevitable. Some addicts never relapse. It is crucial for addicts and those who love them to understand that relapse is not a given. Every addict and every alcoholic writes their own unique story; statistics inform us of the enormous range of outcomes but don't predict the outcome for any single individual. It's worth saying again: some people never relapse. Of course that is the goal. That is what addicts and alcoholics and their families pray for.

One problem with acknowledging that relapse can be part of the process of recovery may be that it seems like a Get Out of Jail Free card for addicts—permission, or at least an excuse, to relapse. It is not a Get Out of Jail Free card. Quite the contrary. It cannot be repeated enough times: every relapse is potentially lethal.

In New York City, an addict in recovery for twelve years felt that she had, as she informed a friend, licked her addiction. "Thank God," she said, "I no longer have to live with the monkey on my back." She had a good job and, after a history of failed relationships—victims of her addiction—a solid marriage. She had two children, a son and daughter, both of whom she adored. She often showed off their photographs: a bright-eyed girl, age 12, with doe eyes and pigtails, and a handsome boy, 8, posing in a Little League uniform. One weekday night in early 2005, she went out to a meeting and never came home. Later her husband learned that his wife ran into an old friend who was smoking a joint. He passed it to her and she accepted. Why did she accept it? He will never know. Then she accepted a snort of cocaine. Afterward, she drove to the neighborhood of her former drug dealer where she scored heroin, which more than a decade earlier had been her drug of choice. She injected it, overdosed, and died. For her, relapse was not a part of recovery.

One more time: addicts do not have to relapse. Some don't. You, or your loved one, may never relapse.

If treatment is conceived of as an ongoing process that sometimes includes one or more relapses, rather than as a cure, a more realistic notion of success emerges. A relapse can feel less hopeless for the addict and their family if they know that it is relatively common and it can ultimately lead to long, uninterrupted, periods of recovery.

It may be unrealistic to expect every addict to stay sober forever after one or two or three or however many tries at sobriety, but it's important to keep in mind another statistic: "Over half make it. They do reach a state of sustained recovery," says Michael Dennis, the research psychologist.

The good news about relapse is that it often leads not only to a new period of recovery, but recovery has a new character—a new urgency. An addict has learned more about themselves and their illness. Addicts who return to recovery may start out discouraged, but often they discover that the rewards of sobriety are greater than they ever could have imagined.

THE SCIENCE OF RELAPSE

Given the high risk, why do those in recovery relapse? If only there were just one reason. If only it were predictable. Even after rehab or multiple rehabs, many things can facilitate this return to drug use. One of the goals of rehab is to prevent relapse by teaching addicts to avoid situations that may trigger a relapse—the people, places, and things that remind an addict of the drug. As Charles O'Brien, of the Center for Studies of Addiction, says, "When a person who has this disease is exposed to cues, or stimuli, that remind them of or previously have been associated with the use of the drug, there is an uncontrollable reflex that happens very, very quickly. The person doesn't have the ability to stop it. It may happen before they are even conscious of it." Ongoing recovery requires addicts to stay away from triggers as much as possible. "Addicts must learn to recognize situations that could lead to relapse and avoid them," NIDA's Nora Volkow explains.

"I never meant to get high," says Randy, a meth addict in Sacramento. He had been sober for two years. "I can tell

Managing Craving

Anna Rose Childress, PhD

Research associate professor, Department of Psychiatry, University of Pennsylvania School of Medicine

You can get help with managing craving, and there is much ongoing research aimed at the development of more effective anticraving interventions (for food, drugs, sex, gambling, etc.).

Both anticraving medications and anticraving behavioral strategies may be helpful to inhibit or "Stop!" drug craving. Many of these medications have been well studied; others are in the early stages of testing.

Five things to do about craving
When you have an episode of craving:

1. Try to view the craving in a matter-of-fact way. Having a craving does *not* mean that you are unmotivated—or that you are doomed to relapse.

2. Learn about your craving triggers, and how to manage them. This will be an important part of your recovery from addiction.

3. Try anticraving behavioral strategies, such as the "five-minute contract" (making a contract with yourself not to act on the desire for the next five minutes, and then engaging in a distracting activity in the meantime). Many urges are short-lived—you will find they are weaker if you can "surf through" the first few minutes.

4. Find a trained treatment professional to help you work through the behavioral techniques that may be helpful in managing cravings. Though treatment manuals are available that offer behavioral tools, the guidance of a trained professional may be invaluable for getting the most out of your treatment efforts.

5. Consider an anticraving medication. Craving can erupt quickly and feel overwhelming, making it difficult to put to use behavioral anticraving strategies, even well-learned ones. An anticraving medication may give you a better chance to use the tools you have learned. Some FDA-approved medications for alcohol and heroin addiction may have a beneficial effect on cue-triggered craving; medications for cue-induced cigarette craving and cue-induced cocaine/methamphetamine craving are the focus of many ongoing research studies. Several medications that may work for more than one type of craving, offering "one-stop shopping" for those with more than one addiction, are already under study or in the early research phase.

you about it now, but at the time I had no idea what had happened to me. Believe it or not, it started with a TV show. There was this great music—the Stones—and this guy was drinking a martini. Martinis had been my drink. The next thing I knew, I was high again after two years sober. I went down quickly. Pills, then meth, and then one day I got into a screaming fight with my wife and I thought, *How did this happen? How did I start using again?*"

The answer is a process known as cueing that originates in the skewed "Stop and Go" system of the addicted brain (see Chapter 2). When an addict—even one who is working to recover—encounters a certain trigger, or cue, the "Go!" system overwhelms the part of the brain that's telling them, "Stop! This is a very bad idea!" Studies have shown that addicts respond to cues on a visceral level. "It's as if a switch is turned on," says Edythe London, PhD, a professor of Psychiatry and Biobehavioral Sciences and Molecular and Medical Pharmacology, at the David Geffen School of Medicine at UCLA. "They may or may not be aware of it."

A cue can be anything from the smell of a chemical reminiscent of crack burning in a pipe to the sight of a particular street corner. The trigger can also be something essential to the addicted person's life: one man in recovery realized that his addiction was triggered by the deadline pressure of his chosen profession as a journalist, and was prompted to start a new career. Many people in recovery move away from their old neighborhoods to escape known triggers.

Some addicts or alcoholics associate the drug with sex. "Arousal can be a powerful cue," says Rawson. "People who associate a drug with sex may be doing fine in treatment until they find themselves sexually stimulated by anything from a strip club to a sexual situation or an X-rated video." He recalls a patient who had been in recovery for a year but relapsed on cocaine after driving by a strip club he had visited when he was using. That one night he overdosed and died.

"The motor starts running even for someone who had no intention of using drugs," Rawson explains. "The patient sees, smells, or experiences something that reminds them of the drug. They don't then say to themselves, *Remember what*

What If Relapse Happens?

Thomas McLellan, PhD

Co-Founder and CEO, Treatment Research Institute

There is no cure for addiction, but it can be effectively managed. Even effectively treated individuals will confront unexpected situations upon return to their home environment that will produce potentially intense periods of craving to reuse alcohol and other drugs.

Lapse: Reuse of alcohol or drugs at least once following treatment occurs in at least 50 percent of those who complete treatment. The most dangerous period for lapse is the first three to six months after completing formal treatment.

Relapse: A return to excessive or problematic use is less common, occurring in approximately 20 to 30 percent of those who complete formal care in the prior year.

Treatment preparation

It is critical that patients, their families, and friends are prepared for the possibility of lapse or relapse before it happens, to keep that problem from becoming a full-blown relapse. Planning during the treatment process is among the best clinical practices to forestall or detect a lapse. Patients who complete effective addiction treatment should expect to:

→ Recognize they have a problem that will require continued management and monitoring.

→ Learn and practice some of the fundamental skills needed to recognize and overcome the urge to use drugs or drink when these situations emerge.

→ Be engaged into a continuing care program such as AA and receive regular monitoring of substance use through urine screening or a Breathalyzer.

→ Receive periodic phone calls or in-home visits from a counselor following treatment to monitor recovery.

Post-treatment preparation

To prevent and contain relapse, the family should agree to fully participate in planned continuing care activities. There are steps that can be taken by family and all concerned others:

→ Have copies of the continuing-care plan prominently displayed to reduce ambiguity and promote full communication and response.

→ Early during formal treatment, ask the recovering addict to describe, in writing, some of the very early signs and behaviors that could lead to lapse and relapse. (For example, "I will begin seeing my friend Jimmy." "I will not do my homework." "I will not attend AA meetings.") Monitor these early warning signs post-treatment.

→ Ask the affected family member early on what they think should be done when relapse signs emerge. Immediately following completion of formal treatment, use the responses to develop a contract regarding the plan for actions upon detection of any of these signs. Be prepared—before the relapse happens—to take the type of actions contracted.

→ Receive and display the results of post-treatment urine screens. Praise good results.

→ Monitor and support changes that are consistent with a drug-free lifestyle. In other words, catch them doing something good and then encourage it appropriately.

happened last time? You lost your job, almost lost your life. Those thoughts are not part of the mix. They are beyond thought."

Researchers use brain imaging to better understand how these cues activate the reward circuit of the brain. "What we noticed is that the system can be activated when we show pictures that are as short as 33 milliseconds," says Childress. "So what's really difficult here for the 'Stop!' system is that the message doesn't even have a chance to get up to the frontal lobes for them to weigh in. It's coming in under the radar before you have a chance to mount a defense."

Scientists such as Childress have been studying how medications can be used to slow the response of the pleasure pathway. She explains, "The hope is that you would have a chance for the frontal lobe to do its thing. To be able to weigh in and have a chance to put into place good decision-making." Medications have become a valuable tool to control craving for some drugs and alcohol, but they are best used in conjunction with counseling and behavioral therapies that encourage the good decision-making.

PREVENTING RELAPSE

Part of the process of an effective rehab program and ongoing recovery work is to teach addicts about cues and to train them to, first, be aware of them, and, second, avoid them. However, it is not possible to avoid every trigger. Nor is it possible to avoid traumatic life events—deaths, relationship problems, illnesses—and stress, which also can lead to relapse. An addict relapsed when she learned that her husband was having an affair. Another addict relapsed when her mother was diagnosed with cancer. A teenage boy relapsed when his only friend moved away. Triggers can be smaller events, too—normal, everyday frustrations that everyone faces, but that can be too much for an addict. "You want to watch for a variety of states that can lead an addict to relapse," says Frank Vocci, PhD, director of the Division of Pharmacotherapies and Medical Consequences of Drug Abuse at the National Institute on Drug Abuse. "It can be a big thing or a small thing. We teach them that it can be something simple: they can be hungry, angry, lonely, or tired—everyday states like that."

Good treatment programs teach addicts how to reframe situations that previously may have led them to relapse and interrupt or retrain their normal reactions. "If they are angry or having a bad day, get them to talk to a counselor, a significant other, or a therapist," says Vocci. "They can go to a meeting. A user can be taught to call an AA sponsor or drug counselor, go to a meeting, or make other healthy choices."

Stephen Shoptaw, PhD, a research psychologist at UCLA's Integrated Substance Abuse Programs, has developed specific cognitive and behavioral therapies that are designed to help addicts who associate meth with sex to reframe their responses to arousal. "You teach them to look at their own thinking," Shoptaw says. "They learn to recognize when their thinking is heading in the wrong direction. They stop it and change it."

RETRAINING THE BRAIN

In relapse prevention, addicts also learn about priming, the mechanism that leads a single slip to become a full-blown relapse. The goal is to counteract what is often the initial reaction to a slip. "Often, after a use, besides the neurobiological effects, there are affective and cognitive responses," UCLA's Ling says. "It's, 'Dammit, I did it again! I swore I wasn't going to do it.' Shame, remorse, anger. Sometimes, instead of shoring themselves up and saying, 'That was just a slip, I can do it,' they say, 'I've done it now, started to relapse,' and it becomes a self-fulfilling prophecy. Cognitive behavioral training can have someone instead think, *I used last night but it doesn't necessarily mean that I have to relapse. I have a great probability to relapse, but what can I do?* If they reframe the incident, they may then stop the relapse on their own."

Retraining behavior and responses isn't easy. Rawson says it is particularly challenging for some addicts because "they don't have a large repertoire of other behaviors." It works, though. Training addicts to reframe their reaction to cues or to interrupt the process of priming creates substantive change. Time, practice, and reinforcement are required, but experts say that new and healthier responses to cues and priming can become automatic and normal. It works.

There are millions of examples. It works one day at a time.

As addicts go forward with their recovery one day at a time, there are other opportunities to increase the chances that they will stay sober. For addicts with co-occurring mental illnesses, it is an opportunity to continue to fine-tune diagnoses and treatments for the disorders. According to Dennis, a benefit of time in recovery is that clear of drugs, people can be more thoroughly diagnosed and treated for problems such as anxiety, depression, or bipolar disorder.

Also, clear and drug-free, even after multiple relapses, addicts may for the first time begin to face the traumatic experiences and pain that may have caused them to turn to drugs in the first place. It's one of the challenges of recovery. You get sober, but at first you don't necessarily feel hopeful and optimistic. You may feel defeated and bleak because you can be returned to the place of pain from which you fled, or tried to flee, with drugs in the first place. "It's Groundhog Day all over again," scientist Gantt Galloway says. "Until you fix it. Only then will you get what addicts who have gone through it—through whatever it took to be well—have gained." It is why sometimes recovery can require traditional psychotherapy, psychiatric medication, or other treatments for co-occuring disorders.

AFTERCARE

Various types of aftercare and ongoing care help addicts to stay sober. After inpatient programs, addicts should transition into a comprehensive outpatient program for as long as possible. Many addicts are helped with outpatient programs alone. Ideally the outpatient program would begin with four or five day or evening sessions a week, tapering off to three times a week, and finally once a week. An outpatient program should continue for as long as possible—at least three months, but six months is preferable. A person may even require a year or more in an outpatient program. Also if possible, family participation in these programs ups an addict's chances of success.

Drug testing is another useful component of outpatient and aftercare programs. For many reasons, people who are addicted—especially young people—frequently fail to

Recognize Relapse Triggers

When a dependent person stops using drugs, they are in "remission." Remission means that a disease has abated, not that it has been cured. Addiction experts tell us that recovery is difficult. Many people encounter triggers that lead them to relapse and use a drug again once, a few times, or even regularly, in a slide back to dependency.

Perhaps one of the biggest threats to sobriety comes from social pressure. Going to parties or other places where people are likely to drink and use drugs can tempt those in recovery. Certain cues also function as triggers, such as revisiting environments in which drug use occurred, or even listening to music that is associated with using.

Less overt triggers involve emotions that may lead to using. Interpersonal conflict and strong emotional states are common relapse triggers. Arguments with partners, friends, or coworkers can create stresses that might lead someone to consider using again. Major life events (such as losing a job) and lifestyle factors (demanding daily obligations) can also lead to feelings of depression, loneliness, and anger—and trigger relapse. Paradoxically, psychologists have also identified positive emotional states as triggers in some individuals who may wish to enhance that good feeling by drinking or using drugs again.

With so many potential pitfalls, it should be no surprise that the majority of people in recovery experience at least one brief relapse, although returns to dependence are less common. Frank Murphy, PhD, director of Psychological Services at the Caron Treatment Centers, says recognizing this may help those who do relapse stay on the path to recovery. Understanding what has triggered a relapse helps addicts meet temptation in the future.

tell the truth about their using habits, even when they are making a recovery effort. Urine testing can verify which treatment approaches work and which do not, so doctors, counselors, and parents may fashion a plan that is tailored to meet an individual's specific needs.

"One of the things we try to encourage for continuing care, particularly in the first ninety days after treatment, is to keep up on the urine monitoring," says Dennis. There are simple-to-use, over-the-counter urine tests that are effective and that can be administered at home by parents. Urinalysis is a quick and effective way to determine if a person is using—and, if so, how heavily.

Dennis recommends that parents let their child know from the outset that they will be tested, and that if they test positive, they will return immediately to treatment. "By testing a couple of times a week, you will know the minute they relapse," he says. "That pressure, from knowing that they're being monitored and knowing what the consequences will be, helps them stay clean."

Meanwhile, for the initial months or sometimes years of recovery, many adults find it far easier to stay in recovery if they live in halfway houses. They resume their lives (or start over, depending on the damage in their wake) but have a safe place to come home to—a safe place with ongoing support. Some halfway houses hold recovery meetings and some have ongoing group therapy or even family therapy. At halfway houses, both counselors and fellow residents help addicts to stay sober and rebuild their lives by teaching them life skills and supporting their efforts to return to school or work. Like outpatient programs, halfway houses may be useful for three to six months, but many people require a year or more. Some people stay in halfway houses for two to three years.

For most if not all addicts and alcoholics, twelve-step meetings—AA and NA—are essential. "I breathe a sigh of relief when I hear someone is going to twelve-step meetings," says Galloway. "It's not essential for everyone, but for many addicts, getting into recovery in twelve-step programs is a transformative experience that reflects a transition from hell to earth." Dozens of research studies confirm that twelve-step support groups offer the most effective sobriety

How to Enhance the Odds for Recovery

William L. White

Senior Research Consultant, Lighthouse Institute, Chestnut Health Systems

Things you can do to enhance your recovery odds

→ Don't use—no matter what!

→ Choose a treatment program that offers a rich menu of continuing care services and actively use these supports.

→ Find a recovery support group and stay actively involved. Make meetings a priority, get a sponsor, build a sober social network, and apply recovery program principles to the problems of daily living.

→ If you do not have a living environment supportive of recovery, investigate the growing network of recovery homes.

→ Involve your family members in recovery support groups and activities.

→ Become an expert on your own recovery and take responsibility for it.

Things families can do to support the recovery of a family member

It has long been known that addiction can negatively affect all family members and disrupt family relationships, but recent studies have shown that recovery from addiction can also exert great strain on family members and family relationships. At the same time, family relationships have to be readjusted to the realities and demands of recovery. Here are several things family members can do to help speed these adjustments:

→ Educate yourself on the recovery process for individuals and families.

→ If your recovering family member is living with you, provide a sober environment to support that recovery.

→ Seek professional and peer support (from a group such as Al-Anon) for your own physical and emotional health.

→ Support your family member's involvement in treatment aftercare meetings and recovery support groups.

→ Help the recovering family member with assistance in locating sober housing, employment, child care, transportation, or other recovery support needs.

→ Assertively reintervene in the face of any relapse episode.

maintenance programs available, and regular attendance at twelve-step meetings is the greatest predictor of a stable, long-term recovery. For those who don't feel comfortable in traditional twelve-step programs, it is important to look for other support groups, whether a church or school-based recovery program, gender-based groups, family support groups, or life transition groups. The important thing is to continue to go to counseling or meetings to help maintain sobriety.

For how long? For some, forever. At these meetings, it's not uncommon to hear people talk about their recovery in terms of decades. Nonetheless, they always say they did it and continue to do it the same way someone does it who is celebrating their first week of sobriety: one day at a time.

One day at a time. It is a simple concept, sometimes maddeningly so. But it works. It works for addicts. It works for their loved ones. Get through today. One day at a time, days add up. Data say the more time you have staying sober, the more time you will remain sober. The good news is that over time these changed behaviors can become automatic—almost as automatic as behaviors that formerly led to using.

Finally, there is another message that comes with recovery. It is a message often repeated by addicts who are in recovery and their families, especially if their recovery is long lasting. While no one would choose to go through this, there is a benefit beyond sobriety—a benefit on the other side of addiction. It is the benefit of a life made fuller by the knowledge of something that people who go through this acquire on the deepest, most profound level: an appreciation of a life that is free of dependence on drugs or alcohol. On the other side of addiction, joy is possible. On the other side of addiction, love is possible. On the other side of addiction, there can be the fullest life imaginable.

Relapse is part of the disease, not a sign of failure.

Explaining Alcoholics Anonymous

Thomas McLellan, PhD

Co-founder and CEO, Treatment Research Institute

For the past sixty years, the most common and often the only form of care for alcohol and other substance-use problems has been Alcoholics Anonymous (AA). There are various other mutual assistance groups (Smart Recovery, Narcotics Anonymous, etc.), but AA is by far the most widely available. AA meetings include frank, open, honest discussion about all aspects of dealing with recovery—both the pains experienced during periods of substance use and the positive experiences that recovery has brought.

There are no fees or charges. The meetings are one hour long. They are chaired by a volunteer who typically begins by telling his/her "story" of personal recovery and then opens the meeting to individuals who raise their hands and ask to "share" either a problem they are having or a positive experience that their recovery has brought them. There is no criticism in AA, and nobody's statements or issues are derided. All issues and comments are treated with respect and confidentiality.

Is AA treatment?
No. AA is simply a mutual help organization. Many of those who have entered into recovery have done so simply by attending AA meetings without formal treatment. Many others have used AA as a form of continuing care to keep them sober following formal treatment.

Is AA a religious group?
No. While spiritual (not religious) elements are part of many groups, this is not universal. Many AA members believe that getting in touch with their spirituality is a key to their recovery—but not all share this view. There is no requirement for spiritual involvement in AA.

Is AA only for alcoholics?
AA is intended for anyone with alcohol problems who has an interest in attaining sobriety and remaining sober, regardless of diagnosis or level of severity.

Is there anything besides just talk?
Yes. Most of those who attend AA meetings meet other recovering people and join them socially for coffee and meals and other events. AA meetings can lead to connections to jobs, affordable housing, etc. In this way, meetings can meet social and day-to-day needs for people in recovery and help with their everyday challenges.

Where can I find an AA meeting?
There is a posted AA directory on the Internet and local schedules are available in most treatment programs. Just about every town has one or more churches that dedicate a meeting room to AA meetings several times per day and per week.

The Twelve Steps of Alcoholics Anonymous

What are the Twelve Steps?

The Twelve Steps discussed in AA meetings and writings involve the steps suggested by the collective experience of those in recovery that lead to development of an honest, helping, forgiving lifestyle—the kind of life that is inconsistent with addiction.

Alcoholics Anonymous was the first twelve-step program, founded in 1935 by a New York stockbroker and an Ohio doctor who both suffered from alcoholism. AA has grown to more than two million recovered alcoholics worldwide.

At the heart of the program are their Twelve Steps:

1. We admitted we were powerless over alcohol—that our lives had become unmanageable.

2. Came to believe that a Power greater than ourselves could restore us to sanity.

3. Made a decision to turn our will and our lives over to the care of God as we understood Him.

4. Made a searching and fearless moral inventory of ourselves.

5. Admitted to God, to ourselves, and to another human being the exact nature of our wrongs.

6. Were entirely ready to have God remove all these defects of character.

7. Humbly asked Him to remove our shortcomings.

8. Made a list of all persons we had harmed, and became willing to make amends to them all.

9. Made direct amends to such people wherever possible, except when to do so would injure them or others.

10. Continued to take personal inventory and when we were wrong promptly admitted it.

11. Sought through prayer and meditation to improve our conscious contact with God as we understood Him, praying only for knowledge of His will for us and the power to carry that out.

12. Having had a spiritual awakening as the result of these steps, we tried to carry this message to alcoholics, and to practice these principles in all our affairs.

Afterword

Susan Cheever

My father leaned over a glass of whiskey at the table as I explained my tears. My boyfriend hadn't called. I knew he was cheating on me. I imagined him kissing someone else. I was a loser. I sat crumpled in the armchair in my parents' dining room. My father went to the kitchen and brought back a tall glass gently clinking with ice and beading with condensation on the outside. The afternoon was hot and the drink looked cool. He handed it to me. "Maybe this will help," he said. Decades later, I can almost taste the cool, slightly viscose, faintly metallic gin and the fizzy quinine of the tonic. My father used to say that he liked to mix drinks "strong enough to draw a boat."

As I sat there and sipped on that suburban Sunday afternoon, the knots in my stomach and heart began to dissolve. I took a few more sips, and a lovely, calm feeling came over me. By the time my father had mixed me a second drink, I seemed to be floating buoyantly in the benevolent summer air. Of course my boyfriend loved me; I remembered the fervor in his eyes. Everyone loved me. This boyfriend was only a college boyfriend, after all. I would have many men in my life. My heart soared with love and longing for men I hadn't met yet and for my boyfriend far away. The world was a magnificent place as I sat there on the gorgeous summer afternoon with my loving father.

Years later, when I read Alcoholics Anonymous co-founder Bill Wilson's description of his first real drink, a Bronx cocktail at a party where he had been writhing in social discomfort, I remembered that gin and tonic on that hot afternoon. Wilson wrote that he had found "the elixir of life." That was how I felt.

An addict's first discovery of a substance, whether it is alcohol, heroin, or cocaine, is an epiphany. Drugs work. Alcohol works. Even if addicts know that their solution to life's problems will inevitably destroy them and anyone close to them, that knowledge seems irrelevant and far away. For an addict, taking the substance is one of the most pleasurable and effective experiences in life. Clumsy people become eloquent. Shy people become confident. Needy people become loveable. Suddenly life seems doable, delicious, and infinitely precious. The things that were impossible before become easy. The situations that once baffled the addict fall into simple pieces with simple solutions.

Most addicts remember their first high with bright vividness. Most begin using the discovered substance, first slowly and then more rapidly, to help overcome the longings and sadness, the awkwardness and self-loathing that is part of being human. After I drank that gin and tonic, I used alcohol to control my moods and attitudes for thirty years, and I only stopped when it stopped working. In fact, after it stopped working it took me years to realize what had happened and years more before I was able to stop drinking.

These days we understand that addiction is a disease. Many people know that addicts can't stop even if they want to—even if they desperately want to. Addicts don't need self-control, they don't require discipline, they need treatment. And, as this book shows, there are many paths to finding a treatment that works for each addict. There is a lot of exciting new scientific research on addiction. We now have a better idea than ever before of what the disease is and how to treat it, but there is still something profoundly mysterious at the heart of all addictions. Most people can be counted on to do what benefits them. Not addicts.

My story is typical. Although I never got arrested for drinking and I never killed anyone, by the time I stopped drinking it had brought me to an intolerable level of despair. I had a husband, two small children, and a solid career, but my life seemed to be an unbearable burden. I felt as if I was being crushed in a vice. My children were wonderful, my husband loving, but I was completely beyond understanding any of that. As it says in the book *Alcoholics Anonymous*, written by the first men to recover from alcoholism in AA, "Alcohol gave me wings to fly and then it took away the sky." I confided in my children's pediatrician, and he suggested that I stop drinking. I agreed to stop.

Back then we were living on the top floors of a dilapidated townhouse on 92nd Street in Manhattan. We had signed the lease with the owner over a bottle of good Cabernet Sauvignon. Each night at twilight, my husband fixed his own vodka tonic. I poured a seltzer and squeezed in some lemon juice. This went on for a few days. But eventually there would be an evening when something had gone wrong. One of the kids had a fever, I got a rejection letter, a friend was bitchy. On those nights when my husband fixed his drink, I opened a bottle of wine and poured myself a glass. My husband smiled indulgently; he liked having company. I had promised myself that I wouldn't drink, but it almost felt as if someone else was opening the bottle of wine and pouring it into the glass. I felt dissociated from the drink, as if it had nothing to do with the texture of my real life and my previous decisions. Sometimes I drank the whole bottle of wine before the trance lifted. Sometimes it lifted right away and I quickly justified my actions. What could be more normal, after all? What could be friendlier than a wife pouring her own innocent glass of white wine to join her husband for a cocktail? White wine was hardly even liquor.

One moment I would be deciding not to drink and the next moment I would be taking a big swallow, and I couldn't really remember what had happened in between. The next morning, with a splitting headache, I started the process all over again. Officially I wasn't drinking, but the cases of wine kept diminishing and having to be reordered. According to my view of the world I wasn't an alcoholic—I couldn't be. My husband was an alcoholic because he drank vodka while I drank wine. My father had been an alcoholic; he got arrested and had the DT's.

I had watched my father struggle and almost die—of a heart attack, of hypothermia, of various alcohol-related ailments. The helpful man who had mixed me that first gin and tonic was eviscerated by alcohol. He kept trying to stop drinking and then starting again. But finally he reached out for real help. He went to a rehabilitation center and emerged a sober man. Something seemed to change at his deepest core. He went to meetings of Alcoholics Anonymous almost every day. He hadn't had a drink for the last seven years of his life when he died of cancer in 1982, and those were wonderful, wonderful years. I loved the father who had been restored to me by sobriety. I wanted my own children to have a sober parent, but no matter how often I vowed not to drink, as evening fell I often found myself with a glass of white wine in my hand.

What changed? I wish I could say that I had a classic epiphany, a moment of truth when I realized that my alcoholism was out of control. That didn't happen. I finally did reach out for help . . . for my husband. I thought his drinking was the source of my problems. I began to call alcoholism counselors, rehab centers, psychiatrists, and hospitals. I went to see anyone who offered help. I told them all about my husband's drinking. Finally one of them asked about my drinking. I answered that I would try treatment if that would help my husband. So, for all the wrong reasons, I began my own recovery.

The moment of truth was more like a slow winter dawn. It took me months to confess that I had a problem with alcohol. It took me another few years to settle into the pattern of help I needed and to have what Wilson called "a change of heart." I haven't had a drink in more than fourteen years now. I take my sobriety a day at a time. I know how lucky I am.

What's odd is that the very buoyancy that hooked me with that first gin and tonic has come to me in sobriety. It wasn't as if the cares of the world were lifted off my shoulders in an instant, but slowly my life has changed so that I feel at home in the world in almost the same way that first gin and tonic helped me feel at home in the world. This is one of the many puzzles of addiction. The substance that gives so much at first—it makes you feel loved, it makes everything possible—in the end robs you of the very things it gives. In a way, I had to get sober to recapture the feelings released by that first long-ago drink.

Resources

The following list is selective and limited largely to national organizations. Additional resources may be found at www.HBO.com/addiction and from your doctor or other healthcare practitioners.

FEDERAL AGENCIES

Addiction Technology Transfer Center (ATTC)
University of Missouri, Kansas City
5100 Rockhill Road
Kansas City, MO 64110-2499
816-235-6888
www.nattc.org
Funded by the Substance Abuse and Mental Health Services Administration (SAMHSA), the ATTC is dedicated to identifying and advancing opportunities for improving addiction treatment.

Center for Substance Abuse Treatment (CSAT)
240-276-2750
www.csat.samhsa.gov
CSAT promotes the quality and availability of community-based substance-abuse treatment services for individuals and families who need them. CSAT works with state and community-based groups to improve and expand existing substance-abuse treatment and recovery services under the Substance Abuse Prevention and Treatment Block Grant Program.

National Clearinghouse for Alcohol and Drug Information
11300 Rockville Pike
Rockville, MD 20852
800-729-6686
www.ncadi.samhsa.gov
This federal agency provides extensive information about addiction prevention, treatment, and recovery. It has a staff of English- and Spanish-speaking information specialists who are available 24/7 to recommend appropriate materials. They also have copies of "Know Your Rights," a guide for people who have had trouble getting help.

National Institute on Alcohol Abuse and Alcoholism (NIAAA)
National Institutes of Health
5635 Fishers Lane
MSC 9304
Bethesda, MD 20892-9304
301-443-3860
www.niaaa.nih.gov
NIAAA provides leadership in the national effort to reduce alcohol-related problems. The web site has extensive resources including fact sheets about a wide range of alcohol-related topics, as well as a variety of publications for researchers and health professionals.

National Institute on Drug Abuse (NIDA)
National Institutes of Health
6001 Executive Boulevard, Room 5213
Bethesda, MD 20892-9561
301-443-1124
www.nida.nih.gov
NIDA's mission is to bring the power of science to bear on drug abuse and addiction. NIDA supports most of the world's research on the health aspects of drug abuse and addiction.

Office of National Drug Control Policy. Parents: The Anti-Drug
800-729-6686
www.theantidrug.com
TheAntiDrug.com was created by the National Youth Anti-Drug Media Campaign to equip parents with the tools they need to raise drug-free kids.

Substance Abuse & Mental Health Services Administration (SAMHSA)
1 Choke Cherry Road
Rockville, MD 20857
800-662-HELP
www.samhsa.gov
SAMHSA is focused on building resilience and facilitating recovery for people with or at risk for mental or substance-use disorders.

Working Partners for an Alcohol- and Drug-Free Workplace

U.S. Department of Labor
200 Constitution Avenue, Room S-2312
Washington, DC 20210
202-693-5919
www.dol.gov/workingpartners
Working Partners for an Alcohol- and Drug-Free Workplace provides facts and figures about addiction to alcohol and other drugs, its costs to the workplace, and strategies for how to establish an alcohol- and drug-free workplace.

PRIVATE ORGANIZATIONS

Addiction Treatment Forum

Clinco Communications, Inc.
124 Jansen Lane
Vernon Hills, IL 60061
847-392-3937
www.atforum.com
Addiction Treatment Forum reports on substance use and addiction therapies, with a special emphasis on medication-assisted recovery featuring research, news, and events of interest to both healthcare professionals and patients.

Addiction Intervention Resources (AIR)

400 Selby Avenue, Suite D
St. Paul, MN 55102
800-561-8158 / 651-222-6740
www.addictionintervention.com
AIR is a national addiction consulting service for families and organizations.

American Council on Alcoholism (ACA)

1000 East Indian School Road
Phoenix, AZ 85014
800-527-5344
www.aca-usa.org
ACA is dedicated to educating the public about the effects of alcohol, alcoholism, and alcohol abuse, as well as the need for prompt, effective, readily available, and affordable alcoholism treatment.

Canadian Centre on Substance Abuse (CCSA)

75 Albert Street, Suite 300
Ottawa, ON K1P 5E7 Canada
613-235-4048
www.ccsa.ca
CCSA is Canada's national addictions agency, with the mission of providing objective, evidence-based information and advice to help reduce the health, social, and economic problems associated with substance abuse and addictions.

Center for Science in the Public Interest: Alcohol Policies Project

1875 Connecticut Avenue NW,
Suite 300
Washington, DC 20009-5728
202-332-9100
www.cspinet.org/booze
The Alcohol Policies Project works with organizations and individuals to promote a comprehensive, prevention-oriented policy strategy to change the role of alcohol in society.

Children of Alcoholics Foundation (COAF)

164 West 74th Street
New York, NY 10023
800-359-COAF / 646-505-2060
www.coaf.org
A parent company of Phoenix House, COAF helps children of all ages from alcoholic and substance-abusing families break the cycle of parental abuse and reduce the problems that result from parental addiction. COAF develops curriculum and other educational materials, writes reports, provides information about parental substance abuse for the general public, trains professionals, and promotes research.

Community Anti-Drug Coalitions of America (CADCA)

625 Slaters Lane, Suite 300
Alexandria, VA 22314
800-54-CADCA
www.cadca.org
CADCA works with community-based coalitions and represents their interests at the national level to address the illegal use of alcohol and other drugs and violence.

Faces & Voices of Recovery

1010 Vermont Avenue, #708
Washington, DC 20005
202-737-0690
www.facesandvoicesofrecovery.org
Faces & Voices of Recovery is a national campaign of people in long-term recovery, families, friends and allies, and organizations that advocate to end discrimination, broaden social understanding, and achieve a just response to addiction as a public health crisis.

Hazelden Foundation
CO3, P.O. Box 11
Center City, MN 55012-0011
800-257-7810 / 651-213-4200
www.hazelden.org
Hazelden provides treatment and continuing care services, education, research, and publications to individuals, families, and communities struggling with addiction to alcohol and other drugs.

Join Together
One Appleton Street, 4th Floor
Boston, MA 02116-5223
617-437-1500
www.jointogether.org
www.alcoholscreening.org
Join Together, a program of the Boston University School of Public Health, is the nation's leading provider of information, strategic assistance, and leadership development for community-based efforts to advance effective alcohol and drug policy, prevention, and treatment. Through extensive online information resources and national policy panels, Join Together helps community leaders understand and use the most scientifically valid prevention and treatment approaches.

Legal Action Center
225 Varick Street
New York, NY 10014
212-243-1313
www.lac.org
The Legal Action Center is a law and public policy organization that fights discrimination against people with histories of addiction, HIV/AIDS, or criminal records, and advocates for sound public policies in these areas.

Marin Institute
24 Belvedere Street
San Rafael, CA 94901
415-456-5692
www.marininstitute.org
The Marin Institute monitors and exposes the alcohol industry's negative practices.

National Association of Drug Court Professionals
www.nadcp.org
www.ndci.org
This organization provides information and technical assistance to people working in drug courts and in the planning, implementing, and enhancement of drug courts. The National Drug Court Institute provides training to drug court professionals.

National Association on Alcohol, Drugs, and Disability (NADD)
2165 Bunker Hill Drive
San Mateo, CA 94402-3801
650-578-8047
www.naadd.org
NADD works to create public awareness of issues related to alcoholism, drug addiction, and substance abuse faced by people with other coexisting disabilities, and to provide a peer approach to enhance access to services, information, education, and prevention through the collaborative efforts of individuals and organizations nationwide.

National Center on Addiction and Substance Abuse at Columbia University (CASA)
633 Third Avenue, 19th Floor
New York, NY 10017-6706
212-841-5200
www.casacolumbia.org
CASA brings together a coalition of professionals from various disciplines to study and combat substance abuse. Its programs vary from policy development and analysis to studies concerning substance-abuse treatment.

National Council on Alcoholism and Drug Dependence (NCADD)
22 Cortlandt Street, Suite 801
New York, NY 10007-3128
800-NCA-CALL / 212-269-7797
www.ncadd.org
NCADD advocates prevention, intervention, and treatment of alcoholism and drug addiction through a nationwide network of affiliates. They also operate a toll-free Hope Line (800-NCA-CALL) for information and referral, as well as a National Intervention Network (800-654-HOPE) to educate and assist the families and friends of addicted people.

The Partnership for a Drug-Free America
405 Lexington Avenue, Suite 1601
New York, NY 10174
212-922-1560
www.drugfree.org
The Partnership for a Drug-Free America is a nonprofit coalition of communication, health, medical, and educational professionals working to reduce illicit drug use and help people live healthy, drug-free lives.

Robert Wood Johnson Foundation
P.O. Box 2316
College Road East and Route 1
Princeton, NJ 08543
888-631-9989
www.rwjf.org
This foundation is the largest philanthropic organization devoted to improving the health and healthcare of all Americans.

PRIVATE, PROFESSIONAL, AND TREATMENT FACILITIES
FEDERAL AGENCY

Substance Abuse Treatment Facility Locator
www.findtreatment.samhsa.gov
SAMHSA provides an online resource for locating drug and alcohol abuse treatment programs. It includes private and public facilities that are licensed, certified, or otherwise approved for inclusion by their state substance abuse agency, as well as treatment facilities administered by the Department of Veterans Affairs, the Indian Health Service, and the Department of Defense.

PRIVATE ORGANIZATIONS

National Association of Addiction Treatment Providers (NAATP)
313 W. Liberty Street, Suite 129
Lancaster, PA 17603-2748
717-392-8480
www.naatp.org
This organization lists professional treatment facilities in every state.

Phoenix House
www.phoenixhouse.org
The nation's largest nonprofit substance-abuse services organization includes more than one hundred drug and alcohol treatment programs at sixty locations in nine states. There are eleven residential high schools for teens, twenty-eight adult residential programs, and an array of outpatient programs, recovery residences, and after school programs.

SUPPORT GROUPS AND ORGANIZATIONS

Al-Anon/Alateen

1600 Corporate Landing Parkway
Virginia Beach, VA 23454-5617
888-4AL-ANON / 757-563-1600
www.al-anon.alateen.org
Al-Anon and Alateen Family Groups offer support and fellowship to relatives and friends of individuals with alcohol problems. Mutual support groups meet worldwide.

Alcoholics Anonymous (AA)

P.O. Box 459
New York, NY 10163
Check your phone book for
local listings
www.alcoholics-anonymous.org
Alcoholics Anonymous offers support and fellowship to individuals with alcohol problems through its Twelve Steps program. AA meetings are completely anonymous and open to anyone of any age who wants to achieve and maintain sobriety.

Narcotics Anonymous (NA)

P.O. Box 9999
Van Nuys, CA 91409
818-997-3822
www.na.org
Narcotics Anonymous is an international, community-based association of recovering drug addicts.

Secular Organizations for Sobriety
SOS International Clearinghouse

The Center for Inquiry-West
4773 Hollywood Boulevard
Hollywood, CA 90027
323-666-4295
www.cfiwest.org/sos
SOS is a non-spiritually-based recovery fellowship that credits the individual for achieving and maintaining his or her own sobriety.

SMART Recovery

7537 Mentor Avenue, Suite 306
Mentor, OH 44060
866-951-5357 / 440-951-5357
www.smartrecovery.org
SMART Recovery is a nonprofit organization offering free face-to-face and online mutual help groups. SMART stands for Self-Management Aid and Recovery Training.

Women for Sobriety

P.O. Box 618
Quakertown, PA 18951
215-536-8026
www.womenforsobriety.org
Women for Sobriety is an organization and self-help program for alcoholic women.

RESEARCH ORGANIZATIONS
FEDERAL AGENCY

Center for Substance Abuse Research (CESAR)

4321 Hartwick Road, Suite 501
College Park, MD 20740
301-405-9770
www.cesar.umd.edu
CESAR conducts policy-relevant research and evaluation studies, disseminates statistical and other information, assists in training students in substance-abuse research methods and policy analysis, and provides technical assistance to agencies and organizations working in substance abuse–related fields.

PRIVATE ORGANIZATIONS

Center of Alcohol Studies

Rutgers, the State University
of New Jersey
607 Allison Road
Piscataway, NJ 08854-8001
732-445-2190
www.alcoholstudies.rutgers.edu
The Center of Alcohol Studies is the first interdisciplinary research center devoted to alcohol use and alcohol-related problems and treatment. Its library, one of the world's largest collections of alcohol research and clinical and professional literature, is open to the general public.

Drug Strategies
1616 P Street, NW, Suite 220
Washington, DC 20036
202-289-9070
www.drugstrategies.org
Drug Strategies is a nonprofit research institute that promotes more effective approaches to the nation's drug problems and supports private and public efforts to reduce the demand for drugs through prevention, education, treatment, law enforcement, and community initiatives.

Ensuring Solutions to Alcohol Problems
George Washington University
2021 K Street, NW, Suite 800
Washington, DC 20006
202-296-6922
www.ensuringsolutions.org
A health initiative at the George Washington University Medical Center, Ensuring Solutions works to reduce the burden of untreated alcohol problems on communities, businesses, families, and individuals by providing information and tools to increase access to effective and affordable screening and treatment.

National Development and Research Institutes (NDRI)
71 West 23rd Street, 8th Floor
New York, NY 10010
212-845-4400
www.ndri.org
NRDI is a research and educational organization dedicated to advancing scientific knowledge in the areas of drug and alcohol abuse, treatment and recovery, HIV, AIDS and HCV, therapeutic communities, and other related areas of public health and criminal justice.

Research Society on Alcoholism (RSOA)
www.rsoa.org
RSOA serves as a communications point for scientists and addiction field professionals to share and disseminate information and research findings.

Treatment Research Institute (TRI)
600 Public Ledger Building
Philadelphia, PA 19106
215-399-0980
www.tresearch.org
TRI is a nonprofit research and development organization dedicated to reducing the devastating effects of alcohol and drug abuse on individuals, families, and communities by employing scientific methods and disseminating evidence-based information.

Center for Substance Abuse Prevention (CSAP)
5600 Fishers Lane
Rockwall II Building, 9th Floor
Rockville, MD 20857
301-443-0365
www.prevention.samhsa.gov

CSAP provides national leadership in the federal effort to prevent alcohol, tobacco, and other drug problems. CSAP promotes a structured, community-based approach to substance-abuse prevention by designing and implementing public education programs.

PRIVATE ORGANIZATION

American Council for Drug Education
164 West 74th Street
New York, NY 10023
800-488-DRUG
www.acde.org
An affiliate of Phoenix House, ACDE is a substance-abuse prevention and education agency that develops programs and materials based on the most current scientific research on drug abuse and its impact on society.

Glossary

Addiction A chronic disorder that includes craving for drugs or alcohol and a compulsion to use them; inability to control substance use; and continued use in spite of negative consequences. Other symptoms can include tolerance, physical and psychological dependence, and withdrawal.

Aftercare Also known as continuing care. An outpatient program following rehabilitation that helps a person maintain changed behavior, support healthy living, monitor threats to relapse, and, if relapse occurs, reengages the patient.

Alcoholism An addiction to the consumption of alcoholic beverages. For a more in-depth definition see Alcohol Dependence.

Alcohol/drug abuse A maladaptive pattern of alcohol/drug use leading to clinically significant impairment or distress as manifested by one (or more) of the following in a twelve-month period: alcohol/drug use that interferes with the ability to fulfill major obligations; use in situations that are physically hazardous; recurrent, alcohol- or drug-related legal problems; continued use despite adverse social or interpersonal consequences.

Alcohol/drug dependence A maladaptive pattern of alcohol/drug use leading to clinically significant impairment or distress, as manifested by three (or more) of the following conditions in a twelve-month period: tolerance; withdrawal symptoms; impaired control over drinking or drug use; preoccupation with alcohol/drugs; less time spent on important social, occupational, or recreational activities; and use of alcohol/drugs despite adverse physical or psychological consequences.

Cognitive Behavioral Therapy (CBT) A short-term, focused approach to helping people with substance use disorders to stay abstinent. Very simply, CBT attempts to help patients recognize situations when they are most likely to use drugs or alcohol, avoid these situations when appropriate, and cope more effectively with a range of problems and problematic behaviors associated with substance abuse.

Conditioned cues A multitude of stimuli (sights, sounds, smells) that trigger drug cravings.

Co-occurring disorders A condition where a person has both a substance use disorder and a psychiatric disorder at the same time. Between 30 and 60 percent of adults with drug or alcohol addiction have a concurrent mental health diagnosis, and 40 to 60 percent of adolescents and young adults in drug and alcohol treatment programs also need attention for psychiatric problems.

Depressants Drugs include barbiturates (amobarbital, pentobarbital, secobarbital), benzodiazepines (Valium, Ativan, Xanax), chloral hydrate, and paraldehyde. The most commonly used, by far, is alcohol. These substances produce a soothing sedative and anxiety-reducing effect and can lead to dependence.

Dopamine A brain chemical, classified as a neurotransmitter, found in regions of the brain that regulate movement, emotion, motivation, and pleasure.

Hallucinogens A diverse group of drugs that alter perceptions, thoughts, and feelings. They include LSD, mescaline, psilocybin ("mushrooms"), and phencyclidine (PCP).

Inpatient treatment A treatment program in which people stay overnight at a hospital or treatment facility, for a few days to several months, to participate in rehabilitation and recovery.

Multi-Systemic Therapy (MST) A family-oriented, home-based program that targets chronically violent, substance-abusing juvenile offenders, age 12 to 17 years. MST uses methods that promote positive social behavior and decrease antisocial behavior, including substance use, to change how youth function in their natural settings.

Neurotransmitter A chemical produced by neurons to carry messages to other neurons.

Opiates Powerful drugs derived from the poppy plant. These include heroin, opium, codeine, oxycodone (OxyContin), Vicodin, and others.

Outpatient treatment Programs in which people live at home and attend treatment sessions during the day. Most programs provide individual counseling and/or a support-group session led by a professionally trained group leader.

Overdose A drug dose that is large enough to be toxic.

Recovery Changes in behavior and outlook made by the addict to abstain from drinking and drug use. Recovery is much more than simply abstaining from alcohol or drugs—it involves active, continually evolving behavioral changes.

Relapse When referring to substance abuse, this term means that a person who has not been using any drugs or alcohol, and is committed to continuing this pattern, returns to excessive or problematic use of alcohol or drugs. A lapse or "slip" is when a person returns to use after a period of abstinence that does not lead to full relapse.

Stimulants A class of addictive drugs that speed up the body's central nervous and circulatory systems. These include amphetamines, cocaine, dextroamphetamine, methamphetamine, and methylphenidate (Ritalin).

Therapeutic community (TC) Drug-free residential communities with treatment stages that reflect increased levels of personal and social responsibility. There is also a focus on changing negative patterns of thinking and behavior through individual and group therapy, community-based learning, confrontation, games, and role-playing

Tolerance A condition in which higher doses of a drug are required to produce the same effect as experienced initially.

Twelve Steps Programs designed to assist in the recovery from addiction, especially a spiritually oriented program that requires individuals to surrender their self-reliance and adopt a practice of reliance on God or a higher power. The phrase is derived from the name for the twelve guiding concepts of Alcoholics Anonymous.

Withdrawal Physical changes occurring when a person stops or suddenly decreases heavy use of alcohol or other sedative drugs, or opioids. Withdrawal symptoms may include shaking, sweating, rapid pulse, and agitation. Hallucinations or convulsions may also occur with alcohol and other sedatives.

Contributors

Susan Cheever is the bestselling author of twelve books, including five novels, the memoirs *Note Found in a Bottle* and *Home Before Dark*, *My Name is Bill*, a biography of Bill Wilson, the cofounder of Alcoholics Anonymous, and most recently, *American Bloomsbury*. She is a director of the Corporation of Yaddo, a member of the Authors Guild Council, and teaches in the Bennington College MFA program and at the New School.

Katherine Eban, a medical journalist and Alicia Patterson fellow, has worked for the *New York Times*, the *New York Observer*, and ABC News. Her articles have also appeared in other publications, including *The Nation* and *Vanity Fair*. She is the author of *Dangerous Doses: A True Story of Cops, Counterfeiters, and the Contamination of America's Drug Supply*.

Susan Froemke has more than twenty-seven nonfiction films to her credit, including *Grey Gardens* (1976) and the 2001 Academy Award®–nominated *Lalee's Kin*, an HBO film that was also honored at the Sundance Film Festival. A four-time Emmy® winner, Froemke won a 2001 Grammy® for her work as director and producer of *Recording the Producers: A Musical Romp with Mel Brooks*. Before starting her own company in 2003, Froemke was the principal filmmaker at Maysles Films, Inc.

John Hoffman, vice president of HBO Original Programming, has spent the past eleven years creating, producing, and supervising documentary programming for HBO, including the ADDICTION project, *Hacking Democracy*, the Emmy®-nominated *Last Letters Home: Voices of American Troops from the Battlefields of Iraq*, and *In Memoriam, New York City, 9/11/01*. Before coming to HBO, Hoffman produced and created the children's television series *Allegra's Window*, and served as executive director of AIDSFILMS, where he produced six multi-award-winning films, including *AIDS: Changing the Rules*.

Katherine Ketcham is the co-author of thirteen books, including *Broken: My Story of Addiction and Redemption* with William Moyers, and the bestselling titles *Under the Influence* with James Milam, *The Spirituality of Imperfection* with Ernest Kurtz, and *Teens Under the Influence* with Nicholas Pace, MD. She lives in Washington with her husband, Patrick Spencer, and their three children.

Sheila Nevins, president of HBO Documentary Films, is responsible for overseeing the development and production of all documentaries and family programming for HBO, Cinemax, and their multiplex channels. During her tenure at HBO, she has received seventeen Primetime Emmy® Awards, twenty-four News and Documentary Emmys®, and twenty-five Peabody Awards. Nevins has also been honored with a Personal Peabody in 2001 and an Emmy® Lifetime Achievement Award in 2005 for her contributions to the art of the documentary.

David Sheff is the author of *Beautiful Boy: A Father's Journey Through His Son's Meth Addiction*, based on his award-winning *New York Times Magazine* article, "My Addicted Son." His other books include *Game Over*, *China Dawn*, and *All We Are Saying*. His work has appeared in several publications, including *Fortune* and *Rolling Stone*.

Larkin Warren is a freelance writer and editor whose articles and essays have appeared in *Esquire*, *Good Housekeeping*, *Glamour*, the *New York Times*, and *AARP—The Magazine,* among others. She has collaborated on four published autobiographies and is currently at work on a novel.

EXPERT CONTRIBUTORS

Samuel B. Bacharach, PhD, is the McKelvey-Grant Professor at the Cornell University School of Industrial and Labor Relations and the director of Cornell's Smithers Institute for Alcohol-Related Workplace Studies. In addition to his work in alcohol studies, Bacharach is the author and editor of more than twenty books on management, organizational behavior, and industrial relations.

Deborah Beck, MS, is a drug and alcohol treatment consultant and president of the Drug and Alcohol Service Providers Organization of Pennsylvania. She serves as policy cochair of the State Associations of Addiction Services, and is on the boards of the National Alliance for Model State Drug Laws and the Pennsylvania Recovery Organizations Alliance.

Kathleen T. Brady, MD, PhD, specializes in addiction psychiatry. She is director of the Clinical Neuroscience Division, director of the Women's Research Center, and associate director of the General Clinical Research Center at the Medical University of South Carolina. Brady is also currently president of the American Academy of Addiction Psychiatry and director of the Southern Consortium of the National Institute on Drug Abuse's Clinical Trials Network.

Mady Chalk, PhD, is the director of the Center for Performance-Based Policy at the Treatment Research Institute. For many years, Chalk was the director of the Division of Services Improvement in the Federal Center for Substance Abuse Treatment/Substance Abuse and Mental Health Services Administration.

Anna Rose Childress, PhD, is a research associate professor in the Department of Psychiatry at the University of Pennsylvania School of Medicine and the director of the Brain-Behavioral Vulnerabilities Division at the Center for Studies of Addictions. She conducts research funded by the National Institutes of Health/National Institute on Drug Abuse on the motivation for drug use and relapse.

Thomas J. Crowley, MD, is a professor and director of the Division of Substance Dependence at the Department of Psychiatry, University of Colorado School of Medicine. His research addresses the combination of substance dependence and conduct disorder in adolescents. Crowley has published more than one hundred scientific reports and book chapters.

Michael L. Dennis, PhD, is a senior research psychologist and the director of the Global Appraisal of Individual Needs (GAIN) Coordinating Center at Chestnut Health Systems. He is currently chair of the Society of Adolescent Substance Abuse Treatment and Effectiveness (SASATE) and is a past chair of the Joint Meeting on Adolescent Treatment Effectiveness (JMATE).

Mathea Falco, JD, is president of Drug Strategies, a nonprofit research institute that promotes more effective approaches to the nation's drug problems. The author of *The Making of a Drug Free America: Programs that Work* and numerous articles, Falco comments frequently on drug policy in the media and in public speeches across the country.

Scott Farnum, MS, MPA, is currently department head of Pharmacological Therapies at the Hill Health Center in New Haven, Connecticut. He also serves as a process improvement coach for the Network for the Improvement of Addiction Treatment (NIAT). He has more than twenty-five years of clinical and management experience in the mental health and addiction fields.

Robert F. Forman, PhD, is a clinical scientist at Alkermes, a biotech company in Cambridge, Massachusetts, that develops addiction medications and advanced pharmaceutical delivery systems, and is adjunct assistant professor at the Center for Studies of Addiction, University of Pennsylvania School of Medicine.

A. Thomas McLellan, PhD, is a professor of psychiatry at the University of Pennsylvania and co-founder and CEO of the Treatment Research Institute, a nonprofit research and development institute. McLellan is internationally recognized for his research into treatment effectiveness for substance abuse patients. He has published more than four hundred articles and chapters on addiction research.

Douglas B. Marlowe, JD, PhD, is the director of the Division on Law and Ethics Research at the Treatment Research Institute and an adjunct associate professor of psychiatry at the University of Pennsylvania's School of Medicine. He is a member of the board of directors of the National Association of Drug Court Professionals.

Robert J. Meyers, PhD, is a research associate professor of psychology at the University of New Mexico's Center on Alcoholism, Substance Abuse, and Addictions, and is in private practice. He has coauthored five books on addiction, including *Get Your Loved One Sober: Alternatives to Nagging, Pleading, and Threatening.*

Richard A. Rawson, PhD, is the associate director of the UCLA Integrated Substance Abuse Programs in the Jane and Terry Semel Neuropsychiatric Institute, David Geffen School of Medicine at UCLA. He has worked with the U.S. State Department on large substance abuse research and treatment projects, exporting U.S. technology and addiction science to Mexico, Thailand, Israel, Egypt, South Africa, and the Palestinian Authority.

Paula Riggs, MD, is an associate professor in the Department of Psychiatry at the University of Colorado at Denver and UCD's Health Sciences Center. She is the author of numerous publications and educational articles and monographs in the field of adolescent treatment research.

David Rosenbloom, PhD, is a professor of public health at Boston University, where he directs Join Together, a program that helps communities throughout the country prevent and reduce alcohol and drug problems, and the Youth Alcohol Prevention Center. Rosenbloom is the principal investigator for the National Institute on Alcohol Abuse and Alcoholism Center for the Prevention of Alcohol Problems in Young People.

Mitchell S. Rosenthal, MD, is president of Phoenix House, a private, nonprofit organization that operates nearly one hundred treatment and prevention programs. A pioneer in the drug-free treatment of substance abuse, Rosenthal has been a White House advisor on drug abuse, a special consultant to the Office of National Drug Control Policy, and chairman of the New York State Advisory Council on Substance Abuse.

Paul N. Samuels, JD, is director and president of the Legal Action Center, a nonprofit public interest law firm specializing in legal and policy issues involving alcohol and drug use, AIDS, and criminal justice. Samuels has served on numerous national and state advisory groups.

Nora D. Volkow, MD, was appointed director of the National Institute on Drug Abuse (NIDA) in May 2003. She is recognized as one of the world's leading experts on drug addiction and brain imaging. Volkow has received numerous awards for significant scientific and public service achievements. She was recently included in *Newsweek*'s "Who's Next 2007."

William L. White is a senior research consultant for the Lighthouse Institute at Chestnut Health Systems in Illinois. White has authored or coauthored more than 270 articles and monographs and twelve books. His book, *Slaying the Dragon: The History of Addiction Treatment and Recovery in America*, received the McGovern Family Foundation Award for the best book on addiction recovery.

Elizabeth Whitmore, PhD, is an associate professor of psychiatry at the University of Colorado School of Medicine. She is director of Synergy Outpatient Services, a large substance-abuse treatment program for adolescents in Denver.

Mark Willenbring, MD, is director of the Treatment and Recovery Research Division of the National Institute on Alcohol Abuse and Alcoholism at the National Institutes of Health. He works to stimulate new directions in research on health services and on treatment and recovery, and to disseminate new research findings in order to facilitate their adoption.

Credits

TEXT

Chapter 1 Written by Katherine Eban with additional contributions by David Sheff, Larkin Warren, and Chris Jozefowicz, except pg. 37 adapted from "Myths of Addiction," written by Dr. Carlton Erickson, PhD, of the University of Texas Addiction Science Research and Education Center. Reprinted with permission.

Chapter 2 Written by Larkin Warren with additional contributions by Elizabeth Dougherty and Lynora Williams.

Chapter 3 Written by Larkin Warren with additional contributions by Elizabeth Dougherty and Max Dickstein, except pg. 111 CRAFFT © Children's Hospital Boston, 2001. Reproduced with permission from the Center for Adolescent Substance Abuse Research, CeASAR, Children's Hospital Boston.

Chapter 4 Written by Katherine Ketcham with additional contributions by A. Thomas McLellan, PhD, Max Dickstein, Chris Jozefowicz, and Lynora Williams, except pg. 121 AUDIT © World Health Organization, 1993; pg. 122 DAST-20 © 1982 by Harvey A. Skinner, PhD and the Centre for Addiction and Mental Health, Toronto, Canada. Reproduced with permission.

Chapter 5 Written by David Sheff with additional contributions by Max Dickstein.

Chapter 6 Written by David Sheff with additional contributions by Katherine Ketcham and Chris Jozefowicz, except pg. 225 The Twelve Steps, reprinted with permission of Alcoholics Anonymous World Services, Inc. (AAWS) Permission to reprint the Twelve Steps does not mean that AAWS has reviewed or approved the contents of this publication, or that AAWS necessarily agrees with the views expressed herein. AA is a program of recovery from alcoholism only—use of the Twelve Steps in connection with programs and activities which are patterned after AA, but which address other problems, or in any other non-AA context, does not imply otherwise.

ILLUSTRATIONS AND GRAPHICS

pg. 58 © 2006, MediVisuals Inc; pg. 60 Netter medical illustration used with permission of Elsevier; pg. 61 © 2006 Catherine Twomey; pg. 72 Jennifer Fairman.

Information graphics by mgmt. design

PHOTOGRAPHS

Jacket, pgs. 20, 52, 84, 118, 166, 204, Albert Watson/HBO; pg. 7 The Partnership for a Drug-Free America; pgs. 8, 9, 63, 65, 82 courtesy of Brookhaven National Laboratory; pg. 72 courtesy of the Department of Psychiatry and Behavioral Sciences, Stanford University School of Medicine; pgs. 50–51, 74–75, 94–95, 117, 164–65, 186–87, 210–11 courtesy of the HBO ADDICTION project.

MELCHER MEDIA

Produced by Melcher Media Inc.
124 West 13th Street, New York, NY 10011
www.melcher.com

Design by mgmt. design

HOME BOX OFFICE in association with THE ROBERT WOOD JOHNSON FOUNDATION, THE NATIONAL INSTITUTE ON DRUG ABUSE and THE NATIONAL INSTITUTE ON ALCOHOL ABUSE AND ALCOHOLISM Present "ADDICTION" Produced by JOHN HOFFMAN and SUSAN FROEMKE; Co-Producer MICAH CORMIER; Edited by PAULA HEREDIA; Production Executive SUSAN BENAROYA; Executive Producer SHEILA NEVINS; Segments Directed by JON ALPERT, JOE BERLINGER, KATE DAVIS, SUSAN FROEMKE, LIZ GARBUS, CHRIS HEGEDUS, DAVID HEILBRONER, EUGENE JARECKI, ELLEN GOOSENBERG KENT, BARBARA KOPPLE, ALBERT MAYSLES, D.A.PENNEBAKER, ALAN RAYMOND, BRUCE SINOFSKY, JESSICA YU.

Acknowledgments

We are greatly indebted to both the National Institute on Drug Abuse (NIDA) and the National Institute on Alcohol Abuse and Alcoholism (NIAAA) for all the support they have given us through the three years it took to produce ADDICTION. We are proud to have NIDA, NIAAA, and the Robert Wood Johnson Foundation as our co-presenters.

The entire ADDICTION project comes from the spirit and vision of Sheila Nevins, president of documentary programming for HBO. We are indebted to our chairman and CEO, Chris Albrecht, for continuing to foster an environment at HBO that allows projects like ADDICTION to flourish. Every department at HBO has gone above and beyond in their efforts to extend the reach of ADDICTION to as large an audience as possible. We greatly appreciate their invaluable contributions.

Special thanks to all those who helped shape and guide our thinking about addiction: Samuel B. Bacharach, PhD, Ruben Baler, PhD, Deborah Beck, MS, Ann Bradley, Kathleen T. Brady, MD, PhD, Victor A. Capoccia, PhD, Deni Carise, PhD, Mady Chalk, PhD, Anna Rose Childress, PhD, Tim Condon, PhD, Thomas J. Crowley, MD, Elisabeth Davis, MPH, Michael L. Dennis, PhD, Gaya Dowling, PhD, Mathea Falco, JD, Scott Farnum, MS, MPA, Robert F. Forman, PhD, Larry Gentilello, MD, Eric Goplerud, Anara Guard, Jerome Jaffe, MD, Bankole Johnson, MD, PhD, Carol Krause, Petros Levounis, MD, Ting-Kai Li, MD, Jan Lipkin, Lynn Madden, MPA, CHE, Douglas B. Marlowe, JD, PhD, David M. McDowell, MD, Eileen McGrath, JD, A. Thomas McLellan, PhD, Robert J. Meyers, PhD, Lucinda Miner, PhD, National Association of Drug Court Professionals, National Drug Court Institute, Charles O'Brien, MD, PhD, Don Perks, Christopher Policano, Richard A. Rawson, PhD, Paula Riggs, MD, David L. Rosenbloom, PhD, Mitchell S. Rosenthal, MD, Paul N. Samuels, JD, Ann Staton, MPH, Pat Taylor, Nora D. Volkow, MD, Susan Weiss, PhD, William L. White, MA, Mark L. Willenbring, MD, Judge Robert P. Ziemian

Additional thanks to John Baker and Rob Meyer.

A very special thanks to Jane Potenzo, who has played such an important role in producing the Expert Advice columns for this book and for the HBO ADDICTION web site.

The book would not have been possible without Leigh Haber and Mia Carbonell at Rodale and the dedicated team at Melcher Media: Charles Melcher, publisher; Bonnie Eldon, associate publisher; Duncan Bock, editor in chief; Betty Wong, editor; and Lindsey Stanberry, assistant editor.

Melcher Media would like to thank Beth Adelman, Emily Anderson, David E. Brown, Lina Burton, Alicia Cheng, Daniel Del Valle, Max Dickstein, Jane Frazier, Sarah Gainer, Sarah Gephart, Rachel Griffin, Keach Hagey, Andrea Hirsh, Eric Helmuth, Jane Koropsak, Chris Krogermeier, Lauren Nathan, Alessandra Rafferty, Lia Ronnen, Holly Rothman, Jessi Rymill, Edie Sullivan, PhD, Alex Tart, Shoshana Thaler, and Megan Worman.

Index